Lars Oxelheim (Ed.)

The Global Race for Foreign Direct Investment

Prospects for the Future

With 23 Figures and 43 Tables

Springer-Verlag

Berlin Heidelberg New York
London Paris Tokyo
Hong Kong Barcelona
Budapest

Professor Dr. Lars Oxelheim
The Industrial Institute for Economic and Social Research
Industrihuset, Storgatan 19, P.O.Box 5501
S-114 85 Stockholm, Sweden

ISBN-13:978-3-642-78311-1 e-ISBN-13:978-3-642-78309-8
DOI: 10.1007/978-3-642-78309-8

Softcover reprint of the hardcover 1st edition 1993

2142/7130-543210 – Printed on acid-free paper

Preface

The contents of this book are the proceedings of the *Elof Hansson Symposium* held in Gothenburg in September 1991. The symposium was organized by the School of Economics and Commercial Law at Gothenburg University. The members of the programme committee were Göran Bengtsson and Lars Korn, both representing the Elof Hansson Foundation; Lennart Hjalmarsson, Lars-Eric Nordbäck, Lars Nordström and Lars Oxelheim, professors at the School of Economics and Commercial Law at Gothenburg University. The symposium was generously sponsored by the *Elof Hansson Foundation*.

The symposium consisted of presentations by a number of researchers as well as practitioners. Dr Curt Nicolin, chairman of Asea Brown Boveri (ABB) delivered the practitioner's view in a keynote speech and also chaired a panel discussion. The revision of the academic papers that followed the symposium benefitted from opinions brought forward in this discussion. Due to time restrictions, some of the papers included in the volume were presented at the symposium as only brief comments in the panel discussion. Nevertheless, these papers were invited to complement the papers that were more fully presented to facilitate the assessment of the complex race for foreign direct investment.

As editor, I would like to thank the contributors for all their efforts devoted to improve the quality of this volume. I am also grateful to Solveig Helgeson, who acted as secretary of the symposium and of the work with this book. My thanks also go to Kerstin Edvinsson and Anders Larsson for their typing and layout assistance. Finally, I would like to thank the *Elof Hansson Foundation* for its financial support of the editorial work.

Lars Oxelheim

Contents

List of Figures

List of Tables

Introduction

Lars Oxelheim

Foreign direct investment (FDI) has become the prime engine to foster growth and to facilitate the restructuring and internationalization of formerly sheltered areas during the 1980s. This book deals with the future prospects for FDI and provides answers to some critical questions confronting us at the beginning of the 1990s: Will the unprecedented high rate of growth of FDI in the 1980s continue for the rest of the twentieth century and beyond? If so, which will be the major recipient countries, source countries and sectors involved in these transactions?

The book contains nine chapters. The general approach of each chapter is to begin with a review of the factors that prompted the expansion of FDI during the 1980s and then assess their value as driving forces in the future. New factors are finally added to the discussion. The first four chapters deal with general questions such as: Will the restrictions on capital flows be reimposed? What are the future prospects for the world economy? Which ingredients will shape the global competition for investment? What are the likely patterns of FDI to emerge in the next decade? The remaining five chapters are devoted to more specific questions such as: How will increased instability in the financial system influence trade and FDI? What role in future FDI will merger and acquisition (M&A) activities play? What influence will the emerging market economies have on the global distribution of FDI? Will the Japanese continue to be the major foreign direct investors in the future? Will FDI from small and medium-sized firms gain momentum as they become more exposed to international competition and as their customers become increasingly involved in FDI?

In Chapter One, Lars Oxelheim discusses the implications of the liberalization of capital movements that swept over the world in the 1980s. Different forms of integration are discussed. It is emphasized that in a world of perfectly mobile capital, a government's degree of freedom in attracting foreign direct investment in "fair" competition is small. In addition, the incentives for firms to undertake FDI are reduced. The climate for investment is a key component in such a situation. Since it is assumed that enlighted governments fully appreciate inward investment, the creation of a favorable investment setting is put at the top of the policy agenda. Along with the undertaking of further liberalization measures consistent with a respect for market rules, individual governments will try to attract investment by an increasing use of incentives ("carrots") that are more or less incompatible with the ideas of "fair" competition. The implementation of such incentives may spur frustrated governments in other countries injured by such marketing activities to reimpose capital controls. The probability that governments will resort to regulative measures will be high in times of recession.

History shows that periods of war and general distress are followed by periods of extensive use of regulations. The author predicts that the regulation-liberalization pendulum will continue to swing around what he calls the minimum set of regulations required to guarantee the market infrastructure, to promote the soundness of a market and to warrant "fair" competition. He predicts that although some parts of the liberalization of capital movements may be irreversible, FDI activities will still lend themselves to a wave of reregulation. Such a wave may become a reality already in the next global recession. The author also points to some global threats that might initially increase FDI, but may ultimately trigger a wave of reregulation in the absence of a supranational authority in charge of supervising the conditions for foreign direct investment.

Chapter Two deals with the prospects for the world economy in a longer term perspective. Kjell Andersen emphasizes the traditional role of the growth of the labor force and productivity trends in supply-side based projections. He finds, however, demographic factors unlikely to be a decisive factor in this time perspective and focuses instead on productivity. The author notes that since the early 1980s economic policies in the OECD countries–where two thirds of world output originates–and more recently also in most other countries, have favored structural reforms designed to strengthen competitive forces and make the economies more efficient and flexible. He foresees that, although progress in these directions has been uneven, more competitive markets and technological advances would seem likely to generate stronger productivity growth. In the absence of major supply side shocks and political disturbances, there are reasons to expect stronger world economic growth in the 1990s than has taken place the last 15-20 years. Asia, particularly the South Eastern part, is expected to have the highest growth, supported by rapidly expanding intra-regional trade, direct investment and transfer of technology.

Chapter Three provides a framework for an analysis of the international competition for investment. Richard Sweeney emphasizes that domestic and foreign investment go hand-in-hand in an increasingly integrated world. Foreign direct investment is considered an intermediate target to social wealth and welfare. Policymakers may be successful in attracting inward investment, but this does not necessarily mean that welfare is increased. In the assessment of the welfare-implications of different policies to attract inward investment, the author makes a key distinction between investment diverting and investment creating policies. He finds domestic content rules and non-tariff trade barriers to be increasingly adopted, but investment diverting in character and, hence, contributing to reduced welfare in the world. The author issues a warning for using total amounts of FDI to judge success in attracting FDI. The quality of FDI can be more important than its quantity. A little of the right kind of FDI can be better than much of the wrong kind.

Policies within a trading bloc as well as between blocs are discussed. The trading blocks considered are the European Community (EC), North American Free Trade Area (NAFTA) and a potential Far-East bloc. The welfare-implications of the "race-to-the-bottom" policy are analyzed and found to have investment creating effects within, e.g., the EC or NAFTA. However, it may not be used as a competitive strategy for the EC or NAFTA as a whole, since poorer societies such as Eastern Europe or mainland Asia cannot be beaten on these margins. To attract FDI, an EC member must adopt policies that make wages gross of taxes compatible with the productivity of its workers.

The author projects regional trading arrangements to grow in importance during the rest of the twentieth century and beyond. Concern about access to major regional "blocs", such as the European Community, forces international corporations to consider more foreign investment. Governments already manipulate import barriers (for example, with domestic content rules) to induce multinationals to invest and produce locally rather than using imports. These incentives can lead to welfare-reducing misallocation of investment across countries and regional groups. Countries in a regional group are in a contest to attract investment from each other. Intra-group competition can lead to reduced tax rates and regulatory burdens; tightly regulated countries with high tax rates have incentives to try for political agreement on policy harmonization that will reduce intra-group competition.

In Chapter Four, John Dunning discusses future patterns of FDI. The driving forces behind historical patterns of direct investment are emphasized. The persistence of these forces are then assessed and projections provided. The author focuses attention on one of the most remarkable features of the last decade: the growing degree of internationalization of business and the extent to which countries are engaging in two-way investment. With the exception of Japan and France, outward and inward investments have become increasingly more balanced. The author also emphasizes the increased role of cooperative agreements due to, among other things, the steeply escalating cost of R&D and the need to protect and advance one's global competitive position in a turbulent world economy. The future role of the multinational enterprise is also said to be changing to that of an orchestrator of productions and transactions within a cluster or network of cross-border internal and external relationships.

The author assumes that the world's center of gravity will remain in the Triad, that technological development will continue make the world a smaller place, and that governments will still be interested in reaping the benefits of economic interdependence, while at the same time maintaining real political sovereignty. Based on these assumptions, international investment is found to be a major engine not only of growth in the 1990s, but also of integration and world trade. The author suggests that activities of multinational enterprises will be facing a third Golden Age in the 1990s, although it will differ from the past two in that the motives will no longer be to acquire natural resources or to seek out markets. Instead, multinational enterprises will seek to restructure or rationalize existing investment to capitalize on the advantages of regional integration or to acquire new technological or marketing assets in order to maintain or advance a globally competitive position. A development of pluralistic hierarchies of firms is expected to occur.

It is emphasized that the fastest growth of FDI in the 1980s actually occurred in the service sector. The author presents three reasons why the 1990s will see a further increase in the significance of this sector: 1) a rising proportion of services in consumer spending, 2) an increasing service intensity of manufactured goods and 3) the liberalization of cross-border markets coupled with technological advances in telecommunication facilities. As regards the geography of future international investment, the author suggests that the outward pattern of investment will increasingly resemble that of trade in manufactured goods and services. Hence, the share of the U.S. and the U.K. will continue to fall, while that of continental European countries, Japan and the first generation of the Asian tigers–Hong Kong, Korea, Taiwan and Singapore–will increase. Brazil and Mexico are also suggested to be potentially important outward investors in the rest of the twentieth century.

The second half of the book takes up special issues mentioned in the preceeding chapters, and studies them in greater detail. These issues are of functional as well as geographical character, and concern the role of financial instability, mergers and acquisition activities, emerging market economies, Japanese investment, and small and medium-sized firms.

Chapter Five focuses on the role of financial instability in trade and direct investment. Gunther Dufey starts with a discussion of the role and organisation of the international financial system. He concludes that the essence of this system is the interaction of national financial systems. It is emphasized that these markets are not operating in a vacuum, but are imbedded in international monetary arrangements of which the exchange rate regime is one major component. Two concepts of instability are discussed and of these the author chooses to focus on the instability originating from possible increases in the volatility of rates and prices. Three systematic changes that will determine the degree of such instability of the international financial system are then considered. The first is the advance in information technology and data processing which is found to have made financial markets more flexible for users, but also increased the scope for the transmission of external and internal "shocks". Related to this is the second systematic change: alterations in the nature of inter-governmental coordination of regulatory structures and macroeconomic policies. Globalization has changed the way in which governments co-operate. Increased capital mobility has implied a move toward international coordination of macroeconomic and regulatory policies. The third systematic change is the trend of regionalization involving economic and monetary cooperation among countries. This change counteracts the development towards global policy coordination.

As a result of these systematic changes, exchange rates will fluctuate less within trading blocs, but exhibit greater volatility among economic blocs. The overall impact will be more volatility in the 1990s. The author finds the influence of exchange rate volatility on trade and FDI, under reasonable assumptions, to be quite negligible. In addition, it is also emphasized that liberalization as a general feature allows economic entities to cope with macroeconomic risks more effectively.

In Chapter Six, Ingo Walter analyzes the role of mergers and acquisitions in foreign direct investment. It is pointed out that the high frequency of substantial policy changes in the 1980s, reenforced by the reduction in transactions costs associated with international trade and the rapid evolution of the multinational firm, has worked as a catalyst in promoting international specialization, intra-industry trade, and technology transfers. The increased international competition placed a premium on the search for economies of scale and economies of scope, low-cost productive factors and appropriate skill levels. This implied a restructuring that to a significant degree occurred through domestic and cross-border M&A transactions. For the U.S., this meant the fourth merger boom in the twentieth century. For Japan and countries in continental Europe this meant the first.

The chapter contains an analysis of patterns of M&A between 1985 and 1991. Based on an assessment of the permanence of these patterns, the author finds it plausible that the merger market will gain further momentum in the 1990s. He foresees that the European share of global M&A activity will continue to rise through most of the 1990s as the EC-market liberalization initiatives take hold.

Chapter Seven deals with foreign direct investment in emerging market economies. Thomas Brewer emphasizes the strong role of foreign direct investment in domestic capital formation. For the period 1980-1987, the annual FDI flow as a share of gross domestic capital formation was about 6 percent in the emerging market countries as compared to about 3 percent in developed countries. However, there is a great dispersion among countries. Among the emerging market countries India was at the low end (0.1-0.2 percent) and Singapore at the high end (23.4-25.5 percent). In his review of historical patterns, the author finds inbound FDI in some industries in the manufacturing sector to have been of crucial importance to the development of some key economies of Asia and Latin America.

The author begins with a review of the major determinants of FDI in emerging market countries. He divides these determinants into four categories: microeconomic, macroeconomic, macro-political, and micro-political. One important observation regarding the macro-political determinant is a trend toward liberalization in emerging market economies. In terms of micro-political determinants, the importance of creating FDI "issue networks" is emphasized.

The analysis of historical patterns of FDI focuses attention on a long-term shift in the sectoral composition as well as the regional distribution of FDI flows. The author emphasizes that Latin American countries received more than half of the FDI going to emerging market countries at the beginning of the 1970s, while the emerging market countries in Asia took over that role by the end of the 1980s. A strong but somewhat decreasing level of concentration regarding recipient countries as well as source countries is shown. During the 1980s, the ten developing countries hosting the greatest amount of FDI received about two thirds of all flows to developing countries. Three source countries–the United States, the United Kingdom and Japan–accounted for slightly more than two thirds of these flows. The author notices an important change by the end of the 1980s: increased outflows from firms based in Japan to developing countries. Another trend emphasized by the author is the increase in flows of FDI from emerging market countries as source countries.

In his assessment of the prospects for the future, the author predicts that FDI projects in emerging market economies will increase substantially. He predicts a total annual flow in constant 1990 USD of 35-40 billion by the end of the 1990s. The regional distribution will reflect growth patterns. FDI flows are expected to surge as investors are increasingly involved in undertaking market-seeking projects to serve the growing markets. Hence, the bulk of FDI to emerging market countries will go to Asia. FDI in the motor vehicle industry will be substantial, while the author does not believe in any significance of FDI in the service sectors of emerging economies. The Triad economies are predicted to be increasingly dependent on FDI in emerging market countries.

In the previous chapters much evidence has been provided for an increasing role of Japanese foreign direct investment. An in-depth analysis of this issue is provided by Thomas Andersson in Chapter Eight. The author starts with a discussion of five reasons why it is particularly difficult to assess the future prospects of Japanese FDI. He then surveys driving forces behind its past development. In doing so, the author reviews the Japanese success story and some of its international impacts. The internationalization of Japanese firms over time is also discussed.

In the historical analysis it is emphasized that the Pacific Basin has taken over the role of the Atlantic Basin as the core of world economic relations. Japan–the engine of Pacific Asia–expanded its flow of outward investment substantially in the 1980s. In 1989, the share of these investments of total domestic capital formation was above six percent–more than in any other major country. The Japanese success in trade was not matched in direct investment until the late 1970s. The special features of the Japanese home market was viewed as an obstacle to operations abroad. When Japanese foreign direct investment started to gain momentum in the late 1970s it was concentrated to Southeast

Asia. In the 1980s, the composition of Japanese FDI changed markedly in terms of sectors and regions. Southeast Asia remained important, and Thailand and Hong Kong experienced the highest relative increase of Japanese FDI in that area. However, Japanese outward investment became to a large extent directed towards the U.S. Gradually, a considerable friction emerged in the U.S. and by the end of the 1980s, the European Community evolved as a major recipient area for Japanese FDI. The sectoral composition of Japanese FDI moved in the 1980s from mining, natural-resource related investment and manufacturing, towards finance, real estate, transportation, commerce and service.

Japanese foreign direct investment is predicted to remain important in the 1990s. The flow to the United States may stagnate, and Japanese firms already established there will adapt to local requirements and increase exports back to Japan. The growth will occur in Europe–in sectors outside finance and insurance–but particularly in East Asia. As they achieve dominance in East Asia, the most rapidly developing region in the world, Japanese companies are predicted to become even more formidable competitors to western firms.

In Chapter Nine, Pontus Braunerhjelm deals with the prospects for small and medium-sized enterprises (SME) and their foreign direct investment in a globalized or regionalized world. The increasing role of these firms since the 1970s is emphasized. The chapter reviews major structural factors that during the last decades have formed the capabilities and competitiveness of small firm production. Based on this review, and on a case study of Swedish SMEs, prospects and strategies for small and medium-sized firms' engagement in foreign operations are assessed.

The special advantages of SMEs are found to be customization, prompt delivery paired with flexibility and the supply of related services. Small units are also claimed to attain higher cost efficiency as well as have flatter, non-bureaucratic organisations and highly motivated personnel. On the negative side, SMEs often experience heavy financial constraints and a scarcity of management and marketing knowledge. It is also found that in an increasingly integrated world, small firms will no longer enjoy protection from global shocks and disturbances in their home market. Hence, although a firm is operating entirely in its domestic market, it has to incorporate more global concern in its strategy. The author points to facts indicating that the expansion of SMEs is connected with increased heterogeneity in consumer demand and the implementation of new technology, allowing flexibility and high quality production. The expansion is found to be unrelated to sectoral or cyclical factors. With reference to a case study of the Swedish SME sector, the author focuses attention on the fact that Swedish SMEs base their decisions about foreign direct investments on strategic considerations rather than on considerations following the traditional behavioristic school of thought, meaning that FDI by SMEs has occurred in such distant markets as the U.S. and Japan.

The author predicts a continued trend–supported by income effects, technological progress and externalization–towards small units. The success of SME production in industrialized countries will, however, continue at a lower rate as compared to the 1980s. It is also projected that advanced subcontractors, producing systems or operating within niches, will to an increasing degree embark on FDI as their customers establish production abroad. For subcontractors producing low-tech components, FDI will be undertaken in markets where production costs are competitive, indicating increased FDI in Eastern Europe and other semi-developed countries. For small firms the options are almost identical, but the strategy of remaining local is found more relevant. In the adjustment process a large number of SMEs are expected to fail and exit. Networks and network externalities are expected to gain in strategic importance in the future and influence the patterns of FDI. Clustering is likely to occur to a large extent and influence the decisions of SMEs as to where to locate their FDI.

In sum, the dramatic increase of FDI in the 1980s is not an occasional adjustment of corporate "portfolios" of production facilities. The development is forecasted to continue at least during the rest of the twentieth century.The case for FDI should become stronger, particularly as "unfair" incentives ("carrots") and regionalization emerge. The development is expected to be further propelled by a world economic record stronger than that of the last two decades. The highest economic growth will probably occur in Southeast Asia. As an additional support to high FDI levels, the merger markets are expected to gain further momentum. As a potential threat to these prospects some global economic shocks stand out on the horizon at the beginning of the 1990s. The occurrence of any of them may lead to a wave of reregulation that in its most severe form implies decreased FDI.

With the exception of FDI to emerging market economies, the highest growth in FDI during the rest of the twentieth century is expected to come about in the service sector. Inward investment to the emerging market economies should also surge, but predominantly in the form of traditional market-seeking investment. Outward FDI from the U.S. and the U.K. will probably decrease as compared to the 1980s, while that from continental Europe, Japan and the first generation Asian Tigers is likely to increase. Brazil and Mexico are also expected to appear as important source countries. As a distinct feature of the 1990s, emerging market economies will increasingly appear as recipient countries. Asia is expected to receive the bulk of these inward investments. At an overall level, the Triad economies are predicted to be increasingly dependent on FDI in emerging market economies. A continued flow of Japanese investment to East Asia to support her dominance in that area is expected. Japanese FDI in Europe may also increase, while the U.S. market seems to have been saturated. Finally, the success of SMEs is predicted to continue and subcontractors producing high-tech products are expected to engage in more FDI throughout what remains of the twentieth century.

Chapter 1

Foreign Direct Investment and the Liberalization of Capital Movements

Lars Oxelheim

Introduction

In the 1980s a surge of foreign direct investment (FDI) occurred on a global scale with the total value of inflows reaching about USD 185 billion in 1989.[1] The growth came about at an unprecedented high rate during the latter part of the 1980s and the inflow of 1989 was three to four times the average flow in the first half of the decade. The average annual growth rate between 1985 and 1990 was 34 percent. However, growth was rather unevenly distributed. The developing world experienced a drying-up of inflows and its share of global flows fell from an annual average of about 24 percent in 1975-79 to about 14 percent in 1985-89.[2] At the same time, successful economies in Asia siphoned the flows away from the heavily indebted countries in Africa and Latin America. The bulk of the increase in FDI flows in the latter part of the 1980s took place almost entirely between developed countries, with a heavy concentration in the countries of the Triad: the United States, the European Community and Japan. In the aggregate, direct investment flows amounted to well over 1 percent of GNP in fourteen major industrial countries by 1989,

---

[1] A *direct investment* implies a permanent relationship between the investor and the object, and particularly the opportunity for real influence over the object's operation. Investments which do not fit this description are to be classified as *portfolio investments*. The aim of a foreign direct investment according to the IMF definition is to "acquire a lasting interest in an enterprise operating in an economy other than that of the investor, the investor's purpose being to have an effective voice in the management of the enterprise". The definition of foreign direct investment includes extended trade credits from a parent to a subsidiary, acquisition of shares, loans from parent to subsidiary companies, a parent company's guarantee of a subsidiary's loan, and self-financing over and above the normal consolidation requirement. However, exceptions are frequent. Japan and France, for instance, do not count retained profits in a foreign subsidiary as FDI. The common view of the practical minimum of equity for having an "effective voice" in management is a 10 per cent ownership. Again, France, Germany and the United Kingdom use other definitions. Hence, whenever cross-country comparisons are made regarding foreign direct investment, attention has to be paid to differences in definitions.

[2] The figures are based on IMF Balance of Payment statistics. To indicate the general uncertainty surrounding measurements of capital flows it may be emphasized that UNCTC (1992) reports the share of flows to developing countries in the latter part of the 1980s to be about one fourth of global flows.

compared to about .5 percent of GNP in the early 1980s.[3] Since this increase is higher than that for gross domestic investment, it can hardly be attributed entirely to cyclical factors.[4]

The playing field for foreign direct investment changed substantially during the 1980s. Economic integration increased, stimulated by, but also supporting, increased financial integration.[5] The development was propelled by a variety of forces among which improvements in the technology of information and a general wave of deregulation may be seen as the strongest.[6] The deregulation was to some extent just an acknowledgement (de jure) by the authorities that existing regulations had eroded and (de facto) become inefficient. But deregulation was also an expression of a change in the philosophy underlying national economic policy in the 1980s, reflecting a growing insight that excessive controls are not compatible with efficient resource allocation and solid and balanced economic growth. In the 1980s, controls were increasingly seen to discourage financial savings, distort investment decisions and make the intermediation between savers and investors ineffective.

The wave of deregulation that paved the way for foreign direct investment involved a dramatic change in the regulatory environment of national markets. The regulatory changes differed substantially between countries, and the variation concerns e.g., timing, activities of supervisory authorities and content of *external* and *internal* deregulative measures. The abolition of capital controls and a general opening up for inward foreign direct investment is an example of an external measure, while the relaxation of limits on activities in which different firms may engage and the relaxation of rules that discriminate against foreign-owned firms are examples of internal measures.[7]

---

[3] The Group Ten countries plus Austria, Australia and Spain.

[4] For industrial countries in the 1960s, 1970s and early 1980s, the ratio of foreign direct investment flows to GNP followed a pattern similar to that of the share of gross fixed investment in GNP and was clearly related to cyclical factors.

[5] From a conceptual point of view the two forms of integration are overlapping, since they both include foreign direct investment. From a causal point of view it can be claimed that the financial integration was triggered and made inevitable by the increased internationalization of firms.

[6] Deregulation and liberalization are used more or less synonymously in the literature to emphasize relaxation and removal of constraints and barriers that have limited competition, or insulated markets from general economic forces. These two concepts, which embrace efforts made by the market as well as by regulators will be used interchangeably in this book.

[7] At the beginning of the 1990s, privatization programmes in more than 70 countries offered new opportunities for foreign investors, especially in the service sector (UNCTC, 1992).

Once the deregulation had opened up the way for FDI, the growth of FDI was fueled by several structural forces. Increased regionalization and the "outsiders'" fear of increased protection and discrimination, maturing markets for international mergers and acquisitions (M&A), and the increasing role of services, which at the beginning of the 1990s accounted for 50-55 percent of total FDI outflows from most major source countries are the most prominent examples of these forces.[8]

In this chapter we analyze the link between capital controls and the global patterns of FDI. In the 1980s, deregulation and increased FDI proceeded hand in hand. Many of the mainstream theories would have predicted the opposite. Was the increase then just an occasional adjustment of the "portfolio" of production facilities providing no ground for extrapolation, or was it a manifestation of remaining obstacles of more or less invisible character? Moreover, what will happen in the future, when increasing inward investment is on the top of every policymaker's agenda? What elements will be used by governments to attract such investment in an increasingly integrated world?

A "race" for foreign direct investment is anticipated. The choice of word reflects the belief that when the value of inward direct investment is fully comprehended, the competition for inward investment will become intense. In an integrated world, little freedom remains for individual countries to become front-runners in splendid isolation. Rather, the race will be a narrow "elbowing" one where, especially in times of recession, measures that abuse "fair" competition may become common. Since policymakers in general care about being reelected, they are constantly looking for explanations for growth failures. In the absence of a supervisory institution of supranational character, the multiplicity of interpretations of "fair" competition provides such explanations. Under the pretext of being injured by foreign "unfairness", frustrated governments may be tempted to retaliate by reimposing restrictions on capital movements. In this way, a global wave of reregulation might be triggered.

The chapter starts with a review of the major determinants of the general deregulation in the 1970s and 1980s. It continues with a discussion of the case for FDI from the perspective of governments as well as corporations. The competition for inward investment is then discussed in the context of a perfectly integrated world, where international purchasing power parity (PPP) and the international Fisher effect (IFE) prevail. Finally, four potential crises

[8] See UNCTC (1992).

or distortions discernible at the beginning of the 1990s that have the power to trigger a wave of reregulation are discussed.

The Trend Towards Perfect Capital Mobility

The abolition of capital controls has opened up the market for FDI, but it has also paved the way for a race among governments to increase total investment in the nation by attracting foreign direct investment. Hence, in assessing the prospects for future FDI, one relevant question concerns the permanence of the liberalization of capital flows. History shows that periods of regulation are recurrent. The situation at the beginning of the 1990s resembles, for instance, very much the global situation in 1880-1913. Although a large part of the liberalization experienced at the beginning of the 1990s has to be seen as irreversible, the area of foreign direct investment may still lend itself to reregulation. The market for corporate control is much easier to regulate than the market for footloose capital. Hence, the permanence regarding this area is vulnerable to changes in governments' attitudes towards FDI. A related issue with implications for capital flows concerns tax harmonization and its influence on incentives to undertake FDI.

Why Capital Controls?

The label of capital controls covers a very large body of measures. All types of restrictions, though highly diversified, have a common goal: to constrain non-governmental cross-border investment decisions. The IMF Balance of Payment Statistics shows that a large part of these cross-border investments is foreign direct investment. Between 1975 and 1979, the amount of FDI flows from 14 major industrialized countries was twice the flow of portfolio investment, i.e. bonds and equities.[9] A temporary change occurred between 1985 and 1989, when the flow of securities was twice that of FDI due to a heavy increase in investment in bonds. In 1990, the opposite was true again.

In general, the imposing of capital controls has been justified on four grounds:

* they help manage the balance-of-payment crises or unstable exchange rates generated by excessively volatile short-run capital flows.

---

[9] The Group Ten countries plus Austria, Australia and Spain..

* they help ensure that domestic savings are used to finance domestic investments rather than to acquire foreign assets, and to limit foreign ownership of domestic assets.

* they enable governments to tax financial activities, income, and wealth and so maintain the domestic tax base.

* they prevent capital flows from disrupting reform programmes.

In addition, by imposing external regulations governments have paved the way for internal regulations, such as interest rate ceilings and reserve requirements, which have created opportunities for low-priced domestic financing to boost domestic economic recovery.

Efficient capital controls provide governments some degree of freedom in the making of national policy: governments may exert influence on inflation, interest and exchange rates. By "managing" these variables, they may also influence the relative attractiveness of their country to international investors. Depending on which variables policymakers emphasize, they can choose an appropriate policy regime. The role of capital controls in this context is shown by the triangle in Figure 1.1 which describes three optional monetary regimes (corners) based on three policy elements that can only be combined in pairs. The "impossible" triangle produces three policy regimes as paradigms. One combines fixed exchange rates, capital controls and national monetary autonomy (1). The second combines a fixed exchange rate, perfect capital mobility and no autonomy (2), while the third regime is based on a floating rate, perfect capital mobility and national monetary autonomy (3).

A characteristic feature of many small economies with a high degree of openness to international trade has been the strive for a fixed exchange arrangement.In general, they have also opted for monetary autonomy. In order to create this combination, they have had to reduce capital mobility by imposing capital and exchange regulations. Hence, they have opted for corner (1) in the figure. The erosion or abolition of capital controls moved them to corner (2). As a characteristic feature of the monetary turbulence in Europe following the halt in the negotiations on the European Monetary Union (EMU), a row of straddle-vaults from corner (2) to corner (3) has occurred.[10]

---

[10] Since the beginning of the 1980s there is a trend towards increased use of flexible exchange rates. According to the IFS-classification in IMF (1990), 74 percent of the member countries in IMF pegged the value of their currency at that time, while in 1991 the proportion had decreased to 65 percent. During this period, the proportion of member countries with independently floating exchange rates rose from 5 to 18 percent of the member countries.

Figure 1.1. The Monetary Policy Option Triangle.

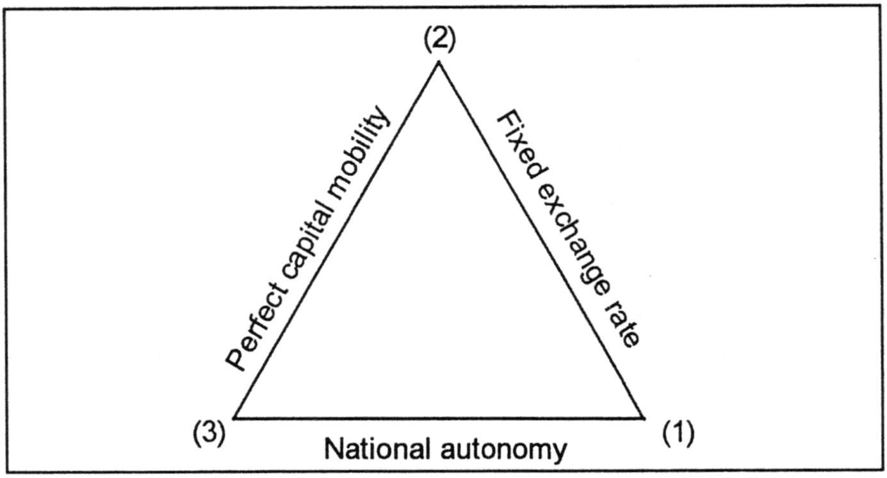

Financial integration is an aggregated measure of capital mobility. The most comprehensive definition of financial integration embraces both direct and indirect integration, as is seen in Figure 1.2. Perfect integration according to this definition means that expected real interest rates on equally risky projects are the same in different countries. Perfect (total) integration presupposes perfect indirect integration, i.e., perfectly integrated goods and foreign exchange markets, and the coordination of economic policy such that relative political risk premiums are zero. During the transition towards a perfectly integrated world, the competition for inward investment will come about in terms of remaining segmentating factors of quantitative character, i.e. deviations from PPP, relative political risk, exchange rate risk and relative taxes[11]. Hence, in a disintegrated world, policymakers may affect the corporate decision about where to locate a production facility by managing a set of international relative prices: exchange rates, relative inflation and interest rates. In general, they can create investment incentives or business opportunities by creating deviations from the international purchasing power parity and the international Fisher effect which express the links between the relative prices.[12] Additional business incentives controlled by policymakers are relative taxes and relative political risk.[13]

[11] Measuring financial integration in terms of capital flows only, either directly or indirectly by looking at rates of return, without going into detail about financial services for instance, is motivated here since capital movements must be seen as the catalyst and indicator of the future integration of all markets.

[12] For a discussion about the role of deviations from PPP and IFE in corporate strategies, see Oxelheim and Wihlborg (1987).

[13] Political risk is an expression for unanticipated policy-induced fluctuations in the rules of the market.

Figure 1.2. Outline of Total Financial Integration under Different Market Assumptions.

Form of integration	Market in country A		Market in country B	Effect on level of total financial integration if this form of integration does not prevail
Political and cultural integration	Politics and culture in country A	<---> ↓	Politics and culture in country B	Political risk premium
Integration of goods markets	Goods market in country A	<---> ↓	Goods market in country B	Deviation from purchasing power parity
Monetary integration	Foreign exchange market in country A	<---> ↓	Foreign exchange market in country B	Premium for exchange risk
Indirect financial integration				The above mentioned premiums and deviation equal to zero
Direct financial integration	Capital market in country A	<--->	Capital market in country B	Market inefficiencies
Total financial integration	Expected real interest rates the same in country A and country B			All above components zero

Source: Oxelheim (1990)

To conclude, in attracting inward investment during the period of transition from a national market to an integrated part of the global market, governments can influence the relative cost of capital by using an adequate mix of interventions. However, the pursuit of "fine-tuning" measures, or rather the investors' perceived threat of such measures being taken in a nation, will increase the relative political risk premiums charged for investing in that country. Hence, when managing the investment climate this way, governments have to consider the sum of political and exchange risk premiums as a constraint.[14]

As integration and harmonization gain further momentum, the opportunities for national governments to create a wedge between the domestic and foreign cost of capital– financial or human –via the traditional macro variables will fade. The measures that remain to be used in "fair" competition are incentives– "carrots"–not covered by the general harmonization and not violating

---

[14] Political interventions in support of the exchange rate might contribute to an increased political risk premium. For example, if taxes are increased to reduce a country's fiscal deficit in order to stabilize the exchange rate, the tax change may cause uncertainty among market participants about future tax policy and, hence, contribute to a higher political risk premium.

international agreements. Governments may also try to attract inward investment by increasing their efforts to reap the benefits from international regulatory arbitrage. This alternative may, however, be perceived as "unfair" from a competitive point of view. In order to make it less provocative, the arbitrage[15] will express itself in qualitative rather than quantitative terms. As a third alternative, governments can choose to take measures that violate international agreements and hope that no retaliation will come about.

The Liberalization of Capital Movements in a Historic Perspective

After the second world war, a period followed when policymakers believed that the best way to heal the economic wounds from the war was to impose various forms of internal and external regulations. A shift in opinion in favor of greater freedom of cross-border capital transactions appeared in the 1950s and manifested itself, for example, in the OECD's adoption of a Code of Liberalization of Capital Movements in 1961. The international deregulation was nevertheless quite modest and even underwent a setback in the 1960s due to balance-of-payment imbalances. Liberalization started to accelerate in the 1970s, gained momentum in the 1980s and is, as of the early 1990s, in a phase of completion. In a global perspective, however, there is an alarming inconsistency in the policy path as most countries implement further liberalization on the tariff side, while at the same time they increase the use of non-tariff barriers and measures that are incompatible with "fair" competition. Regulators are also beginning to realize that the economic problems that appeared in the late 1980s were almost as much a regulatory debacle as a financial one. This will perhaps mean that the 1990s will develop into a decade of regulatory rigor. Regulatory rules on financial institutions are, for instance, hotly debated issues at the beginning of the 1990s.

A brief historic review of the deregulation process in major developed countries may help assess the persistence of current liberalization. An overview can be obtained by looking at the development of reservations to the OECD Capital Movement Code as reported by OECD (1990). Members of the OECD have tried to liberalize capital movements through the application of the

[15] International regulatory arbitrage may express itself in a race between national regulatory authorities in introducing reforms aimed, e.g., at strengthening the competitive position of the financial markets in the countries in which they preside. The competition may concern the easing of interest-free reserve requirements imposed by national monetary authorities on banks' deposit liabilities as well as fiscal regulations in terms of withholding taxes or stamp duties.

principles of the Code, which has been changed only slightly since 1964. Member countries that imposed controls on capital movement operations have maintained reservations or derogations to items of the Code in the areas where restrictions have been in force.[16]

The development of the number of liberalized items, full reservations, limited reservations, general derogations and specific derogations under the Code is shown in Figure 1.3. The development represents a useful, and probably unique, indicator of the progress of liberalization of capital movement operations. The tendency towards reduced reliance on exchange controls is reflected in the number of reservations maintained under the Code. During the period from 1964 to 1990 nearly all OECD countries maintained some exchange controls for at least a brief period. While some countries applied fairly. strict regimes of capital movement restrictions throughout the period, other countries, traditionally more liberal ones, tended to restrict capital movements mainly during periods of balance-of-payments difficulties, exchange rate crises or undesired monetary developments.

In the 1960s, some progress was achieved in relaxing capital controls. The relaxation concerned predominantly long-term capital movements. A group of countries–notably the United States[17], Germany, Switzerland and Canada– already applied fairly liberal policies with respect to capital movements. However, most other countries maintained a substantial number of direct control measures as well as more market-oriented mechanisms– such as two-tier exchange rate systems–which interfered with capital movement operations.

The liberalization did not develop uniformly throughout the period from 1964 to 1990. Rather, the coverage of reservations on the capital outflow side tended to increase up until the mid-1970s. However, some of this increase may be explained by the relatively restrictive position of countries that became members of the OECD in the late 1960s and early 1970s. But the use of control measures also became more common in several countries during the 1960s and

---

[16] Reservations are either "full" reservations or "limited" reservations, where remarks to the reservation specify that a country allows certain capital movement operations under the particular item of the Code to take place or permit transactions up to certain limits. The derogations may be classified as "general" derogations –viz. a special arrangement whereby an economically less strong member derogates from the obligations of the Code–"specific" derogations, which have permitted members temporarily to reintroduce restrictions on already liberalized items because of serious economic and financial disturbances or balance-of-payments problems.

[17] Major parts of the internal deregulation were completed in the early 1980s, while some parts like, e.g., the Glass-Steagal Act, formally still remain, even though they are eroding gradually.

Figure 1.3. Evolving Degree of Liberalization of Capital Movements 1964-90.

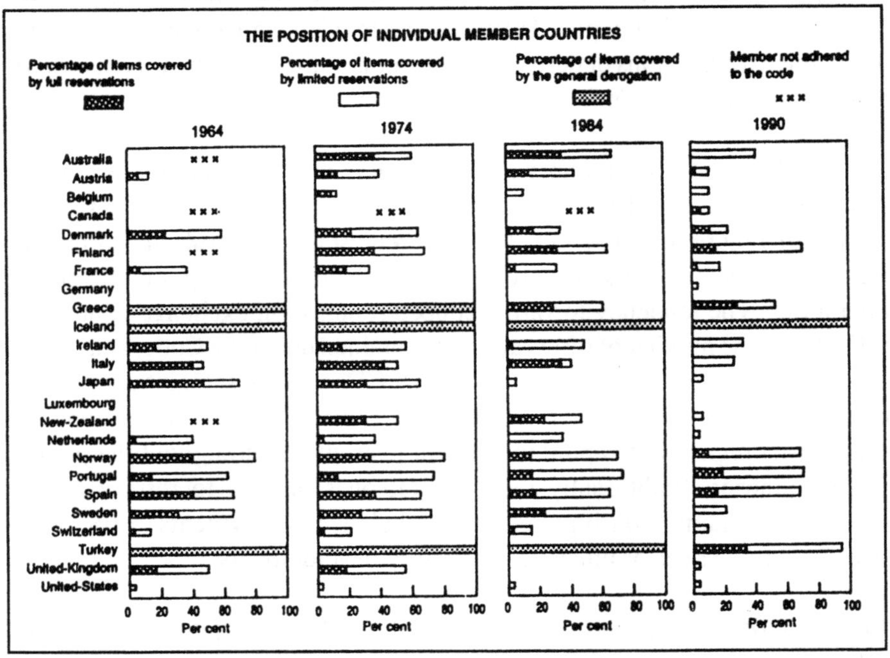

Note: The degree of liberalization–at any point in time–is measured by the number of "reservations" or "derogations" maintained under the terms of the OECD Code of Liberalization of Capital Movements. The presence of a reservation or derogation indicates that the Members concerned may restrict the operations covered by specific "item(s)" of the Code. Certain countries have in the past maintained "general derogations" allowing them to restrict the operations covered by all the items of the Code; only Iceland still does. The diagram illustrates the degree of liberalization of capital movements by reference to the "percentage of items covered" by limited reservations, full reservations or general derogations. Items covered by "full reservations" may be totally restricted, although often less than totally restrictive in practice. Where "limited reservations" apply, the items concerned may be restricted only to the extent specified in "remarks" to the reservation concerned. The interpretation of the diagram has to be cautious as until the 1989 amendment, the Code did not cover all capital movement operations. Most short-term operations, except for commercial credits and loans, were excluded. Furthermore, certain measures–like taxes on transactions and payments, two-tier exchange rate systems and currency deposit requirements–which may impede capital movements, were not considered to be restrictions in the meaning of the Code.

Source: OECD (1990)

early 1970s. A resort to indirect methods of restraining capital movements, which are not immediately considered to conflict with the obligations under the Code, was also common and increased in importance during the period. Control measures were extensively used to minimize the balance-of-payments implications of capital flows. Restrictions on the overall foreign position of financial institutions was one such measure that was used along with the application of reserve requirements, restrictions on interest payments, and other measures designed to discourage or penalize capital flows. These techniques were used even by traditionally liberal OECD-members, for example, by the United States in 1963-1964 to dampen capital outflows, and included a so-called "voluntary restraint" on direct investment abroad, an interest equalization tax and in 1968-70 a reserve requirement on Eurodollar borrowing by banks; and by Germany during 1971-74 with reserve requirements on bank and non-bank external liabilities and disincentives on borrowing abroad by German business.

By the mid-1970s, the liberalization of exchange controls was clearly moving forward. The process was dominated by the almost complete dismantling of capital movement restrictions in the United Kingdom and then in Japan. A number of other countries initiated a gradual reduction of the scope of their exchange controls. However, for some countries reregulation was on the agenda, as in Switzerland in 1978, when a negative interest charge was imposed on deposits of non-residents and their purchase of Swiss stocks and bonds prohibited.[18]

The liberalization process gained momentum in the 1980s during which many developed countries abolished most or all capital controls. Australia and New Zealand dismantled most controls early in the period (1983 and 1984, respectively), the Netherlands removed its last few restrictions in 1986, Denmark completed its external deregulation in 1988, France and Sweden achieved virtually full liberalization in 1989, and Italy and Ireland removed a substantial number of restrictions between 1988 and July 1, 1990, the deadline for achieving free capital movements for most EC countries.[19] During the 1980s, only France, Norway and Finland felt it necessary to suspend temporarily the freedom of operations not covered by reservations.

The liberalization process in the developed world continued towards completion in the early 1990s. More and more countries have opened up their economies to FDI flows, as evidenced by the fact that of 82 changes made in foreign direct investment policies in 35 countries during 1991, 80 were in the direction of increased liberalization.[20] However, in 1992 capital restrictions in some form are still applied in almost half of the countries in the developed world.[21]

---

[18] The restrictions were lifted in 1979.

[19] The EC-commission's 1992 target may, however, be seen as the date for having completed its internal deregulation as well.

[20] See UNCTC (1992).

[21] From IMF (1992) it can be seen that 11 out of 21 developed countries still try to maintain control by the use of capital restrictions.

Moreover, as a preview of what might come, Spain imposed limited foreign exchange controls in September 1992.[22]

Countries in the developed world were not the only ones to liberalize during the last two decades: in a relative sense they have liberalized the least. Newly industrializing countries exhibit the greatest relative liberalization followed by the developing countries.[23] In spite of the high speed of liberalization in developing countries, its completion seems still far away since these countries had a wide use of controls at the outset. In 1992, 114 out of 136 developing countries still maintained capital restrictions.[24]

The nature of liberalization varies, and the process has been less spectacular in areas where special factors motivate restrictions, on e.g., inward direct investment and the ownership of real estate by non-residents. Nevertheless, liberalization has been of considerable importance, especially with regard to the establishment of new enterprises by non-residents and investment in the financial sector. Asymmetries persisted for long periods. The process of liberalizing trade in securities began, for example, much earlier than that of liberalizing borrowing abroad by residents and the admission of domestic securities to foreign financial markets. The liberalization of capital exports seems to have been distributed slightly more evenly across items as a result of the dominance of economic considerations in the formulation of policies on outward capital movements.

As for national approaches to deregulation, two polar-opposite cases can be identified: gradual approach or total abolition in a single stroke. Deregulations since the 1960s suggest that most countries prefer the first mentioned approach over the dismantling of foreign exchange controls in a single stroke, with the timing and the scope of liberalization measures generally being determined by economic fundamentals and market pressures of various kinds. In the countries concerned it was often regarded as politically necessary to proceed step-by-step, analyzing the effects of each phase before carrying the process further. However, liberalization is contagious and, as it advances, the pressures favoring progress gain momentum. Governments may find it progressively

---

[22] Lifted in November 1992.

[23] Based on a study of 46 countries: 20 developed, 5 newly industrializing and 21 other developing countries, 1977-1987 as reported in UNCTC (1991).

[24] Calculated from IMF (1992).

more difficult to justify and administer remaining controls, and are forced to speed up the process. The experience of the late 1980s and the early 1990s also shows that several OECD countries abolished all exchange controls in one go. The need for political support to achieve liberalization led some governments to act decisively before interest groups could organize resistance to measures taken in the general interest.

Japan provides an interesting example of the gradual approach. Japan maintained extensive restrictions in 1964 when it joined the OECD, and embarked on a liberalization programme that year. Nearly all restrictions on capital movements were removed in a gradual process leading up to 1980. The initial phase of the programme focused on gradually expanding the number of sectors open to foreign direct investment, and on providing increased possibilities for both inward and outward securities transactions. Removing the last few restrictions on personal capital movements, which became completely free at the end of 1970, was the last step in the process. The Foreign Exchange and Foreign Trade Control Law of December 1980 marked the completion of the process of liberalizing Japanese exchange controls. Although the process appears rather gradual and smooth, it was closely linked to developments in Japan's economic circumstances. Denmark and France are two further examples of the gradual approach.

The United Kingdom (1979), Australia (1983), and New Zealand (1984) constitute examples of the "single-stroke" approach. Shortly after new governments were elected, all three countries liberalized capital movements more or less "overnight", making a fundamental break with past restrictiveness and the active use of exchange control measures as a policy tool. Exchange controls had long been used to protect the balance-of-payments position and to support the management of the exchange rate while providing autonomy to the domestic monetary policy. Despite the similarities of the single-stroke approach, the decision to liberalize was taken within somewhat different economic circumstances for each country. Being less related to the contemporary economic situation, the decision to remove barriers to capital movements was of a more philosophical nature reflecting a change in attitude and a shift of emphasis away from government intervention towards almost complete reliance on market forces. To a large extent, the dismantling of exchange controls was part of wide-range structural reforms and a fundamental change in the modus operandi of economic policy.

To conclude, liberalization of capital movements in the post-war period has reflected national economic conditions as well as government attitudes.

However, some countries have been forced to liberalize due to spillover from deregulated neighbor countries. Will the completion of a worldwide liberalization then be a stable end-station? Not necessarily. History shows that periods of war and general economic distress tend to be followed by periods of extensive use of regulations. Although "creative destruction" forces governments to acknowledge the inefficiency of regulations by formally abolishing them, the propensity for imposing new regulations remains.[25] Since some areas such as FDI still lend themselves to new regulations, the pendulum will continue to swing over time around a benchmark set of regulations that I would call the minimum set required to guarantee the market infrastructure, to promote the soundness of financial markets and to warrant competition. In a world where national markets are more or less fully integrated, in times of recession nations might start competing to attract investment by providing investors a looser interpretation of the regulations. The risk of reregulation is present.

Tax-Harmonization and the General Scope of Tax Reforms in Major Industrial Countries

We have mentioned relative taxes as one important investment incentive in the hands of policymakers. Competition and the removal of capital controls may interact in many ways with tax incentives with implications for the real economy. Each quantitative measure within the palette of exchange controls has a theoretical tax equivalent with the same restrictive effect. With hindsight, we may find that tax incentives had serious negative implications for the investment in production facilities.[26] One concern developed in the early 1980s that economic distortions resulting from higher taxes imposed additional and unacceptably high efficiency costs on the economy. The pursuit of less discriminatory tax systems became as important a budgetary influence as controlling the overall burden of taxation. In principle, this implied a move towards a system of revenue-raising that minimizes the negative impact of taxation on economic behavior, and resulted in national tax-reforms from the mid-1980s sharing three basic characteristics:[27]

---

[25] See Schumpeter (1942).

[26] In many countries, generous tax deductions have generally been allowed on household interest payments. For long periods, such deductions were allowed not only on mortgage loans but on consumer loans as well. Deductions of this kind channeled domestic savings in the wrong direction, away from productive investment.

[27] For a more complete description see OECD (1987) and OECD (1989).

* A reduction of income tax rates linked to a broadening of the income tax base, a reduction in the number of marginal rates and a lowering of top rates relative to the average rate. In some countries there have also been moves to integrate income and social security taxes;

* A rationalization and broadening of the consumption tax base through a switch to a general expenditure tax (usually VAT);

* A trend towards base-broadening and greater neutrality in the corporate tax system, often accompanied by a switch from household to corporate taxation and/or a better integration of corporate and personal income taxes (including capital gains).

The rationale behind these reforms was that high marginal tax rates threaten work incentives and aggravate the problem of tax avoidance. Moreover, these reforms were motivated by the fact that accumulated tax concessions had rendered tax systems overly complex and inequitable, distorting consumption/saving decisions as well as patterns of investment, corporate finance and production.

Perfect capital mobility will act as a catalyst in the process of tax harmonization, yet governments will probably continue the race to the bottom by attempting to attract investment with competitive tax reductions after the harmonization is completed. Eventually, a wave of reregulation might be triggered, also for tax reasons.

Changing Attitudes Towards Foreign Direct Investment

The attitude of government towards foreign direct investment has changed radically during the last three decades. The liberalization of capital flows is partial evidence of this change. Trends in attitude can be recognized for developed as well as developing countries. For some periods these trends differ between the two groups. In the 1980s, opinions about foreign direct investment were in general so much in favor, that global FDI experienced a surge of unprecedented size.

The shift in attitudes from the 1960s was substantial. In the progressive debate of that decade, FDI was claimed to be a tool of capitalism–a way of getting hold of basic, scarce resources and exploiting cheap labor in the host country. Furthermore, the exploiters were said to pay no tax in the host country, repatriating all cash to the country where they were domiciled. U.S. steel companies investing in Latin America were accused of belonging to this category. Prestige was claimed to be the reason why management preferred to repatriate gains and have them taxed at a higher rate at home. The use of transfer prices was said to be a way of escaping all taxes in the host country whenever such taxes were imposed.

In the 1960s, the prevalent method used by governments in the Third World was to invite *one* leading firm to invest in the country at favorable conditions. The unsatisfactory outcome of this strategy made governments in the 1970s try to increase the technological spillovers from the invited firm by adapting an adequate trade-off between stick and carrot. In the 1980s, most governments had learned their lesson and began to invite more than one firm from each sector in order to enhance competition and ultimately also reap increased benefits from transfers of technology. By the end of the 1980s, FDI had become the principal source of foreign capital in the majority of the developing countries.[28] However, this partly reflected a decrease in net lending by other private sources, especially commercial banks. Many governments in developing countries continue to distrust foreign investors and insist, for instance, on controlling imported inputs for foreign firms. The cases of Singapore and Hong Kong deserve to be mentioned as "success-stories" of how to attract foreign investment. The approach used by these countries is based on a two-way partnership that recognizes foreign investors on the same basis as domestic investors. Moreover, competition among foreign investors is emphasized.[29]

At the beginning of the 1990s the attitudes around the world towards FDI are somewhat diverse. While most developing countries are in favor of inward investment and welcome them in a very concrete manner, the criticism of FDI is clearly being articulated in other countries, for instance in the United States. In the European Community, inward investment is indirectly regulated through the Merger Regulation of September 1990 which makes the "reciprocity of access" an issue to consider in the treatment of non-EC firms. The preponderance of outward investment over inward investment may make the Japanese government reconsider its attitude toward inward investment. The arguments against inward FDI currently raised in many developed countries are based on

---

[28] See UNCTC (1992).

[29] This view is similar to the view expressed in Porter (1990).

nationalism and a fear that foreign investors are buying too extensively into the country's productive assets. On the other side of the coin is the fear that outward investment will reduce investment in the country where the investing firm is domiciled. This argument boils down to a fear of losing domestic jobs and at the beginning of the 1990s is common in small countries, not least in European non-EC countries.

The Need for Supranational Supervision

The future of FDI may be endangered if these arguments are disseminated and allowed to form the basis for policy decisions. However, when the wealth-enhancing impact from these investments are fully understood a new surge of FDI should follow. But, it remains to be seen what supranational institution will actually take on the responsibility that this is comprehended? Unfortunately, at the beginning of the 1990s there is no global institution committed to the task of guaranteeing the liberalization and supervision of foreign direct investment. The OECD, the IMF, the World Bank and the GATT are all potential candidates for this role, but serious drawbacks are attached to each of them in this context. The most important drawback may be that none of them has access to any mechanism of enforcement or punishment when inward investment is regulated, "unfair" competitive measures are used or foreign-owned firms discriminated against.

The share of world trade subject to non-tariff barriers is increasing. The share increased in the OECD countries from 15 percent in 1981 to 22 percent in 1989.[30] By implementing protection measures governments display their inability to subordinate the objective of maximizing short-term political gains to that of maximizing national welfare. At the beginning of the 1990s, a number of bilateral as well as unilateral retaliation programmes exist, such as the "Super 301" norms in the United States.[31] Aggressive bilateralism is blossoming. National campaigns to market a country as host to foreign direct investment have also become common.[32] They are supported by individual governments in the EC as well as by governments in non-EC countries. The race seems to have started.

---

[30] See Grilli (1992).

[31] Included in the Omnibus Trade Act of 1988, which provided U.S. authorities a mandate to identify and to undertake retaliatory steps against countries that rely on "unfair" trade practices.

[32] Campaigns such as "Invest in France", "Invest in Sweden", etc. that are organized and financed by governments.

Foreign Direct Investment from the Viewpoint of Government

The negative attitudes to direct investment — inward or outward — that were ventilated at the beginning of the 1990s are often partial in scope. Although the reasons for FDI are many and complex in character, governments' attitudes towards FDI should be based on a view in which trade and FDI are assessed together. In a historical perspective, the expansion of FDI in the 1980s had its parallel in the trade expansion of the 1950s and 1960s. While the trade expansion was fueled by multilateral trade liberalization, the FDI expansion was to a large extent prompted by the global abolition of capital controls. In the future, trade and FDI should be coupled and share the same position on the international policy agenda.

Trade and investment are closely connected and several different linkages between them can be identified. Ariff (1989) suggests four subdivisions of trade-related FDI :[33]

* Trade substituting–where foreign investment goes into import-substitution activities aimed at the domestic market;

* Trade promoting–where foreign investment takes the form of offshore operations producing for the international market;

* Trade complementing–where foreign investment is directed at providing backup and intra-industry support facilities in the export market; and

* Trade diverting–where foreign investment moves in to take advantage of unfilled quotas under preferential arrangements such as the Generalized System of Preferences.

Although there are conceptual similarities between FDI and trade, inward investment often exposes parts of the host country more directly to international competition by enlarging the tradable sector and reducing the non-tradable sector of the economy. The competition-enhancing role of FDI manifests itself in efficiency gains that may be even greater than those from trade. The role of FDI in provoking efficiency gains may be exemplified by foreign direct investment in the service industry in the latter half of the 1980s.

---

[33] Discussed in an article about the GATT negotiations on trade-related investment measures (TRIMs).

When the value of outward investments is discussed, the size of trade is often compared to the size of foreign investment. At the beginning of the 1990s, such a comparison indicates only a minor role for FDI: world trade being almost tenfold larger than global FDI. However, what matters is not this relation, but rather the relation between local purchases from suppliers and sales to customers generated from FDI in their host markets. For example, in 1987 the total sales by U.S.-owned firms abroad were more than double the U.S. exports.[34] Another indicator of the importance of FDI as compared to trade is the proportion of corporate profits earned through exports as compared to the proportion from sales in foreign markets by overseas subsidiaries. For example, a study of companies listed on the London Stock Market shows that the average proportion of profits earned through exports was 5 percent in 1987, while for the same year 39 percent was generated by their foreign subsidiaries from sales in foreign markets.[35]

To conclude, if a government takes a broader stance in analyzing the country's international competitive position and focuses not only on trade statistics or current account imbalances due to outward investment in a particular year, a positive attitude towards FDI should emerge.[36] Based on such considerations no persistent reversal of what has been achieved in terms of free trade and large flows of FDI should occur. However, this scenario is very vulnerable to shocks and disturbances in the world economy. In times of recession, a greater number of countries will want inward investment and the competition for it will be stiff.[37] Some countries will fail to attract FDI due to inferior domestic economic prospects, others will fall out of the running due to the use of "unfair" competitive measures by competing nations. Hence, many governments will be tempted to implement unfair methods themselves to retaliate or, as an ultimate measure, to reimpose capital restrictions.

---

[34] See Julius (1991).

[35] See Philips and Drew (1988).

[36] Julius (1991) presents an ownership-based "trade" measure that assigns transactions according to country of ownership rather than residence. Using this comprehensive measure she transforms, although with a warning that the result may be somewhat imprecise, the 1986 U.S. trade balance from a deficit of USD 135 billion, based on the location of companies, to a surplus of USD 23 billion, based on their ownership.

[37] This reflects the view that the national value of inward investment might exceed the value of outward investment in the short-term perspective, e.g., by new jobs created through inward greenfield investment.

Inward FDI from the Viewpoint of the Host Government

The major reason for welcoming FDI at a government level is that FDI brings:

* transfers of technology and management skills

* capital inflows with no debt-servicing obligation attached

* new domestic jobs

* domestic production capacity

The first item confronts governments with a delicate problem. They all opt for inward investment with as high a technology content and management sophistication as possible in anticipation of receiving the most qualified transfers possible. However, fear of such spillovers make the foreign investor bring as much knowledge as is needed and no more. The second item is of minor importance and is to be seen more as a complement to external debt than a substitute, since heavily indebted countries attract little FDI.

To assess the value of the third and fourth items a distinction has to be made between greenfield investment and acquisition of assets by foreigners. Both have long-term economic effects. Greenfield investments can provide new jobs or, in the case of an economy close to full employment, raise real wages. Foreign acquisition may have a similar direct effect on the job situation if the acquired asset was under-utilized. However, an acquisition may also have an indirect effect if the invested amount paid to the seller is reinvested domestically. The effect will show up here as a lower marginal cost of capital. In the short term, the two categories of investment may have different implications. Greenfield investment will generate new local jobs almost instantaneously, while acquisition may result in job losses to the extent that the new owners choose to restructure the business.[38]

[38] To the two categories of FDI mentioned, we may add governments' view of FDI as cross-border financial flows. Governments express concern from time to time about the balance of payment effects of FDI. However, the evidence of correlation between the size of the net sign of FDI and the sign of the current account balance is in general weak.

Attracting Foreign Direct Investment

What can a host government do to encourage inward investment? This question boils down to two subquestions: Can anything be achieved by government policies to attract FDI? And if the answer is yes: What constitutes a successful policy in an increasingly integrated world?

The first question can be answered by yes. Appropriate policies appear to be a necessary precondition for attracting foreign direct investment. However, in a study of 46 countries over the period 1977-1987, it is found that by themselves they are not sufficient to improve the ability of most host countries to obtain larger inflows of FDI.[39] Changes in the economic and market conditions are necessary as well. One plausible explanation for this is that liberalizing measures may have neutralized each other as incentives for inward investment since they were undertaken more or less simultaneously on a global scale.

Figure 1.4. Routes to a Foreign Production Subsidiary.

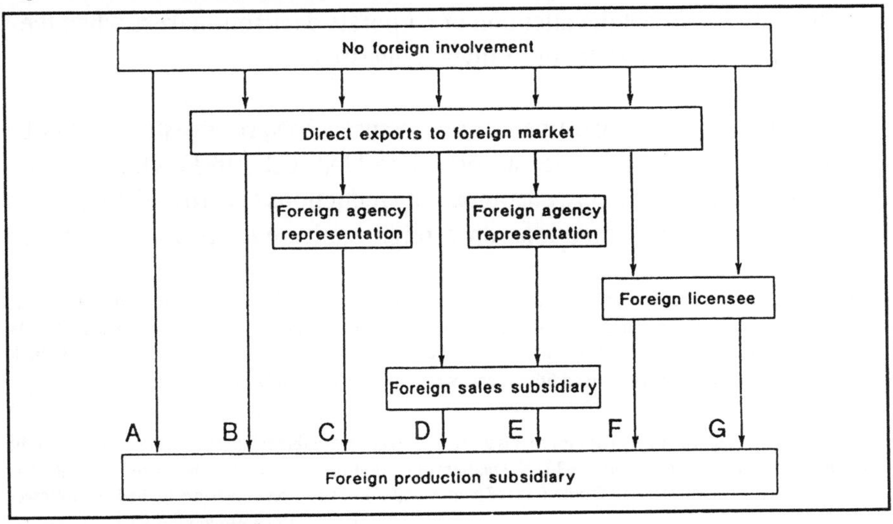

Source: Buckley (1982).

To answer the second question properly, we may briefly review the case for FDI from the corporate perspective along with the experience with past government policies. In designing incentive schemes to promote inward investment, policymakers must consider that corporations may engage in FDI in order to:[40]

---

[39] See UNCTC (1991).

[40] For a detailed survey, see Casson (1987), Chapter 1.

* penetrate foreign markets (market-driven FDI)

* obtain access to raw materials, technology or cheap labor (factor-driven FDI)

* reduce corporate risks (diversification-driven FDI)

* support or substitute exports.

However, in addition to recognizing these motives when designing incentive schemes policymakers also have to make sure that corporations receive their "signals". There are many ways a corporation can approach a foreign market, but most of them imply, as Figure 1.4 shows, some foreign involvement before establishing a foreign production subsidiary.[41,42] Corporations tend to follow the path of internationalization described by the "sequentialist school".[43] Few firms, although probably an increasing fraction, seem to follow routes A or G in the figure.[44] Hence, corporate decisions regarding FDI are based on trade and market experience, which supports the view that policymakers in a particular country may easily get the attention of corporate decision-makers when they change the incentives in favor of inward investment.[45]

The traditional policy instruments used to attract inward investment may be grouped into seven categories according to UNCTC (1991). One category contains ownership policies, encompassing reductions of across-the-board, as opposed to sectoral, limitations on foreign equity ownership. Such broad

---

[41] As paradigms, the decision process can be described as follows: A firm decides to invest in foreign production in a market, if the market 1) is large, 2) has barriers to trade and 3) offers low production costs. A firm decides to produce at home for export, if the recipient market 1) is small, 2) has no barriers to trade and 3) has high production costs. In addition, transportation costs have to be considered.

[42] Buckley (1982) reports frequencies for routes taken by two groups of direct investment in production. With reference to Figure 1.2, only 7 out of 43 U.K. smaller firms (first-time direct investors) opted for route A or G. A somewhat smaller fraction (5 out of 35) of continental European direct investors in the U.K. followed the same route, i.e., omitting the exporting phase on their way to full foreign production.

[43] See Johansson and Wiedersheim-Paul (1975).

[44] The threat of "Fortress Europe" may have urged many firms to locate inside the EC well in time before the completion of the "inner" market. Improvements in the international financial infrastructure have facilitated M&A activities and the route to production abroad without prior export experience from that particular market.

[45] At the beginning of the 1990s, 80 percent of world trade is undertaken by MNEs, 25 percent is intra-firm trade (UNCTC, 1992).

limitations have been explicit in many countries, e.g. China, India, Mexico and several other developing countries, but they have also been implicitly enforced in, e.g., Australia, Japan, Portugal, and Spain until the early 1980s. Extensive liberalization of the ceilings on foreign ownership took place in the 1980s.

A second category of policies contains of tax and subsidy measures. Taxes and subsidies are often combined in one category since a reduction in taxes is seen as tantamount to a subsidy. While France, as was previously mentioned, abolished most government controls on foreign investment entry in 1988, foreign investors continue to liaise with the government on fiscal incentives and taxes. Tax measures and subsidies remain the single most common policy instrument in the overall foreign investment regime.[46]

Policies concerning convertibility of foreign exchange and remittance of earnings constitute a third category. Many countries have eased or eliminated limits on capital repatriation to attract FDI. The major argument has been that a country repels inward investment if it maintains a tight foreign exchange regime. Price control measures represent a fourth category of policies affecting the attitudes of potential inward investors.

Performance requirements, including government mandates which affect the content and composition of the value-added activities within a country, constitute a fifth category. Requirements on minimum exports, local-content, foreign exchange balancing and maximum use of foreign personnel and other kinds of imported inputs belong to this group. By far the most common measures are the first two mentioned requirements.[47] This category is the only one that for the period 1977-1987 shows a tendency towards increased restrictions on FDI, mainly occurring in developing countries.

Sector-specific limitations and incentives may be seen as another category, that most commonly has embraced sensitive industries such as defense, broadcasting, transportation, banking and insurance. Many developing countries, such as India, Mexico, Singapore and Venezuela have begun to offer sector-specific incentives in an attempt to attract specific kinds of investments.

Finally, miscellaneous entry and procedural rules constitute a category of measures that are assumed to impose a considerable cost on a potential FDI.

[46] See UNCTC (1991).

[47] See UNCTC (1991).

Liberalization in this category has meant a shortening or elimination of application procedures.

During the phase of transition, policies belonging to all seven categories may be applied. However, full liberalization means that most of the policy options mentioned above no longer exist. What remains are the policies in the second and fifth category.

Elements of the Race

In a world of perfect total financial integration, expected real rates will be the same on projects that are identical except for currencies and jurisdictions. Hence, no risk premiums exist since perfect monetary, cultural and political integration prevail. The international Purchasing Power Parity and the international Fisher Effect both prevail. In such a world, where regulatory barriers have been removed, taxes harmonized, takeover defenses dismantled, economic policymaking coordinated, accounting principles and disclosure norms harmonized and transaction costs suppressed to a minimum, there is little left for governments to use in the competition for investment. Since the motives for factor- and diversification-driven FDI will have vanished, the corporate investment decision may to a large extent be seen as pure logistics. However, this scenario cannot be completely realized since some incentives will always remain for governments to play with.

Five major groups of incentives in the race to attract inward investment and encourage domestic firms to invest at home can be identified: 1) information advantages, 2) subsidies, 3) looser interpretations of international agreements, 4) cyclical factors, and 5) home-country biased consumers. The incentives can be characterized as inherent, such as language advantages, or created, such as subsidies. They may also be distinguished by whether or not they have a benchmark position. Some types of information advantages are examples of incentives that have a benchmark position, since they vanish when a country reaches the information efficiency of the rest of the world. Subsidies belong in the group of incentives that lack a benchmark position, since the upper limit of what a country can offer is very diffuse.

The first group of incentives is associated with information in general. Some of the advantages within this category are inherent and not easily eliminated in the integration process. The most distinct factor is perhaps language. For instance, the difficulty of the Chinese language may in the future conduce inward investment in China even though the country may be integrated in all the other dimensions mentioned above. The Chinese government may also "help" foreign firms to realize the necessity of being present in China by imposing rules stating, for instance, that all consumer information should be written in Chinese. Governments may turn a language disadvantage into a case for attracting a foreign investment.

Differences in education present another example of an incentive of information character. The incentive is of benchmark type although measurement problems exist. It can be seen as partly inherent and partly created. What is meant here is not differences in people's perception and interpretation of different signals that are related to cultural differences, but rather differences in competence. A government may give priority to education in order to attract inward investment and to persuade domestic firms to invest domestically. Hence, by creating a superior educational system, a country may attract FDI by offering engineers at a competitive wage or rather, in an integrated world, better educated engineers–in excess of what is reflected in PPP–at the same wage as elsewhere.[48] As a by-product of the increased national level of knowledge, the potential for transfer of technology will increase since the rise in knowledge may enhance the competitiveness of local firms and, thus, make foreign investors transfer more advanced technology.

Incentives of information character may also arise from the relative degree of bureaucracy. To attract inward investment, governmental information releases are improved in terms of quality, transparency and reliability. Another dimension of the same incentive belongs to the group of miscellaneous entry and procedural rules and concerns attracting foreign investments by offering a neat way of entry.

The second group of incentives for attracting inward investment consists of different kinds of subsidies. Again, some of the incentives in this category may be seen as inherent–at least in a phase of transition–or rather, perhaps, as inherited from the pre-integration period. They are common in political economies that are characterized by a high political involvement and a high average tax burden, implying that a bulk of social costs are carried by all citizens. Hence, by directing investment to such countries the corporation may

[48] In a study on policies to encourage inflows of technology, Blomström and Kokko (1993) report high educational standard to be an important carrot in the firms' perspective. A major argument for this is the lowering of cost for internal training that it provides.

get free access to the infrastructure, while an investment in other countries may be connected with high fees for the use of highways, telecommunications, etc. Incentives that are inherent can be used by governments in marketing campaigns to attract inward investments. However, they can also choose to create incentives by subsidizing improvements of infrastructure. Transportation, for instance, is highly subsidized in most countries at the beginning of the 1990s and accounts for a substantial fraction of total support.

Among the traditional subsidies we may identify the following instruments: 1) grants, 2) tax concessions, 3) soft loans, and 4) equity participation. Subsidies are generally seen to be incompatible with "free competition under equal conditions". How long they will survive in an integrated world is a matter of negotiation and international transparency of trade and investment conditions.

Grants (excluding supranational grants) are the most important component of total subsidization used by the EC and EFTA countries (Austria, Germany, Iceland and Portugal are exceptions). They are particularly used to subsidize capital formation and current output. Tax concessions are tax-code provisions that favor some sectors or economic activities, such as capital formation, over others. Although international comparisons are of limited value in this context due to incommensurability of data, the relative use of this form of subsidy is known to have been relatively high in the United States and in Germany. Soft loans comprise loans from the government to the private sector at terms more favorable than those obtained on the open market. The use of this form of subsidy has been relatively high in, e.g., Denmark, France and Japan. In Japan, most soft loans have been offered to small and medium-sized enterprises. Governments also offer guarantees on loans as a form of subsidy; this is particularly the case in Iceland, France and Sweden. Government equity participation involves a subsidy to the extent that the rate of return demanded by the government falls below that demanded by private capital markets. Among the EC and EFTA countries, the relative use of this form of subsidy is by far the highest in Austria. (See, CEC, 1990; EFTA 1986, 1987 and 1988; and Ford and Suyker, 1990).

Some reports indicate a declining but still high degree of subsidy in manufacturing. Figures reported in CEC (1990) and EFTA (1988) indicate a decrease in the support as a percentage of manufacturing GDP. Firms in the EC-12 received on average 4.1 percent in 1986-1988 when supranational support is excluded. The EC-10 average for 1981-1986 was 5.1 percent. Firms in Greece and Italy received the largest support, far above the average. In the

EFTA-countries firms received an average support of 1.8 per cent for the period 1984-1987, with a slight decline over the period. Sweden (although coal mining and crude petroleum production were excluded) and Austria exhibit the highest subsidy rates. For the period 1970-86, there is only a very weak tendency, if any tendency at all, of a declining rate of subsidy as a percentage of total government outlays. When Annual National Accounts (OECD) are used with input-output data, the highest figures are found for Sweden and Norway, both with average rates for 1980-86 of about 7 percent as compared to slightly above 1 percent for the United States.

Subsidies are used very differently in the OECD countries. However, most of them are used for sub-sector-specific purposes. The EC-average for 1986-88 (excluding supranational support) for sub-sector-specific purposes was 65.4 percent of total industrial subsidies, based on figures from CEC (1990). The region-specific support came second amounting to 15.6 percent. The average for the EFTA countries (SITC 2 and 3) for 1984-87 was 42 percent. Region-specific and other general support came next, totaling about 20 percent each (see EFTA, 1988). Switzerland exhibits the highest figure of all EC and EFTA countries for Research and Development subsidies (33.9 percent of total industrial subsidies). Denmark is at the top when it comes to environmental subsidies (5.8 percent), while the Netherlands is the country that devotes the largest share of subsidies to small and medium-sized enterprises.

The third kind of carrot for attracting inward investment is the stretchening of international agreements in a favorable way. This can be done by offering softer environmental requirements on production–both in terms of corporate obligations to pay for dysfunctions generated by their production and in terms of softening the minimum requirements on the working environment. In times of severe recession, governments may be tempted to impose environmental requirements on the use of products to stimulate inward investment. Recycling arguments for the use of predominantly scarce resources may be used to claim that products have to be produced in the country where they are consumed.

The fourth kind of incentive includes inherent geographical advantages such as differences in business cycles and seasonal patterns, and other such differences that will remain even as integration becomes more or less perfect.

Finally, a fifth group contains incentives that work via some kind of support to home-country biased consumption and they may be inherent or created. These incentives provide a soft alternative to traditional trade-barriers. Instead of imposing a tax on imports, consumption of goods and services produced domestically is subsidized. One way of doing this, which requires no payments from the government, is to play on nationalistic feelings. This is a provocative alternative, which will make wealth-enhancing global integration crack at a rapid pace.

To conclude, in an integrated world there will remain some acceptable incentives to be used by governments to lure inward investments. However, some tempting incentives that endanger "fair" competition will always be with us, too. They are characterized by being created by policymakers and by having no benchmark position. The major exponent of that group is subsidies. This kind of incentive is predominantly used by low-growth countries and is a characteristic feature at the beginning of the 1990s.[49]

Global Crises That May Trigger a Wave of Reregulation

Although the situation at the beginning of the 1990s is the most liberal in the post World War II period as regards capital controls, the sky is not without clouds. The use of incentives incompatible with "fair" competition increases as the competition for foreign direct investment gets stiffer. In the previous section we stressed that the increased global integration may be threatened in times of global economic distress. The relative frequency with which different incentives will be used depends on the character of the particular shock or distortion that causes the troubles. I will here emphasize four potential threats prevailing at the beginning of the 1990s: 1) an oil crisis of structural character 2) (an aggravation of) the global debt crisis; 3) a systemic financial crisis; and 4) increased protectionism. As a common feature, in their mild form they should all trigger increased FDI, while in their severe form they are likely to increase the propensity of governments to reimpose capital controls.

---

[49] The success of such a strategy is unclear since the use of too generous subsidies may signal future problems in the economy offering subsidies and hence repel rather than attract inward investments.

A New Oil Crisis of a Structural Character

The price of crude oil has swung substantially during the last two decades. In terms of the nominal price per barrel, it has oscillated from about USD 10 to USD 40. In real terms, the price is steadily approaching the level that prevailed immediately prior to the first oil crisis in 1973. It is easy to imagine that these swings may have had an impact on the distribution of wealth between oil-producing and non-oil producing countries, whether they are developed or developing countries. Such swings may have created a redistribution of global wealth that called for adjustment in corporate "portfolios" of global production facilities. Hence, they have actually promoted global FDI.

How large a shock would then be needed to trigger a wave of reregulation? The two oil crises in the 1970s provide very limited information since capital restrictions were extensively used at the time they occurred. But, as we have already noted, the liberalization process continued during the second oil crisis. Hence, what is worthy of concern is rather the structural issue: the uncertainty surrounding the future supply of crude oil. The structural problem is the diminishing number of oil suppliers in the long run and the concentration of these suppliers in a very narrow area in the Middle East.[50] The global supply of oil in the future will become heavily exposed to war. The IMF scenario of USD 65 per barrel during the Kuwait crisis is just a hint of what is to come. A war in the Middle East at the beginning of the next decade would lead to sky-high prices of crude oil, if any supply at all. This would lead to a dramatic redistribution of global wealth and a call for reregulation in many countries in order to keep resources inside a country. Hence, a substantial reduction of FDI flows will follow.

The Global Debt Crisis

Since August 1982, when Mexico announced that it could not service its debts and the global debt crisis became evident, more than 40 countries have experienced similar difficulties. The global financial system has responded in a number of ways. At the organizational level, the first reactions came from the IMF and the World Bank advocating internal restraints. The result was a declining standard of living in the indebted countries and decreasing foreign exchange reserves. The demand for foreign capital became great. To meet that

---

[50] At the beginning of the 1990s, estimated proven global reserves of oil consist to 66 percent of reserves in the Middle East. In terms of remaining years of reserves, estimated at current production/demand situation, it is just Venezuela and Mexico outside the Middle East that will remain important suppliers as from year 2010.

Figure 1.5. Secondary-Market Prices on LDC-Debt.

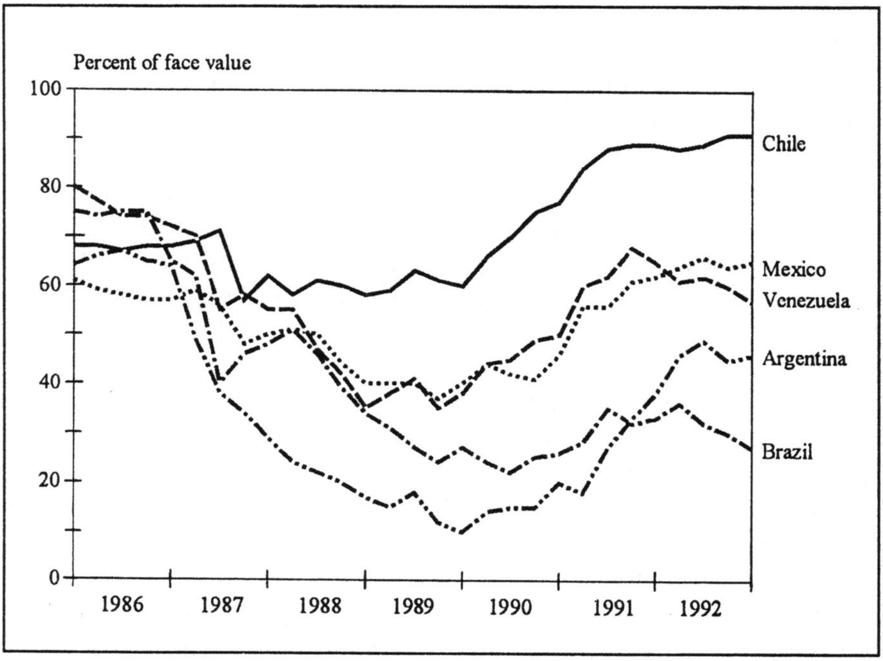

Source: Based on Quotations from Salomon Brothers

demand the "Baker plan" was launched in October 1985. Its success was small and in March 1989 it was followed by the "Brady plan" which included increased emphasis on comprehensive debt relief through market-based debt and debt-service-reduction operations.[51]

At the beginning of the 1990s not much is heard about the global debt crisis. However, the developing countries have seen little relief: they still owe some USD 1300 billion.[52] The global banking system, now in serious trouble for other reasons, may have been rescued, but the Third World remains in the middle of a crisis. This means that heavily indebted developing countries will try anything to improve their more or less impossible situation. When global

---

[51] Bank loans to Mexico, for example, were swapped for tradable bonds that either paid lower interest, or were set at less than the loan's face value. Interest and principal were guaranteed by U.S. treasury bonds held by the Federal Reserve of the United States.

[52] The external debt of developing countries has increased from USD 1095 billion in 1986 to 1313 billion at the end of 1991. The external debt as percent of exports of goods and services has, however, decreased to 118 percent at the end of 1991 after having peaked at 172 percent in 1986.

integration is discussed, this integration actually refers to developed countries and to 10-15 developing countries, while the bulk of the Third World countries has been more or less shut off from the global market. The Third World needs technological upgrading. One possible way for this to come about is through inward investment. The situation at the beginning of the 1990s is that there is a low, but growing interest in investment in these countries. The political and social unrest that characterizes most of these countries cools down the interest of foreign firms, although a political change has recently occurred that might revive their interest.

A solution to the debt crisis will probably reduce the political risk and increase the chance for indebted developing countries to benefit from the technological and managerial spillovers of inward investment. Regarding the change in political attitude towards foreign involvement, there are two indicators that make me believe in a solution that might let the Third World remain on the global business map. One indicator is a general increase in secondary-prices on LDC-debt signaling that the market believes in a solution. The upswing in prices (some major debtor countries are shown in Figure 1.5) has been accompanied by a gradual increase in turnover. The bottom quotations in the figure are in general registered for September 1989 following the decision of J.P. Morgan to "write off" all its LDC-debts and declare unwillingness to provide new capital for heavily-indebted countries. This signal made the market very pessimistic about an ultimate solution to the debt crisis and an average over-night fall in prices of about five percent occurred.

The increasing importance of debt-equity swaps in the provision of capital to developing countries is the other positive sign.[53] The first debt-equity swaps to take place after the emergence of the global debt crisis were in Brazil in 1983,

[53] Debt-equity swaps generally follow a basic pattern, where a bank sells, at a discount, an outstanding loan made to a public sector agency–or sometimes to a private sector enterprise–in an indebted country. An investor, most often a multinational manufacturing company, buys the loan paper at a discount and presents it to the central bank of the indebted country, which redeems all or most of the face value of the loan in domestic currency at the prevailing market exchange rate. The investor then acquires an equity interest in a developing country enterprise with this domestic currency.

followed by Argentina and Chile.[54] International organizations have then become very supportive of the debt-equity swap solution carried out in a controlled and non-inflation-fueling manner.[55] At the beginning of the 1990s there appears to be some scope for mutually welfare-improving debt-equity swaps.[56] Many countries have introduced new procedures in handling debt-equity swaps: e.g. a two-step procedure where the first step is a screening of projects applying for swap-permission and the second step is an auction open to enterprises whose projects have been accepted in the screening. The projects with the lowest bids in terms of face-value to be swapped will receive permission to carry out the transaction. The inflation constraint of the swap-procedure means that most nations just swap small amounts corresponding to an annual rate of some percent of their total debt.[57] Eastern Europe may, for instance, have a potential for welfare-enhancing debt-equity swaps since both debt and equity are in the hands of governments.

To conclude, the global debt crisis may influence the FDI pattern in two ways. If it is aggravated by some type of debtor-cartel, world trade and inward investment to heavily-indebted countries will suffer and a period of external reregulation may follow. If, on the other hand, the interest in debt-equity swaps continues to increase, a relief of the debt crisis and a global increase in FDI will progress together.

---

[54] Some non-residents had been allowed to convert external debt into equity investment at face value and at the official exchange rate as early as 1965.

[55] Two types of debt-equity swaps can be recognized. In the first type, the foreign creditor surrenders his debt claim to the debtor in return for an equity asset. In the second, a domestic resident in the debtor country is induced to exchange his foreign-held asset for a claim against the country's debt, and then to exchange that claim for domestic currency. The second type, used extensively in Chile, for example, can be seen as an attempt from a government to induce citizens to repatriate flight capital.

[56] I am not claiming that this is the ultimate solution to the debt crisis, but together with reform programmes it might contribute quite substantially.

[57] The master-case in terms of swapping while keeping inflation under control, is the "debt-for-nature" swap carried out between Conservation International (CI, a U.S. organization) and the Bolivian government in July 1987. CI purchased USD 650 000 of Bolivia's commercial debt through Citicorp for USD 100 000. In exchange for CI's redemption of this debt, the president of Bolivia agreed to demarcate some 1.5 billion hectares of tropical rain forest as protected area and to establish a USD 250 000 fund in local currency to manage the biosphere reserve. CI also assumed some responsibility for managing the area. In December 1987, the World Wildlife Fund concluded an even larger "debt-for-nature" swap with Ecuador. The concept behind the Ecuador deal was, however, different from the Bolivian concept. The face amount in the Ecuador swap was converted into local currency bonds linked to the rate of inflation. The interest on the bonds were then used to finance a variety of conservation projects in Ecuador.

A Systemic Financial Crisis

At the beginning of the 1990s widespread national financial crises have created concern about systemic risk.[58] Problems arising in one set of institutions may be propagated and their effects felt far from their origin.[59] What makes exposure to systemic risk a problem demanding ever greater respect in financial markets in the early 1990s are interdependence among market participants,[60] required time constraints for settlement,[61] and unsettled large-amount transactions.

A concern has also emerged over the way financial transformation took place and, more specifically, for the interaction between markets and policymakers. There are few indications that policymakers have been successful in reducing the scope and magnitude of a national financial crisis. In reference to interest rate liberalization, for instance, one may argue that authorities should have anticipated the vulnerability of the banking system to such a liberalization and taken precautionary action before the liberalization was implemented. This could have been carried out by, for instance, a close review of the soundness of the domestic banking system and the adequacy of the bank super-vision mechanism. One may also argue that authorities in several countries have aggravated the effects of the global financial crisis felt in their national market by forcing BIS capital-adequacy requirements on the domestic banking industry.[62] In the long run, there may be benefits from such harmonization. In the short run, however, common minimum standards to allow some degree of

---

[58] A plausible sequence of events of a crisis in the whole financial system starts with a shock in a single national securities market. Enforced by the rooting in one market, the shock is then transmitted to other national and international securities markets, and then to the whole global financial system of which they are parts. The ultimate consequence may mean the demise of the global financial system and tremendous effects on the real-world economy.

[59] A continuing advance in the technology of information and data processing with implications on cross border financial transaction meaning that value-creating transactions migrate to jurisdictions that are more conducive to economic enterprize.

[60] Kanda (1992) claims that the traditional understanding of systemic risk as a combination of credit risk and liquidity risk is analytically insufficient and therefore suggests an unbundling of systemic risk into four sub-risks. These are pure credit or default risk, interdependence risk, time risk and large-amount risk. Time is important because payment and other transactions are subject to a relatively short-time constraint, and some mechanical breakdown or one bank's failure will give rise to a liquidity problem for other banks. A large transaction amount causes a liquidity problem to the extent that it remains unsettled.

[61] Settlement and clearance are frequently taken for granted: yet it is precisely there that default and systemic risks manifest themselves in a crisis.

[62] The BIS-capital adequacy requirement, which is also in accordance with an EC-directive, states that a bank's equity must exceed 8 percent of its assets from January 1, 1993. During the years immediately preceding that date, rules implying a gradual approach to these figures have been applied in most industrial countries.

freedom in the transitional stage would have been preferable to identical regulation. The crisis in the U.S. thrift industry may be seen as another example where different elements in the transformation process have interacted in an unfortunate way.[63] In that case, the existence of deposit insurance schemes as a safety net generated moral hazard problems once the thrift industry became deregulated.

From past experience, we can identify the conditions conducive to financial fragility. They appear as combinations of factors like: a real economic shock, such as the 1973 oil price increase; a major change of regime, such as the shift from fixed to flexible exchange rates; a sharp tightening of monetary policy following earlier relaxation; heavy debt accumulation by major classes of borrowers or intense competition between financial intermediaries in new instruments leading to underpricing of risk premiums and concentration in high-risk assets.[64] It is easy to visualize the crucial role of politicians behind each of these factors. Hence, a structural oil crisis of the kind that was previously mentioned will increase the systemic risk. As a transitory problem, the machinery for managing crises may also be inappropriate for the kinds of problems that can emerge.[65]

To conclude, national financial markets have become so closely interlinked that a disruption occurring in one market can hardly be prevented from spreading to others. Supranational authorities have expressed concern about systemic risks and are working on improving supervision of financial markets. However, the art of financial engineering has made their task more or less impossible. The capital adequacy rules are both blunt and arbitrary. Moreover, the timing of their implementation increases rather than decreases the systemic risk. Hence, the risk of a break-down of the whole global financial system and a dramatic setback of economic integration is not negligible. The easier access to information realized by the progress in information technologies justifies such fears.[66] The worst-case scenario would mean a return to a world of barter trade.

---

[63] The S&L (savings and loan) crisis.

[64] See, for instance, Kanda (1992).

[65] According to the Minski hypothesis, it is not just a matter of transitory problems but recurrent *selfenforcing* crises.

[66] One more reason for concern is that progress in information technologies has reduced the "filtering" of information in a way that may cause destabilizing effects on financial markets, at least until the market participants learn how to deal with the new situation. It may, for instance, lead to greater market impact of false but sensational news as compared to accurate but unspectacular news.

Increasing Regionalism

Revolutionary technological changes in telecommunications, electronic trading and data processing, have increasingly strengthened linkages between national markets by contributing to enhanced transparency of their potential incompatibility. Since international compatibility is a crucial test for the survival of a market, governments have increasingly felt the pressure to adjust regulations and macroeconomic policies to external forces.[67] This pressure has provided additional reasons for individual governments to look for regional cooperation that may provide a rationale for unpopular economic policy measures. The cooperation may also provide an insurance against a prolonged crisis in the international financial system, since individual governments can rely on the "survival" of the larger entity.[68] Regionalization of trade is not necessarily a bad thing. It does not automatically lead to lower global welfare, but trading blocs carry risks that should not be underestimated. Regional trade arrangements may easily attract "wrong" kinds of investment and have strong negative consequences on global trade and welfare.

The ongoing increase in regionalism should cause concern in that it may distort rather than pave the way to perfect integration. At the beginning of the 1990s, regionalism is on the policy agenda everywhere. The Triad-regions built up around the nodes of Japan, Germany (EC) and the United States (NAFTA) can easily develop into fortresses and bring us back to a segmented global market.[69] The prolonged negotiations in the Uruguay Round - eight in a series of international trade negotiations conducted within the GATT framework - signal problems for free world trade. On the positive side, i.e., if negotiations are concluded successfully; for the first time rules will be provided for the global trade in services and intellectual property rights. In addition, more stringent rules concerning the use of unilateral remedies against partners' trade practices such as antidumping and countervailing actions will be made explicit.

---

[67] The development of the Euromarket in the 1960s as a response to the introduction of capital controls in New York should have provided a lesson for national authorities.

[68] For a further discussion, see Chapter 5.

[69] In 1990, intraregional trade in goods accounted for 61 percent of total trade in goods of the European Community (up from 56 percent in 1980), 41 percent for Asia, including Japan (up from 37 percent) and 35 percent for North America (up from 27 percent) according to UNCTC (1992).

Regional economic integration of the kind that has emerged during the last ten years, involving both the world's largest economies as well as selected developing countries, have an increasing value in explaining patterns of FDI. When future FDI patterns are discussed in Chapter 4, regional integration is found to be a major explanatory factor. In this context, it can be emphasized that "too much" investment from countries outside the regional blocs may create frustrated source-country governments. To the extent that the investments are triggered by anti-dumping rules, minimum-local-content requirement rules, etc., applied by the region, they will increase the risk of a global wave of reregulation of capital flows.

Concluding Remarks

In a world in transition towards integration, the diminishing interest of corporations to engage in FDI might be revitalized by a government's provision of conventional incentives to attract inward investment. In this pre-phase of the race, the competition for inward investment will also take the form of a gradual elimination of remaining distortions and a lowering of taxes.

The competition for inward investment will probably become intense. As the state of perfect total global integration approaches, the degree of freedom in policymaking will decrease, and the use of incentives–inherent or created–will become a prominent feature of the competition for FDI. A "race" for investment will commence. When the world economy is booming, the implementation of incentive schemes will probably be low, since they challenge the foundations of "fair" competition. The incentives used in boom times will be predominantly soft; i.e. of a quality rather than a quantity character, aimed at enhancing general productivity of a country by improving, for instance, the quality of its educational system and infrastructure. However, some incentive measures may also be welfare-decreasing to the extent the purport of international commitments are streched to appear as an incentive for inward investment, e.g., lowering the environmental requirements on production. In times of recession, fueled by nationalism, the use of "hard" incentives, such as cash-flow related activities, e.g. the offering of grants and loans under favorable conditions, is likely to increase.

Within a balanced-budget framework, the only constraint on the use of subsidies in a tax-harmonized world is the availability of fiscal resources. It is important to note, however, that only the tax rate and base are harmonized. By giving priority to subsidies for attracting inward investment, some other tax-financed projects have to be postponed in the short-term perspective, but more resources may become available in the long-term perspective with the potential enlargement of the tax-base that new investments offer. In an integrated world, access to global saving is free and governments may find it tempting in times of economic distress to finance subsidies through loans, making the upper limit of their efforts to attract investments a more subtle question.

In periods of long recession or high turbulence in the world economy due to various shocks, there is a palpable threat that the use of incentives conflicting with the tradition of "fair" competition will be too extensive and lead to trade and investment wars. The major threats are incentives that are created by governments and have no benchmark position. In the worst case scenario, the risk is obvious that governments will reimpose capital controls and that global welfare will take a giant leap backwards. To prevent this scenario from coming true, the creation of a supranational institution with the task of supervising competition with regard to FDI as well as trade has to be given high priority among policymakers around the world.

References

Ariff, M. (1989), "TRIMs A North-South Divide or a Non-Issue?", *World Economy*, September.

Blomström, M. and A. Kokko (1993), "Policies to Encourage Inflows of Technology through Foreign Multinationals", *NBR Working Paper*, March.

Buckley P.J. (1982), "The Role of Exporting in the Market Servicing Policies of Multinational Manufacturing Enterprises: Theoretical and Empirical Perspectives" in Czinkota, M.R. and G. Tesar (eds), *Export Management - An International Context*, New York.

Casson, M. (1987), *The Firm and the Market: Studies on the Multinational Enterprise and the Scope of the Firm*, Oxford: Basil Blackwell.

CEC (1990), *Second Survey on State Aids in the European Community in the Manufacturing and Certain Other Sectors*, Brussels: Office for Official Publications of the European Communities, Commission of the European Communities.

EFTA (1986), *Economic Committee Working Party on Government Aids, Final Report*, Geneva: European Free Trade Association.

EFTA (1987), *Government Aid in 1985 and 1986*, Geneva: European Free Trade Association.

EFTA (1988), *Government Aid in 1987*, Geneva: European Free Trade Association.

Ford, R.P. and W. Suyker (1990), "Industrial Subsidies in the OECD Economies", OECD Department of Economics and Statistics, *Working Paper*, No 74, January.

Grilli, E.R. (1992), "Challenges to the Liberal International Trading System, GATT and the Uruguay Round", *Banca Nazionale del Lavoro, Quarterly Review*, No. 181, June.

IMF (1990), *Annual Report on Exchange Arrangements and Exchange Restrictions*, Washington: IMF.

IMF (1992), *Annual Report on Exchange Arrangements and Exchange Restrictions*, Washington: IMF.

Johansson, J. and F. Wiedersheim-Paul (1975), "The Internationalization of the Firm - Four Swedish Cases", *Journal of Management Studies*, 12, October.

Julius, D. (1991), "Foreign Direct Investment: The Neglected Twin of Trade", Group of Thirty, *Occasional Paper*, 33, Washington.

Kanda, H. (1992), "Systemic Risk and International Financial Markets" in Edwards, F.R. and H.T. Patrick (eds.) *Regulating International Financial Markets; Issue and Policies*, Kluwer Academic Publishers.

OECD (1987), *Taxation in Developed Countries*, Paris: OECD.

OECD (1989), *Economies in Transition - Structural Adjustments in OECD Countries*, Paris.

OECD (1990), *Liberalization of Capital Movements and Financial Services in the OECD Area*, Paris: OECD.

Oxelheim, L. (1990), *International Financial Integration*, Heidelberg: Springer Verlag.

Oxelheim, L. and C. Wihlborg (1987), *Macroeconomic Uncertainty - International Risks and Opportunities for the Corporation*, Chichester: John Wiley & Sons.

Phillips and Drew Fund Management (1988), *Pension Fund Indicators: A Long Term Perspective on Pension Fund Investment*, London: Phillips and Drew Fund Management, September.

Porter, M. (1990), *Competitive Advantage of Nations*, New York: Free Press.

Schumpeter, J.A. (1942), *Capitalism, Socialism and Democracy*, New York: Harper & Row.

UNCTC (1991), *Government Policies and Foreign Direct Investment*, Series A, No. 17, New York: United Nations Centre on Transnational Corporations.

UNCTC (1992), *World Investment Report*, New York: United Nations Centre on Transnational Corporations.

Chapter 2
Prospects for the World Economy

Kjell Andersen

Introduction

There are important economic factors that point to stronger economic growth in the1990s than during the last l5-20 years. But I need hardly stress that there is great uncertainty. Our knowledge of how the economic system is functioning is incomplete. In addition to the uncertainties related to economic factors discussed later, it is difficult to assess the implications of the political upheavals of the last few years. The liberation of the Eastern European countries, the breakdown of the Soviet Union, the advance of islam, and the possible proliferation of nuclear weapons may contribute to political, ethnic and religions conflicts and create new security problems. These conflicts and problems may in turn affect economic developments. In the following, however, I have assumed that political factors will not exert major adverse effects on the world economy.

Longer term projections usually start with an examination of the supply side, i.e. the growth of the labor force and productivity trends. Demographic projections suggest that the population of working age (15-64 years) will grow more slowly than earlier. However, demography is unlikely to be a decisive factor for the growth of activity since the participation rate–the proportion of people of working age participating in the labor force–is likely to rise and since there is a pool of unemployed that can be drawn upon. I shall therefore start with a discussion of the outlook for productivity.

Productivity Growth

Productivity growth is a matter of fundamental importance. It constitutes an important part of the growth of productive capacity, it is the basis for higher standards of living, and it serves to reduce inflationary pressures. As is seen from Table 2.1, a surprising feature of the last fifteen years has been a marked slowdown in productivity growth. In OECD countries combined, total factor

Table 2.1. Productivity in the Business Sector in OECD Countries.
Per cent change per annum

	1960-73	1973-79	1979-90
Total factor productivity	2.8	0.5	0.8
Labour	4.1	1.4	1.5
Capital	- 0.5	- 1.6	- 0.7

Source: OECD (1992).

productivity–a weigthed average of labor and capital productivity–fell from nearly 3 per cent a year in 1960-73 to 0.5 per cent in 1973-79. Although picking up somewhat, it has remained low also in the 1980s (0.9 per cent). Labor productivity showed an even sharper decline, falling from an annual average of 4.1 per cent in 1960-73 to 1.4 per cent in 1973-79 and rising only slightly to 1.5 per cent in the 1980s. Capital productivity has been falling throughout, but less rapidly in the 1980s than in the previous decade.

The decline in recorded productivity growth may in part be due to measurement problems. These are greatest in the service sectors. In most countries the weight of these sectors in the economy is growing. Under-recording may therefore have increased over time. But more fundamental factors have also been at work.

* First, the diminution or disappearance of certain *positive* factors which were important in the "Golden Age" up to the early 1970s. This applies for instance to the re-allocation of resources from low productivity sectors (like agriculture) to high productivity sectors (like industry), the liberalization of international trade, and the catchup of other countries with the United States, the technological leader.

* Secondly, the appearance of certain *negative* factors, including growing government interventions and higher taxes which have meant that most OECD economies have been functioning less well than earlier, reflected inter alia in stronger inflationary pressures. These pressures, which were accentuated by the two oil price chocks in 1973-74 and 1979-80, led to a tightening of economic policies, lower profits and investment, and therefore slower introduction of new technologies.

Productivity growth, although recovering somewhat, has as noted remained low in the 1980s. But there are in my view reasons to expect an improvement in the years ahead. I shall discuss four factors pointing in that direction.

Lower Inflation and Better Profitability

The first is the situation at the outset of the decade. In the OECD-countries (which account for around two-thirds of world output) much of the 1980s was a period of correction after the inflationary and other distortions that had marked the 1970s–and much was corrected. Two developments are of particular importance. The first is that inflation has been significantly reduced. Figure 2.1 shows that, in the major OECD countries, inflation came down in the 1980s and, unusually, remained low during the cyclical upturn in the last few years of the decade. Better price stability increases confidence in a stable economic development, improves the basis for business planning and investment decisions, and contributes to both higher and more efficient investment.

The second factor is the restoration of business profitability. Measured by the share of profits in value added, profitability in the seven major OECD countries (the G 7) has at the beginning of the 1990s regained the level of the 1960s. Measured by the rate of return on invested capital, profitability is also high, although still somewhat lower than in the pre-1973 period. At the same time, balance sheets have improved in the sense that corporate debt in most OECD countries outside the United States, particularly in Europe, has been significantly reduced. The improved profit situation is a matter of fundamental importance. History shows that a reasonable rate of profit tends to be associated with high investment and strong growth.

In these two respects– inflation and profitability–we have got off to a good start, and the improvement has already contributed to a brisk recovery of investment and activity. Business fixed investment in the OECD area increased by around 10 per cent in volume in both 1988 and 1989 and continued to rise in 1990. Moreover, the share of machinery and equipment–the main vehicle by which new techniques are being introduced–has been higher than earlier, probably foreshadowing stronger productivity growth. Business fixed investment levelled off in 1991 and has remained weak in 1992, but this is a normal cyclical weakening in response to tighter policies and higher interest rates. A recovery of investment growth is likely as the business cycle turns up again, probably in 1993.

Figure 2.1. Output Growth and Inflation in Six Major Industrial Countries. [1]

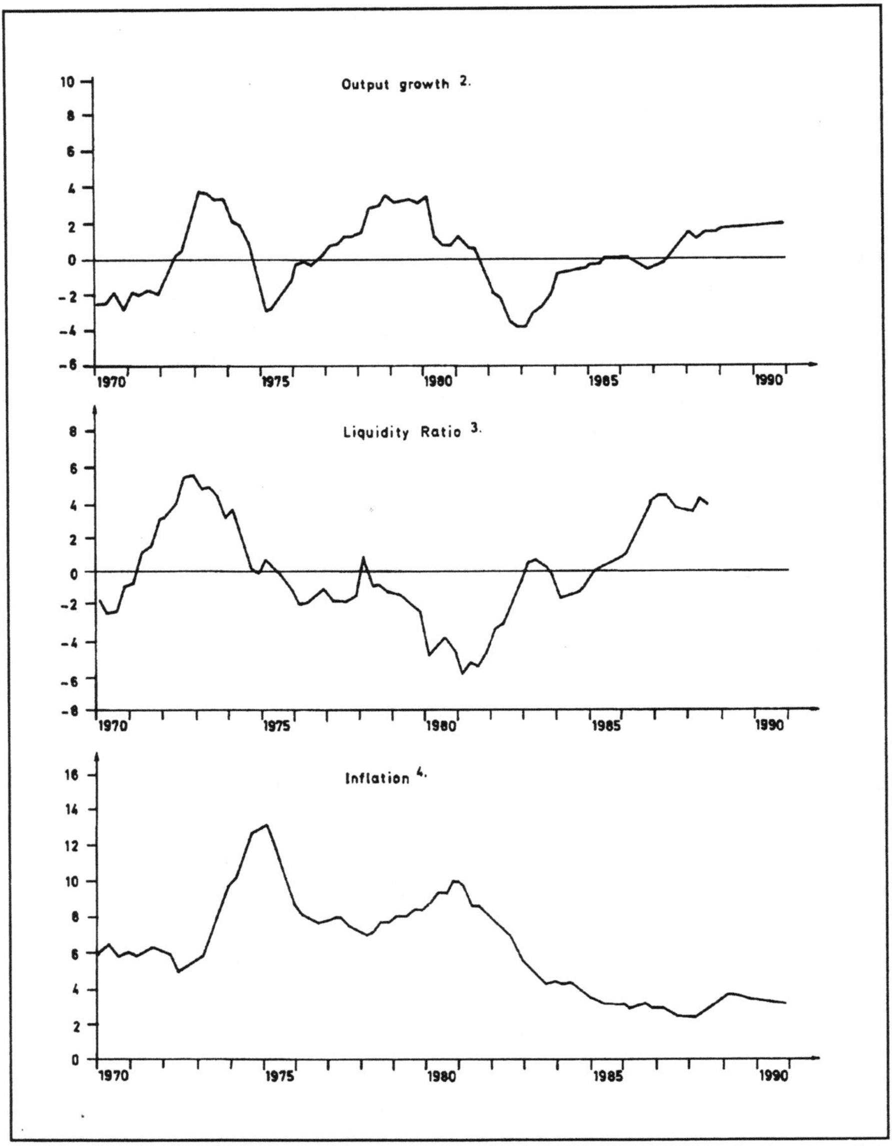

[1] The weights used for aggregation are a moving average of the 12 previous quarters of the U.S. dollar values of respective GNPs.

[2] Output growth is calculated for each country as the percentage deviation from the trend over the period 1970 01 to 1988 03.

[3] The liquidity ratio (M/GNP) is calculated for each country as the percentage deviation from the trend over the period 1970 01 to 1988 03. Broad money (M) is defined as M2 (United States, France, Italy, and Canada), M2 + CDs (Japan), or M3 (Federal Republic of Germany, and United Kingdom).

[4] Rate of change in the GNP/GDP deflator over the same quarter of previous year.

Source: IMF (1991).

Given the liberal policies pursued almost everywhere, there is reason to believe that inflation will remain relatively low and that a reasonable rate of profitability will be maintained. If so, important pre-conditions for stronger economic growth will exist.

The New Liberalism

Following the development towards dirigism and socialism during much of this century, the last ten years have seen a marked change towards liberalism, by some characterized as a "capitalist" revolution. The movement is general, not only affecting the OECD countries, i.e. the Western industrialized world, but also the Eastern and Southern parts of the globe. All OECD-countries irrespective of the political colour of governments–Mitterand and Gonzales as well as Major and Kohl–liberalize their economies: they deregulate and privatize, they reform tax systems and they reconsider welfare provisions. They do this with a view to increase incentives and improve the functioning of the economy, believing that this is the best way to achieve sustainable non-inflationary growth and high employment. There is reason to believe that the new policy emphasis will be maintained. It would be surprising if it did not contribute–perhaps importantly–to greater efficiency and better economic performance generally, although much will of course depend on the speed with which economic reforms will be introduced.

Let me add a comment on one particular aspect of structural reform, namely the efforts made to reduce the relative size of public expenditure, both purchases of goods and services and transfer payments. The efforts made to these ends include measures designed to make the public sector more efficient, to privatize certain government activities, to cut or abolish subsidies to business, and reduce the abuse of the social security system. Success in reducing government expenditure will in turn enable lower tax rates, with positive effects on incentives and resource allocation. There is reason to believe that these efforts will have a favorable impact on productivity growth. A rough indication of this can be seen from Figure 2.2: on average, the countries with the strongest increase in public expenditure in relation to GDP over the last twenty years were the ones which experienced the sharpest slowdown in productivity growth.

Figure 2.2. Public Expenditure and Total Productivity.

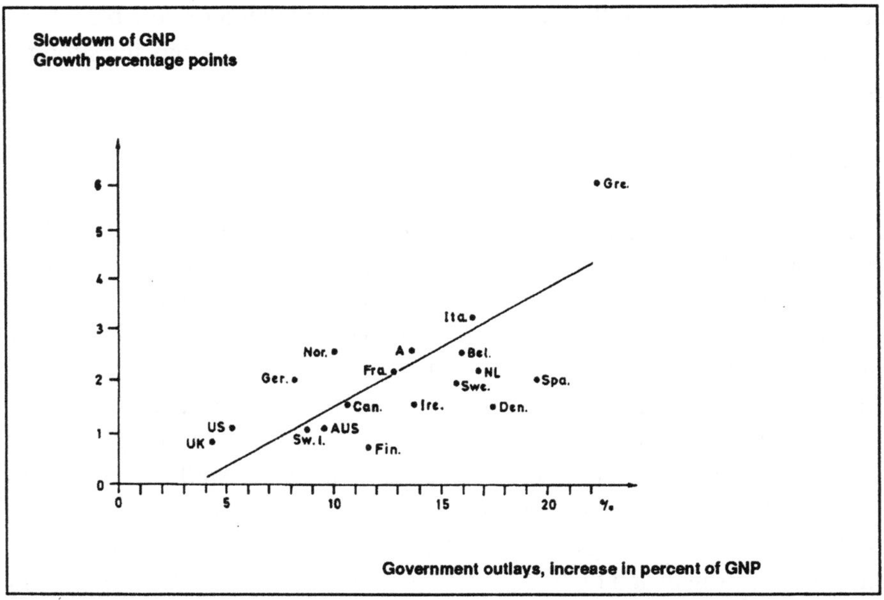

Source: OECD.

Economic Integration

Internationalization has accelerated over the last decade. Despite the increasing use of non-tariff barriers, in particular by OECD countries, trade has continued to outpace production by a large (albeit narrowing) margin. Financial markets now operate worldwide, international investment flows have multiplied, companies are spreading their production activities across the globe, and cross-border alliances and joint ventures have speeded up the dissemination of new technologies. Internationalization has meant stronger competition and, presumably, greater efficiency. There is reason to believe that this tendency will continue.

Regional integration is growing both in breadth and depth. The EC, originally consisting of 6 countries, now include 12, and additional candidates for membership or association are appearing: the EFTA countries and some of the Eastern European countries. The implementation of the Single European Market represents an important deepening of the integration process. The removal of restrictions on the free movement of goods, services, capital and labor in a market of 340 million people represents a particularly important manifestation of the new liberalism. The perspective–rather than the actual implementation–of the internal market has already created renewed dynamism in Europe, contributing to the revival of investment and economic activity in the late 1980s. As the internal market is being implemented during the next few years, and probably extended (in one form or other) to comprise additional countries, competitive forces will be strengthened and economic performance improved in the whole of Europe.

Australia and New Zealand concluded a free trade area agreement already some years ago, and recently a similar agreement was concluded between the United States, Canada and Mexico. Here again, stronger competition is likely to improve productivity growth. Various suggestions have been made for the creation of closer regional cooperation in Asia, but so far no formal agreements have been concluded.

Information Technology

The fourth point is technology. Rapid progress is being made in many areas: information technology, bio-technology, materials technology, space technology and nuclear technology. I shall confine myself to some remarks about information technology (IT) since this is by far the most pervasive and influential in terms of its impact across all sectors of the economy.

IT, defined as the combination of computers, microelectronics, and telecommunications, represents a new generic technology perhaps as revolutionary as the steam engine and electricity in their times, and will probably–like them–lead to fundamental changes in the technical-economic system. Like electricity, IT is already being applied in all areas of economic life: production, trade, transport, and communication. Underlying the rapid diffusion of IT is the continuing dramatic improvement in large-scale integration of electronic circuits with the continuing reduction in costs which this permits, and a parallel development in communication technology, where fibre optics have made possible similarly dramatic improvements in costs and performance.

Why is IT so important? Its main advantages may be summarized as follows.

* It permits savings of inputs (labor, capital, materials and energy) and it improves the quality of products and processes. On-line monitoring of output quality has already led to striking improvements in products as diverse as television sets and automobiles.

* Secondly, and perhaps more important, is the possibilities it offers for instantaneous and low-cost transmission, processing and storing of information. This makes it possible to integrate the various operations in *individual enterprises* (planning, design, production, purchasing, marketing and administration) as well as to link up the networks of a *group of enterprises* (e.g. suppliers of components and assembly-type firms; or producers, wholesalers, and retailers).

* Thirdly, it provides greater flexibility in the production process, a flexibility enabling rapid changes in models and design, and providing a greater variety of products at low costs.

But if IT is so advantageous, and given the fact that investment in IT equipment has been growing rapidly over the last twenty years or more, why is that we have not seen a greater reflection of this in the growth of productivity?[1] As already noted, there may be a problem of measurement. The statisticians are not able fully to catch the increase in output, particularly the quality improvements that are taking place. But the main point is a more fundamental one: we have not yet been able to exploit the potential offered by IT. Many are disappointed with results of their investments in the new technology. The efficient use of IT requires new skills as well as changes in the internal organisation and management of enterprises, changes that are not obvious, that may be costly to implement, that imply trial and error and therefore take time. Moreover, change is not popular, and is therefore resisted.

Experience suggests that enterprises typically go through two phases. In a first phase, certain individual operations are automated and costs fall, but the organisation of the production process is not changed. The operations affected become islands of automation in an otherwise unchanged process. Gradually, however, the need to go further and change the manner in which the individual units of the enterprise cooperate and interact arises. It is only when this second phase–the re-organisation of the enterprise–is implemented that the full efficiency gains of the new technology are realized.

It is therefore not surprising that it takes time to make full use of the new technology. Something similar happened with electricity. The key technical

---

[1] Or to rephrase Professor Solow, the Nobel Price winner: "We see the computers everywhere except in the productivity numbers".

innovations were made between the 1860s and the 1880s. And with the establishment of effective generating and transmission systems in the 1880s and 1890s, there was a rapid diffusion of applications of electricity throughout the economy. But there was no observed increase in productivity. Then as now the efficient use of the new technology required organizational changes in firms, modifications in factory layout, and changes in skills and attitudes of engineers, managers and workers. As suggested by Figure 2.3, it was not until the 1920s that there was a significant increase in productivity.

The analogy between electrification and computerization helps to illustrate the long time-scales involved in any type of technical change that affects a very broad range of goods and services, and where many products and processes have to be redesigned to realize the full potential of the new technology. It is likely that a major unused productivity potential in the form of unexploited IT-efficiency remains today. Many experts argue that we are only at the beginning of the profound changes in the technical-economic system that will be generated by IT. In view of the strong competitive pressures that exist in most markets, and as new age groups in the labor force with more adequate skills and attitudes grow up, we may over time see a broadly-based acceleration of productivity growth, although the speed of this process is uncertain.

Figure 2.3. U.S. Manufacturing - Total Factor Productivity.

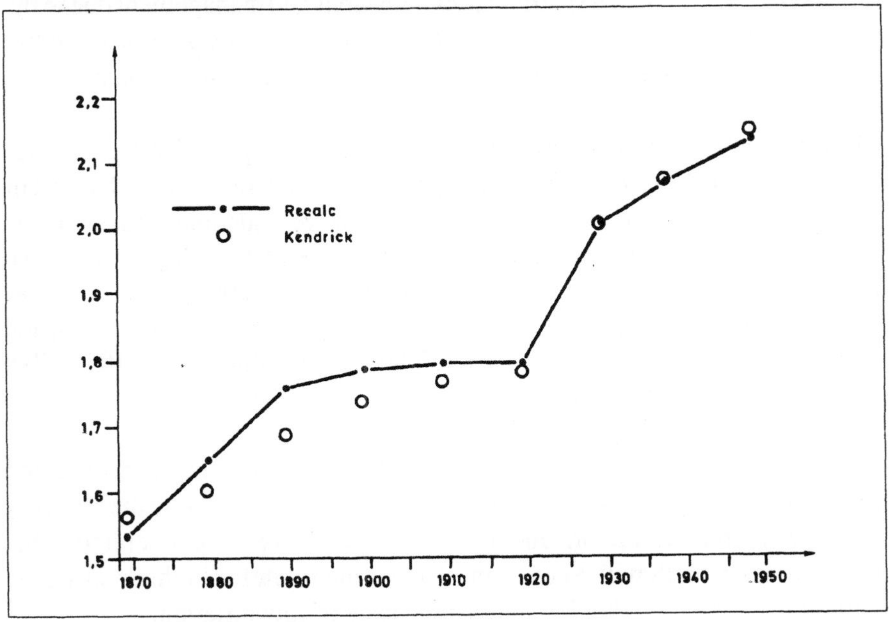

Source: *Unpublished OECD document.*

Risks and Constraints

I have argued that there is a potential for stronger productivity growth in the 1990s and beyond, than in the 1980s. But will conditions be such that this potential will be utilized? I shall briefly discuss the main risks and constraints that could create difficulties in this respect.

The Inflation Problem

A first risk is that inflationary pressures will necessitate the maintenance of restrictive fiscal and monetary policies, entailing slow growth of demand. As already noted, inflation has been significantly reduced in the 1980s, particularly after the fall in oil prices in 1986. Inflation has picked up somewhat in the last couple of years, but the acceleration can mainly be ascribed to cyclical factors such as higher raw material prices, and has already been reversed. How robust will the lower rate of inflation be if unemployment, as everybody would hope, should decline in the 1990s. In my view there is reason for cautious optimism on this point, for two reasons.

One reason is that unemployment is still high, and in Europe quite a bit higher than the equilibrium rate, i.e. the rate which stabilizes inflation (the so-called NAIRU; the non-accelerating inflation rate of unemployment). High unemployment, and the change in attitudes of both labor and management due to the protracted period of difficult labor market conditions and low profitability after the first oil price shock, should exert a dampening influence on inflation.

The other reason is the interaction between actual and expected inflation. Price expectations are heavily influenced by past experience. In the OECD model of the world economy price expectations in the wage equations consist of the cumulative experiences over a number of years. The average lag for the seven largest countries varies from one to three years. The implication is that as inflation comes down, inflationary expectations also decline (with a lag), and this will improve the unemployment-inflation relationship (i.e. NAIRU falls), making it easier to maintain low inflation.

There is obviously great uncertainty on this point. It is, however, encouraging that the rise in wages in the late 1980s remained moderate despite the recovery of activity and the fall in unemployment. Moreover, the likelihood that productivity growth will recover, means that the room for higher real wages will increase, thus facilitating the maintenance of low inflation.

In addition to the risk of increased union militancy, there is also the risk of higher oil and other raw materials prices. On this point, the World Bank–one of the main experts in the field–is relatively optimistic for the next decade[2], projecting a one per cent average annual increase in real primary commodity prices. Other experts are less optimistic, particularly with regard to oil prices, pointing to the narrowing of unused capacity in the oil industry in the last few years, and to the fact, as was emphasized in Chapter 1, that oil consumers rely heavily on imports from a few unstable societies in the Middle East. In the event of a tendency for oil prices to rise sharply, one could perhaps hope that one would be able to handle the situation better than during the two earlier oil price shocks. In OECD countries, oil stocks have been built up and contingency planning for handling a crisis situation exists. Nevertheless, there is great uncertainty in this area as well.

Financial Fragility

Financial market liberalization, which was a widespread phenomenon in the first half of the 1980s, has contributed to a weakening of banks balance sheets. First, securitization has increasingly enabled high quality corporate borrowers to raise funds directly in the market, reducing the average creditworthiness of the remaining pool of borrowers seeking intermediate credit. Second, increased competition has squeezed banks' profit margins. Third, the removal of credit restrictions has increased the overall availability of credit, including that for speculative purposes.

These forces have induced banks in some countries to expand credit in the direction of higher risk (higher yield) activities, while at the same time contributing to higher asset prices. The risks inherent in this situation have been increased by recession or slower economic growth. In Japan the marked fall in stock and real estate prices has reduced the banks' own capital. At the same time there is the need for banks to fulfil the capital-adequacy criteria proposed by the Bank for International Settlement. It is difficult to determine to what extent financial fragility problems will materialize and what adverse consequences they may have for economic activity. It is fairly clear that banks have restricted the growth of credit. The Federal Reserve has estimated that there has been an important shortfall in the credit expansion in relation to "normal" in 1991 and 1992. Measures have been proposed to ease the banks' situation, so we do not know to what extent this so-called credit crunch will

[2] See World Bank (1988).

continue. Although the capital and profit situations of U.S. banks have improved, the possibility that commercial bank prudence will affect the economy beyond the immediate future cannot be excluded. The fragility problem will be further discussed in Chapter 5 in this book.

On the other hand, the U.S. current external deficit–a much discussed source of possible financial market instability in recent years–has fallen significantly from a peak of USD 160 billion (3.6 per cent of GNP) in 1987 to an estimated USD 40 billion (0.7 per cent of GNP) in 1992. The improvement has been influenced by the fall in imports associated with the recession, but is essentially the result of the strong rise in exports in response to the fall in the dollar up to 1987, and its subsequent relative stability against a trade-weighted average of other major currencies. If the current value of the dollar is broadly maintained, the U.S. export performance should remain good. The risk of a "hard landing" for the dollar has therefore been reduced.

Protectionism

As already noted, the last 15 years or so have seen an increase in non-tariff barriers, including the use of subsidies and volontary export restraint. This stands in sharp contrast to the moves towards liberalization and deregulation of the domestic OECD economies and within regions. It is a sad fact that the GATT negotiations–the Uruguay Round–failed to conclude a new agreement as planned by the end of 1991. Of decisive importance was the process of reforming agriculture, for which there are compelling domestic arguments as well. Here almost no progress has been made in implementing the principles adopted in the OECD. Total support to agriculture–i.e. the transfers from taxpayers and consumers to farmers–is estimated to have reached the record level of USD 300 billion in 1990. By way of comparison: total official aid of OECD countries to developing countries amounts to less than USD 50 billion.

The GATT negotiations continue, and OECD Ministers in July 1991 agreed that the talks must be brought to a satisfactory conclusion before the end of that year. One might think that the movement towards more liberal trade and foreign investment regimes in a growing number of developing countries, and the similar tendency already apparent in some of the countries in Central and Eastern Europe, would put pressure on OECD countries to bring the Uruguay Round to an happy end. But there is obviously no guarantee that they will. At the beginning of 1993 they still continue. Moreover, the refusal of France, supported by one or two other countries, to improve marginally the access of

Eastern European countries to EC markets for certain agricultural products (notably meat) is not a good omen. A breakdown of the negotiations could spark off a trade war between the U.S., Japan and the EC, with adverse effects on trade and economic growth. It would nevertheless be surprising if the interests of relatively small sectors (essentially agriculture) would be allowed to put the satisfactory development of the whole world economy at risk. One may therefore hope that reason will prevail so that a relatively liberal trading system will be maintained.

The Environment

Environment problems have come to the forefront in the public debate in recent years. The concept of a "sustainable development" has played an important role. It implies that economic developments must be compatible with the maintenance of the ecological system. This is a vast subject on its own. Suffice it to say in the present context that measures to protect the environment is likely to be given greater weight in economic policy formation than in the past, and that economic growth as traditionally measured may be affected. Much, however, will depend on the kind of measures taken. It is generally agreed that greater reliance on the price mechanism–introducing or increasing environmental charges–will increase the efficiency of environmental policies. Moreover, in many areas a high degree of international cooperation, encompassing also the developing countries is essential, although perhaps not easy to accomplish. If environmental policies evolve in these directions, it should be possible to reduce the conflict between economic growth and the maintenance of the ecological system.

The Outlook for Economic Growth and its Geographical Pattern in the 1990s

Drawing things together, what sort of rate of economic growth could one expect in the 1990s? And with what sort of geographical breakdown? It is obviously hazardous to offer numbers. Nevertheless, for what it is worth, and assuming that a reasonable degree of political and financial stability will be maintained, my idea is that the OECD area should be able to achieve an average annual rate of growth in the 3-4 per cent range. My view is based on two broad considerations. During the "Golden Age", activity in the OECD area expanded at an average annual rate of 4.5 to 5 per cent. But there is general agreement that this was an exceptionally *favorable* period for reasons mentioned earlier.

It is also agreed that the last 15-20 years when the growth rate fell to little more than 2.5 per cent, was a particularly *unfavorable* period. The two oil price shocks strengthened inflationary pressures and reduced economic growth. Much of the 1980s was a correction period with tight demand management and active structural policies to reduce inflation and public budget deficits, restore profitability, and improve the functioning of markets. In the short run, these policies were bound to limit the rate of economic growth. But now that much has been corrected, and various factors and policies discussed earlier point to stronger productivity growth, it should be possible to do better than during the last 15-20 years. As a rough approximation it may be reasonable to assume that the rate of expansion in the 1990s will lie somewhere between the rates experienced in the two earlier periods, i.e. between 2.5 and 5 per cent–or 3-4 per cent if we narrow the range somewhat.

The **United States** has had a weak productivity performance during the last 20 years (less than 1 per cent a year). This has raised doubts about the competitiveness of U.S. industry and the economy's ability to grow. The low rate is related to the strong rise in the labour force and little or no productivity growth in the services sectors. There are, however, serious measurement problems in these sectors, and a major part of services is not traded internationally. It is mainly developments in the manufacturing industry which is decisive for a country's competitiveness. In this sector productivity increased by 4 per cent annually in the 1980s. This is much more than in the two previous decades, and more than in major competitor countries such as Canada, Germany and France. And the difference in performance vis-à-vis Japan was reduced. The strong increase in exports and the regain of market shares since 1987, after the fall of the dollar to a more realistic level, is a manifestation of U.S. competitiveness.

Nevertheless, there are obvious weaknesses in the U.S. economy. The household savings rate is low (3-4 per cent) or around a quarter of the Japanese rate, and the federal budget is in large deficit. The rate of business investment (15 per cent of business value added) is lower than in most other OECD countries and only about half the Japanese rate. It is widely recognized that there is a serious and growing problem with regard to the education, skills, and overall quality of the work force. There is a lack of social innovation, as suggested by the fact that Japanese companies operating in the United States and using American labor, obtain much higher productivity than U.S. firms in the same branches.

It is not clear that this situation will change quickly. On the other hand, history indicates that Americans can bring about rapid change once they become really exercised by a problem. All in all, it may be reasonable to expect an average annual rate of growth of 2.5-3 per cent, broadly in line with past experience.

In **OECD Europe** economic performance improved significantly in the late 1980s. Despite the cyclical weakness of the early 1990s, there is little mention of Eurosclerosis these days. The internal market has created renewed dynamism both inside and outside the EC. The restoration of profitability has contributed to the recovery of business fixed investment. Stronger competition, a move towards larger units of production, and better exploitation of information and other technologies are likely to generate stronger productivity growth. The labor force is growing more slowly than earlier, but high unemployment provides room for higher employment.

It has been generally assumed that Europe is lagging behind the United States and Japan in the technological area. A recent study[3], however, argues that this assumption is based on incomplete and erroneous information. It is true, it says, that Europe spends a smaller proportion of its value added on R&D, and that, apart from software, its technological position in electronics is weak. But Europe is in a strong position in chemicals, pharmaceuticals and nuclear energy, is ahead of the United States in metals and automobiles, and ahead of Japan in aerospace and in technologies for the exploitation of raw materials. The study concludes that, like the United States and Japan, Europe has both relative strengths and relative weaknesses. The situation may therefore be less bleak than generally assumed.

A main uncertainty in OECD Europe concerns inflation. But in line with what has been said earlier, there may be reason for cautious optimism on this point. If so, OECD Europe might be able to achieve an average annual rate of growth in the 3-4 per cent range, more than the 2.5 per cent recorded since the beginning of the 1970s.

Eastern Europe and the former Soviet Union. It is obviously uncertain what will happen in these countries. In addition to the task of developing democratic societies, they are faced with an unusual combination of formidable economic problems: establish market economies with free price formation and private ownership; modernize infrastructure and production facilities; bring monetary

---

[3] See Patel and Pavitt (1989).

and fiscal policies under control and restore a degree of price stability. All this will necessarily take time, and something will depend on the assistance they will receive from the West. I also recall that post-revolutionary situations are rarely stable.

Prospects for successful transition to market economies appear to be best in Hungary, the former Czechoslovakia and Poland. Systematic economic reform has been under way for several years in Hungary, since 1989 in Poland and since 1990 in Czechoslovakia. Comprehensive programmes have by now been put in place in these countries. The programmes combine macroeconomic stabilization through tight fiscal and monetary policies with price liberalization and the opening of the trade regime to provide the incentives for the necessary change of the productive structure. At the same time privatization has been initiated and financial markets have been introduced to enhance responsiveness to these incentives. There are indications that these programmes are starting to produce results. The private sectors appear to be growing rapidly, exports to OECD countries (particularly Europe) have expanded strongly, and the rapid increase in foreign direct investment in Hungary and Czechoslovakia suggests that foreign investors are becoming increasingly confident in the prospects for these countries. Foreign direct investment in Poland has been small to date, possibly due to political instability. These three countries may be able to get on to a dynamic growth process in the latter part of the 1990s. The main risk of a less favorable outcome is rapidly rising unemployment which may undermine the present consensus on the reform process.

In the other countries the old command system has largely withered away, but little has so far been done to lay the foundations for future growth by ensuring macroeconomic stability and by advancing with the institutional requirements of a market system. Bulgaria and Romania have set out to implement ambitious reform programmes. But the situation in the former Soviet Union remains confused. The nature and size of a future union, if any, is unclear. Market economic reforms are being debated in all new nations emerging from the former union. But it remains to be seen whether these reforms can be implemented.

There is little basis for quantitative projections for the Eastern countries. Output fell in all countries in 1990 and 1991, and stagnation or continued decline may be likely in the near term. Subsequently, assuming that comprehensive stabilization and reform programmes are implemented and that political stability will be maintained, fairly rapid recoveries can be expected as the countries catch up with production and management practices in the West. But it cannot be excluded that, in some countries at least, something similar to Latin American situations will prevail for some time, i.e. that policy reforms will be incomplete, large and inefficient public enterprises will continue to dominate, and progress will be hampered by high inflation and lack of external creditworthiness.

Asia. In the post-WW II period Asia has experienced two waves of growth. The first was the rise of Japan to a world economic power in the 1970s. The second was the emergence of the "four tigers" South Korea, Hong Kong, Taiwan and Singapore as important trading nations in the 1980s. A third wave is now developing in the ASEAN countries[4], stimulated by foreign direct investment and rapid growth of intra-regional trade. Moreover, China with 1.1 billion people achieved a 9 per cent annual rate of growth over the past decade, influenced by more liberal policies, and India (750 million people) grew at a 5-6 per cent rate.

An extrapolation of past trends is not warranted. China is politically unstable. The most advanced economies may attract "Western" illnesses in the form of more difficult labor-management relations and associated social conflict. There are tendencies in this direction in South Korea. Nevertheless, it is the economic dynamism that dominates.

In Japan the present cyclical weakness–reinforced by a degree of financial instability–should soon be replaced by renewed growth. In the longer run Japan will probably continue to do well. The labor force is likely to rise very slowly, but in most other respects growth conditions are favorable: a high rate of savings, dynamic business managers, a high rate of investment with strong emphasis on research and development, a well-educated, mobile and hard-working labor force, and a high degree of social consensus. Although some of this may change, both the authorities and private observers expect an average annual rate of real GNP growth of the order of 4 per cent, in line with experience in the 1980s.

South East Asia is also characterized by high rates of savings and investment, active attitudes, and a strong emphasis on education. Growth may well remain high (in the 6-8 per cent range) underpinned by rapidly growing intra-regional trade, direct investment and transfer of technology. The situation in China is still unclear. For the time being the emphasis is on ideology, but allowing

[4] The main ones are Indonesia, Thailand, Malaysia, and the Philippines.

relatively liberal conditions in the coastal areas. Despite historical antipathies stemming from intra-regional hostilities and warfare, there is reason to believe that the complementarity between China's natural resources and Japan's capital and technology over time will result in stronger cooperation and rapid development in China. India, for a long time a dirigiste economy on the Soviet model, is now liberalizing. Most of Asia is still poor. With 55 per cent of the world population, it accounts for only about a quarter of world output. Its weight in the world economy has been growing in the past two decades, and is likely to continue to do so in the 1990s.

Latin America has a great economic potential, but the debt burden and inappropriate - i.e. dirigiste and inward-looking - economic policies constitute serious obstacles to better performance. Fortunately, there are indications that the new liberalism is spreading also to Latin America, including its two largest economies Brazil and Argentina. Moreover, good growth in the rest of the world, and better access to OECD markets as–hopefully–the Uruguay Round is brought to a happy conclusion, will stimulate exports and ease the debt burden. Latin America may therefore do better in the next decade than in the last one.

Africa is poor, with serious debt and development problems. But its weight in the world economy (about 3 per cent) and the impact of what is happening there on the global economy is small. It is a tragic situation which can only be changed by better economic management, debt reduction, and population control.

Concluding Remarks

Even in a long statement, I have had to be very selective. I have mentioned demographic developments only in passing, and environmental problems could have deserved more emphasis. I do think, however, that I have discussed the fundamental features which will affect economic growth of the world economy in the 1990s. On balance, and reflecting in large measure probable improvements on the supply side and, thus, stronger productivity growth, my conclusion is that there is reason for a certain degree of optimism. With respect to economic growth, Asia in particular but also Europe should do well. There is a large potential in Eastern Europe and the former Soviet Union, but stabilizing and transforming these countries to market economies will take time. With good luck and generous assistance from the West–particularly in the form of competence and technology transfer and greater access to Western markets–these countries could become an important new dynamic element in the world economy in the latter part of the 1990s. But the possibility of less satisfactory developments more in line with recent Latin American experiences obviously exists.

Finally, I should also like to stress the uncertainties relating to political factors and how they will impinge on economic developments. The falling apart of the Soviet Union and the Yugoslav Federation, and the emergence of a great many small independent nations with important problems of ethnic and religious minorities, may well be a source of conflict and continuing local warfare. Given the large differences in living standards between OECD countries and Eastern and Southern countries, migration pressures are likely to grow. It is difficult to judge how these developments will affect economic growth in OECD countries, but they obviously increase the uncertainties attached to any forward-looking assessment. Hopefully, they will not prevent the positive features I have discussed to materialize.

References

IMF (1991), *World Economic Outlook*, May, Washington D.C.

OECD (1992), *Economic Outlook*, 51, June, Paris.

Patel, P. and K. Pavitt, (1989), "European Technological Performance: Results and Prospects", *European Affairs*, Summer.

World Bank (1988), *Price Prospects for Major Primary Commodities*, November, Washington D.C.

Chapter 3

The International Competition for Investment

Richard J. Sweeney

Introduction

Since the industrial revolution, countries have been in an international competition for investment, whether or not they know it or consciously adopt the policies that have such large influence on the competition's outcome. Part of this competition is for domestic investment and part for foreign investment; in the present world of high and growing interdependence and integration among industrialized countries, the two types of investment often go together. Policies favorable for domestic investment very often attract foreign direct investment (FDI); similarly, policies that make domestic investment unattractive often discourage inward FDI and encourage outward FDI as home companies and residents look abroad for better uses of capital.

Political changes currently being made will have major effects on this international competition for investment. Some of the political decisions are at the level of individual countries; some of the most important decisions are at the level of trading blocks. This paper often uses the European Community and Sweden as examples; Sweden is often said to be the most multinational country in the world, had the world's highest outward FDI in 1991 (in substantial part to the EC), has applied for EC membership and will almost certainly enter, perhaps by late 1995. More important, current EC policies and the outlines of future policies are substantially clearer than those of other trading blocks that are more potential than actual now. Policies adopted by the EC as a whole and by EC members will surely be important determinants of the international competition for investment, as will reactions by the rest of the world. EC policies may, for example, facilitate formation of rival trading blocks in the Americas and the Far East. Though a variety of economic and political motives were behind negotiations among Canada, Mexico and the U.S. for a North American Free Trade Area, and still are behind the growing integration of the economies of Japan and some of the Asian "tigers," there is no doubt that these moves are partly in response to current and anticipated EC policies. Similarly, these moves in the Americas and the Far East present the EC with important issues. Many observers fear, and some predict, the emergence of hostile, protectionistic trading blocks centered on the EC, NAFTA and Japan and the tigers; other observers suggest that trading blocks with low internal barriers might negotiate for low protection across the blocks, leading to a more liberal economic order.

Analysis of the policies of any one block is complicated. For example, analysis of EC policies and their effects on investment requires both discussion of EC and its members' policies and thus is more complicated than if the EC's policies or a single member's policies could be considered in isolation. Further, many of the policies that have major effects on investment are aimed at other issues, with the effect on investment sometimes overlooked or considered of secondary importance. In addition, there is substantial diversity among both the EC's current and prospective members. For example, some of Sweden's interests are aligned with those of rich EC members and also smaller members; though some of the issues facing Sweden are also faced by all EC members, some important Swedish issues are less relevant to larger EC members and also to poorer members.

Block-Wide Policies and Foreign Direct Investment

Think of two stages in the decision to invest in a country in a trading block. First is the decision to invest in the block. Given this decision, the second stage is to choose one country from possible block locations. In the first stage block-wide policies play an important role, and block-member policies in the second. This section discusses the effect on investment of block-wide policies, taking EC policies as a concrete example, but also referring to NAFTA and a possible Far East trading block. The following section discusses the effects of block-member policies: in some places it takes as an example some Swedish policies relative to EC policies, in other places it uses EC members' policies or focuses on countries in the Americas and the Far East.

It is hard to assess the net effect of EC policies on investment, particularly because some policies are still being negotiated; difficulties are greater and conclusions more speculative when considering outcomes for NAFTA and a possible Far East block. Nevertheless, the direction of influence of some EC policies is clear.

The EC as a Fortress

Since at least the mid-1980s, a substantial but unknown part of EC inward FDI has aimed to get behind EC tariff walls,[1] anticipating both the benefits of 1992's single market[2] and the possibility the EC will become even more protectionistic.[3] FDI motivated by the lure of the single market is "investment creating". This investment is a response to new opportunities and the attractiveness of locating new capital in the EC. On the other hand, fear of tariff walls is "investment diverting"; it forces investment that would be more profitable and productive outside the EC to locate in the EC where conditions are less attractive for these particular investments.[4] The diverted investments are the wrong type for the EC; instead of requiring the resources and particularly the labor skills the EC offers, it is illsuited and provides inferior jobs and uses of other resources. FDI with both motivations will surely continue. Confusion about investors' two goals–to take advantage of the single market and to get behind tariff walls–and about the differences between investment-creating and -diverting policies may make the stimulus to FDI from tariff walls look advantageous to EC nations. Similarly, there is much discussion of the possibility that a completion of NAFTA will stimulate Japanese investment in Mexico, particularly but not only in autos, to avoid current possible future U.S. protectionism against Japanese home-island production. In addition, one

---

[1] "Tariff walls" is shorthand for protection. Much more powerful forms of protection exist: quotas, voluntary export restraints, voluntary import requirements, exclusionary distribution systems, and many more of these destructive nontariff barriers.

[2] It is well understood that the creation of a single market at the end of 1992 will not see major changes in the EC; many of the single-market laws, institutions and regulations came into effect along the way to the single market. It should be noted, though, that single-market institutions and regulations are evolving over time, and it is not possible now to predict with any certainty how some key issues will be resolved; for example, the social charter accepted at the Maastricht negotiations in December, 1991, must be given content over time.

[3] The Economist (Aug. 24, 1991, p. 57) argues that two of the driving forces behind FDI in the 1980s were "companies positioning themselves in the EC before the creation of the single market [and] ... Japanese companies' efforts to dodge rising costs at home and growing protectionism abroad." Thus, some of Japan's outward FDI to East Asia can be interpreted as a natural attempt to escape rising Japanese costs; some, however, can be interpreted as an attempt by Japanese firms to make their products "Thai" rather than "Japanese" and thus avoid some EC and North American protectionism.

[4] For a discussion of the concepts of investment creation and diversion, see Sweeney (1992). Grubel (1990) applies the concepts of trade creation and diversion to analyze the EC; Viner (1950) originated the concepts of trade creation and diversion to analyze customs unions.

interpretation of Japanese outward FDI to the Asian tigers[5] is that this is in part a foothold to start an Asian trading block should NAFTA and the EC prove particularly hostile to Japanese products.

Investment that is diverted from abroad has bad consequences. Protected markets misallocate resources as domestic industries produce goods obtainable more cheaply from abroad. This hurts consumers and also firms denied cheaper inputs from abroad. Even agricultural protection hurts: manufacturing and service industries must pay more to attract labor and capital from agriculture and its subsidized incomes, and the higher food prices lead workers to demand higher wages.[6] Further, tariff walls may reduce competition in the protected market,[7] one likely effect of voluntary export restraints on imports of Japanese autos to the EC. Closely related, protection that spares domestic industries allows them to fall farther behind.

Some observers argue that so far, the effect of EC protectionism has been to increase investment in the EC. At present, it is not clear how protectionistic the EC will be by the end of the twentieth century. If the EC turns to greater

---

[5] The "Asian tigers" are usually taken to refer to Hong Kong, the Republic of Korea (South Korea), Singapore and Taiwan, and more recently to include Thailand. Certainly this is not a homogeneous group, either in terms of political systems or economic policies. Hong Kong is well known for its liberal trading and investment policies and, more recently, for its currency board approach to monetary discipline. In contrast, South Korea has substantial restrictions on imports and FDI. South Korea has a handful of large conglomerates (the Chaebols) that dominate the economy, and try to offer a Japanese approach to company loyalty and long-term employment; Taiwan, in contrast, relies on much smaller firms on average, with production and employment more fluid. None of these countries meets U.S. or Western European standards of democracy, though political freedoms appear to be increasing in some.

[6] Higher food prices reduce employees' real wages; from the point of view of non-agricultural employers, this is an upward shift in the labor supply curve, leading to reduced employment and higher real wages from the employers' viewpoint, lower real wages from the employees'. The Economist (Aug. 10, 1991) reports that for agriculture the "EC's total subsidy stood at $81 billion" in 1990. 59% of Swedish farmers' income came from subsidies, mostly "financed directly from consumers' pockets through artificially inflated prices.... the cost of food has increased much faster than inflation." Swedish reforms adopted in July 1991 "pledged to establish a free market within" Sweden. "By 1995, there will be no price supports....The one source of protection...will be variable levies that block imports....these will be lowered to keep pace with falling domestic prices." During the Uruguay Round GATT negotiations, the U.S. put strong pressure on the EC to reform its Common Agricultural Policy. In May, 1992, EC members agreed to some far-reaching changes; in particular, a shift in emphasis from price supports to income maintenance policies, which should make clearer to EC voters the cost of EC agricultural protectionism. These EC concessions in turn strengthen the hand of the U.S. administration to reduce its government intervention in U.S. agriculture. It is even possible that Japan may someday allow imports of rice.

[7] As an example, see Levinson's (1991) discussion of the effects on competition of trade liberalization in Turkey.

protection, it may get a larger amount of FDI as foreign firms try harder to get inside the tariff walls.[8] This is diverted rather than increased investment from a world viewpoint. Because the investment is not voluntarily located in the EC, but forced there by the threats of protectionism, it is not as well-matched to EC resources and labor skill as voluntary investment would be; this results in inefficient and lower paying use of EC resources and labor. Further, FDI attracted in this way crowds out other FDI and domestic investment that would be better suited to EC conditions; it is not clear if total investment in the EC rises or falls as a result, but the mix of investment that results is clearly less suited to EC conditions. Similarly, if the world breaks into trading blocks, or the probability of this increases, EC and U.S. firms can be expected to increase their FDI in the Asian tigers; non-Japanese Asian markets are the fastest growing in the world, if still substantially less rich than the U.S. and the EC.

There are possible dynamic compensations for the costs of protection. Foreign firms that become domestic firms through their inward FDI may provide stimulating competition for the host-country and host-block firms. These firms may compete in many industries once behind the tariff wall; for example, the start-up costs a firm pays to get into the EC in one line will typically reduce its start-up costs in other lines. In addition, foreign firms and their FDI may help the host country catch up with the rest of the world in some lines; this is the hope that Japanese car production in the U.S. may force or allow U.S. firms to adapt Japanese approaches to the U.S., for example, an emphasis on quality and team work.

For policymaking purposes, these possible good dynamic consequences of protection deserve little weight. Achieving these benefits requires the right amount of protection, on the right products or industries, at the right time;[9] it is a version of the debate over industrial policy. Opinion is divided on the controversial industrial policy issue; many observers agree, however, that using tariff walls to induce good outcomes presupposes both a substantial degree of government intelligence and foresight and that governments find it politically possible to do what is good rather than harmful. There is some

---

[8] The effect on FDI is not entirely clear. If it appears that the EC is adopting policies that keep out foreign goods but will also lead to stagnation, the attraction of getting behind the tariff walls may be offset by the market being less attractive than otherwise. Thus, for low levels of protection, increases in protection likely stimulate inward FDI, but for high levels of protection, increases reduce total investment in the area (Sweeney 1992).

[9] These dynamic arguments abstract from the well known static optimum tariff arguments, and from the possibility of tariff warfare.

evidence that government policies are not made this way. Instead, policies have a large component of special-interest political power.[10] It is often easier to impose protection where it is harmful instead of where it arguably makes sense. For example, current EC and U.S. farm policies have no intellectually respectable defense. Further, agricultural policy did not start out as the current mess; it got that way through the incremental political process in democratic nations. Though the analytical case can be made for the strategic use of trade policy, there is little hope in practice that strategic use of tariff walls will improve results.

The "Race to the Bottom"

Within any trading block, there will be a competition among members to gain an advantage over the other members by offering more attractive policies; conversely, some members will have strong interests in seeing imposed block-wide restraints on such member competition. It is widely recognized that the single market in "Europe in 1992" implies much policy harmonization across members, whether through community-wide agreements or market pressures on countries diverging from the community average. One example is tax policies. Pressures to conform to the average levels of taxes present painful dilemmas for countries with high taxes and social expenditures. Some countries must reduce profit, income, sales and value added tax rates to remain competitive in sales and production; otherwise there will be pressure for their residents to buy more abroad, industries to flee, FDI to go elsewhere in the block, and brain drains to strip away highly productive people. Some view this pressure on government policies as a "race to the bottom," to see who will have lowest tax rates, lowest social expenditures, least protection of the environment, and so forth.[11]

---

[10] The power of special-interest groups is well understood for the democracies in the EC, the U.S. and Japan; an example is agricultural policy. It is also true of Mexico, which is only now moving away from one-party rule, as well as Taiwan and Thailand, where authoritarian regimes provide substantial economic benefits for important groups. One (at least partial) explanation for the Thai military's deep involvement in the national government is the ways high-ranking military officers use government influence to further their business affairs.

[11] The FDI literature has long recognized that differing national tax rates have an effect on the allocation of FDI across countries (Root and Ahmed 1978). Many studies of the states of the U.S. find it hard to detect the effect of differential tax incentives; however, Benson and Johnson (1986) detect such effects and argue that earlier studies were not well formulated to detect these effects.

The race to the bottom is more often to be welcomed than feared; it is investment creating. Some governments compelled to cut tax rates, and thus social expenditures, are appropriately disciplined by the market; like firms, governments need competition. With a given level of block-wide protection, the more the member governments compete, the more investment is created. Some in the U.S. fear that in a NAFTA, U.S. production will be hurt not only by lower Mexican wages but also by Mexican jurisdictions offering lower tax rates and less stringent regulation.[12] This competition within NAFTA would be investment creating; the following section argues that rich countries with high skill labor can be successful without adopting the same standards as low-wage poorer countries.[13]

Countries cutting tax rates to stay competitive make the EC as a whole more attractive for investment and hence raise FDI to the EC. The pressured countries may, however, find that their policy responses go only part way towards keeping them competitive and may find a decrease in their inward FDI and total investment along with a rise in structural unemployment as a result of this competition. These countries may then pressure the EC and its members to adopt policies to divert investment from outside the EC. Further, these countries may adopt more expansionary fiscal and monetary policies, and may pressure other community members to do the same;[14] such expansionary policies are ultimately futile for employment, but may lead to substantial inflation.

---

[12] Some argue that corruption is more wide-spread and severe in Mexico than in the U.S. Corruption acts like a tax rate and thus tends to offset the advantage an area gets from lower tax rates.

[13] In principle, too much investment creation can harm welfare; there is an optimum level of investment, with deviations on either side reducing welfare. The text's point is that rich countries need not be driven to inoptimally high levels of investment because of competition with poor countries.

[14] German reunification led to massive transfers of resources from Western to Eastern Germany, much of the transfers through the central government's budget. This led to higher inflation in Germany and to higher interest rates. Some members of the European Monetary System vocally suggested that the Bundesbank should take action to reduce German interest rates so that the other members could reduce their rates. It is quite possible that such pressures would be even stronger on a European central bank under the proposed European Monetary Union; one argument put forward for joining the EMU is that members would have more influence over the central bank's policies than they now have over the Bundesbank. Redburn (1992) argues that the French government views EMU as an opportunity to have more influence over a European Central Bank than it does over the Bundesbank. It quotes Valery Giscard d'Estaing, former president of France, as saying "I want to see France seize this opportunity which is handed to it on a silver platter to be the country which organizes the introduction, the management, the instruments and the market for the ECU."

The race to the bottom cannot be a competitive strategy for either the EC as a whole or NAFTA as a whole. Neither group can compete with Eastern Europe or mainland Asia on wages gross of taxes[15] or on relaxed environmental standards; these poorer societies, driven by necessity, cannot be beaten on these margins. Instead, both the EC and NAFTA must rely on policies that encourage competition and high productivity within their areas.

Strategies for Reducing Intra-Block Government Competition

Block members with high taxes and social expenditures relative to other members face pressures to cut their tax rates but fear they may still be less attractive than other member countries for FDI and investment in general. This leads the pressured countries' governments to search for ways to reduce competition from other block-members' governments.

At least one motive for the negotiations on an EC social charter was to ensure that the poorer EC countries could not undercut the richer by too much on wages, working conditions, social expenditures and so forth; similarly, Community-wide minimum environmental standards protect high-standard members from being undercut too much by lower-standard members. A strict charter, environmental regulations, etc., will divert FDI within the EC from low-wage, low-productivity countries to high-wage, high-productivity countries that also tend to have high tax rates and social expenditures, along with more stringent environmental standards. A strict charter, stringent environmental standards, etc., will also reduce inward FDI to the EC by making the EC less competitive with the rest of the world. It is in the interest of poorer EC members, the EC as a whole, and the world as a whole to keep agreements such as the social charter from becoming inoptimally stringent. High-tax,-expenditure, -standard countries that attract diverted investment through stringent EC-wide standards will pay by having to buy goods at higher than necessary prices, by having investment less well suited to their work forces, and by financing higher transfers to the poorer members hurt by the standards.[16]

[15] Tax rates on wages are high in some Eastern European countries, though the average wage rate gross of taxes is low. These high tax rates can make low-wage labor uncompetitive because of labor's low productivity.

[16] At the December, 1991, Maastricht conference, Spain managed to extract increased funds for less developed members as the price for agreeing to the changes in the EC. As part of the negotiations, Spain agreed to the social charter (only the U.K. did not); the principles of the social charter appeared ideologically compatible with the views of the socialist Spanish government. Clearly, the social charter serves to divert investment from Spain. By May, 1992, Spain was taking substantial and painful steps to try to meet the convergence criteria for membership in the European Monetary Union. In particular, Spain had to make sharp cuts in its inflation rate and its level of public borrowing relative to GDP. On the one hand, the investment diversion Spain suffered from the social charter made these attempts more difficult and painful; on the other hand, the transfer payments from the other EC members ameliorated some of the pain. It is not at all clear that this tradeoff was on net beneficial for Spain.

A number of U.S. labor unions objected to NAFTA negotiations with Mexico on the grounds that Mexican workers enjoy poorer working conditions and lower social benefits than American workers, and that Mexican environmental standards are less stringent than the U.S.'s.[17] The Clinton administration has make special efforts to protect the environment and also work conditions; these will be major issues in any fight over Congressional acceptance of the NAFTA treaty.

Domestic Content Rules

The U.S. and Canada have had serious problems over the domestic content of Japanese autos produced in Canada but with major use of Japanese-produced components. The U.S. administration's position has been that these autos do not have large enough Canadian content to qualify under the Canada-U.S. free trade agreement. Such issues are inevitable in customs unions, free-trade areas or single markets; they are especially likely to arise from diverted investment, where outsiders are tempted to chisel on the compulsion of tariff walls and have as little domestic content as possible.

An open issue for the EC's single market in 1992 is the minimum percentages of EC value added that certain goods must contain. Domestic content rules clearly have elements of protection, sometimes serving as a second line of protection's defense. An example is autos and whether Japanese makes manufactured in the U.K. to get around EC protection are nonetheless to be counted against voluntary export restraints that the EC will inevitably force on Japan to protect French and Italian automakers.[18] Domestic content rules are sometimes defended as inducing technology transfer; the dominant effect is likely protection. Domestic content rules often induce FDI as foreign firms set up host-country operations to satisfy the rules, rather than simply buying

---

[17] The alliance between unions and environmentalists on the NAFTA is one of convenience; on many domestic issues, such as natural resource exploitation and commercial and residential construction, the two groups differ sharply..

[18] As of May, 1992, EC and Japanese negotiators seem to have agreed on the number of autos produced in Japan that will be imported into the EC over the next decade. There has been no explicit agreement on how many Japanese-make cars will be produced in the U.K., but EC negotiators apparently have received assurances on the level of Japanese investment in auto factories in the EC, and thus on the levels of Japanese-make cars that will be produced in the EC. The result is thus effectively an agreement on the number of Japanese-make cars (whether produced in Japan or the EC) that will compete with EC-make cars.

components from host-country firms. These rules reduce world and EC welfare however they are met; if they induce inward FDI to the EC, they crowd out better domestic investment and FDI, and stimulate EC outward FDI.

Non-Tariff Barriers

The list of the world's non-tariff barriers (NTBs) is enormous and growing; if adopted by the EC, NAFTA or a potential Far-East trading block, most NTBs will initially[19] raise total investment in the block and perhaps inward FDI for the block, but will harm both the block and the world. One example is EC health and safety standards used to keep out U.S.-produced beef. No doubt there are some valid health issues; to the extent these standards are protectionistic, they increase EC beef production and investment in agriculture, though EC agriculture investment is already far too large. Similarly, if the EC adopts devices such as the French port-of-entry regulations for Japanese VCR's, production and investment are diverted to the EC at the cost of world and EC efficiency.

The Policy Mix Within a Trading Block

It is useful to think of a trading block as facing two polar mixes of policies. To be concrete, consider the EC. In one mix, poorer EC members like Spain, Portugal and Greece adopt wage, welfare and environmental standards closer to the levels of the higher-income members; this puts the poorer countries at a disadvantage and is investment diverting[20] for them by reducing the flow of investment from the high-income members to the low and diverting the flow of inward FDI to the EC from the low-income members to the high-income members. The high-income members may also resist political and market pressures to reduce tax rates. Both groups of members are likely to find investment diverted out of the EC and a rise in structural unemployment. Both groups may then press for EC-wide protection policies; such policies would divert investment from the outside world and reduce EC unemployment, possibly leaving the total level of EC investment the same as otherwise. The investment mix in the EC would not be as beneficial as otherwise and the

---

[19] As a footnote above discusses, with high enough levels of protection, increases in protection will eventually reduce investment; see also Sweeney (1992).

[20] There seems little doubt that efforts to raise the poorer countries' wages and working conditions to those of richer members are unrealistic and will divert investment from the poorer members. It is likely that some increase in poorer members' environmental standards will raise these countries' welfare and may also attract more investment; for example, tourism depends in part on environmental conditions.

overall level of world investment would be lower. Members may also press for more expansionary monetary and fiscal policies; the scope for such EC-wide policies will depend on institutions like an EC central bank that are now being negotiated, but such policies ultimately have little effect on structural unemployment and may have severe consequences for inflation. The replacement of investment that is driven out by too-stringent environmental polices and high-tax policies with investment forced in by protectionist policies results in damage for the world and the EC as a whole.

At the other extreme, members may choose EC-wide policies that do not attempt to keep investment from flowing from high-income members to low-income members. High-income members might reduce their tax rates to stay competitive with the rest of the EC and the world. In this case, most members of the EC would see an increase in investment and a reduction in structural unemployment; the increase in investment would be created rather than diverted investment. The world and the EC as a whole would be better off. The outcome for high-income members would depend on their willingness to fight for investment by creating a business environment with tax and other policies attractive relative to other members and the rest of the world. Of course, the high-income countries need not cut their social expenditures or environmental standards to the level of poorer members'; the high-income countries offer a package that is different from other members', as the following section discusses.

Block Member-Country Policies

Inward FDI to any one member country of a block depends on inward FDI for the whole block and also the distribution of investment across the block. For concreteness, consider the EC, currently the best defined and most discussed block; also take Sweden, which has applied to the EC and will almost surely be admitted, perhaps as soon as late 1995. The EC might have zero net FDI while Sweden has positive inward FDI if other EC countries invest in Sweden or if foreigners reduce their holdings in other EC countries while building them in Sweden. In the previous section, it was argued that there has been and will be substantial investment in the EC to get around tariff walls (and NTBs) and to take advantage of the opportunities offered by the EC single market. Every EC country competes with other members for investment from non-EC sources as well as for investment by EC members. The more the EC approaches a true single market, the less are investment location decisions determined by access to a particular EC country. Instead, competition for investment turns on factor prices gross of taxes, infrastructure, transportation and transactions costs, taxes (net of subsidies), and factor productivity.

Each member country must adopt a strategy for this competition, consciously or not. The best strategy recognizes both what the country wants and has to offer. FDI by itself is an inappropriate goal, either to have or to avoid. Instead, an appropriate goal is to increase the country's wealth and welfare.

Investors' FDI decision depends in major part on being able to acquire factors at prices low relative to their productivity. With integrated capital markets, the cost of capital is much the same around the world,[21] differences coming only from government taxes or subsidies on raising funds. Hence, labor is the major factor-market determinant of non-resource-based FDI.[22] As is well understood, it may pay to locate in a high-wage country that has workers and executives so productive that unit labor costs are low; it may pay to locate in a country where workers are not very productive but low wages make unit labor costs low. Changes in unit labor costs, based on compensation relative to productivity, occur all the time.[23] It is not worth saying more than to reiterate what is well known: to attract FDI, an EC member must adopt policies that make wages gross of taxes compatible with its workers' productivity. For example, Sweden must see to it that its people are so productive that the country is justified in having high wages gross of taxes; Swedish wage policies must not price highly productive Swedish labor out of the world market.

[21] This statement means that for a given project, the cost of capital will be much the same for any firm considering the project. Similar projects in different countries can have very different costs of capital. In particular, government policy can raise the cost of capital by increasing the project's systematic risk. Further, even with the same systematic risk and cost of capital, the same project can have very different net present values in different countries because of different expected cash flows, depending in part on government policies.

[22] Even a country with abundant non-renewable natural resources is, over the longer run, in competition for non-resource-based FDI; income from non-renewable resources is more like depreciation than net national income, no matter how a country's national income accountants may treat the flows. Kuwait, for example, realizes that its oil wealth will someday be gone and is consciously trying to acquire an investment portfolio that will generate returns to replace oil income. Much of this portfolio is not in Kuwait; the 1991 Iraqi invasion of Kuwait justifies caution regarding the geographical location of Kuwaiti wealth and serves as a lesson to other Gulf portfolio managers.

[23] Variations in nominal exchange rates change unit labor costs across countries, as measured in a common currency. Often such changes can be large and long lasting.

U.S. experience may be useful. San Francisco in some ways is a tourist town–attractive to visit but with high living costs; many firms feel compelled to locate where amenities are less but costs are lower. Orange County in Southern California is an attractive but expensive place to live suburban life. A firm employing high skill, high wage people who want and can afford high-price amenities may sensibly locate in Orange County; if the firm also employs lower skill workers commanding only lower wages, attracting these workers will be difficult because of high living costs. To be sure, if these lower skill workers were earning high wages, they might well spend some of their larger incomes on Orange County amenities; with their actual incomes, they look elsewhere for work.[24]

FDI, Wealth and Welfare

To make the general points of the discussion more concrete, take the case of Sweden, which has long had important multinational companies, and has been in the top ranks of national income per capita in the post-WWII period. Consider what makes a country risk. First, a country is likely to be rich if its residents own a lot of productive high-return capital, as does Sweden. For a country's wealth in capital, it does not matter whether its capital is located there or abroad; for wealth purposes, owners of the country's capital should seek the best uses and returns for it, at home or abroad. In this sense, the substantial Swedish outward FDI in 1991 can be viewed as an attempt for managers to seek the highest valued use for Swedish capital. Second, a rich country generally enjoys high demand for its resources, principally labor services but also entrepreneurship, land and natural resources.

Sweden has high skill, high wage labor. To maintain high wages, Sweden must aim for high-productivity jobs. This means attracting and keeping firms interested in high skill labor. In manufacturing, these jobs typically focus on high quality output, demanding more intelligence, flexibility, adaptability and creativity than required of lower skill workers. Employers of these higher skill workers are hiring something akin to skills needed in the high skill end of the services market. Increasingly, the demand for high skill labor is in services or service-like manufacturing rather than in assembly-line manufacturing (for

---

[24] This discussion simplifies by omitting commuters; many workers do not live near their jobs, but instead commute. Ceteris paribus, a firm must pay workers higher wages than otherwise to attract commuting workers.

example, the classic Henry Ford assembly line for U.S. autos) or heavy industry (for example, big steel).

Many argue that FDI's benefit is that foreigners provide more capital for workers to use, thus raising demand for labor services. This view, often adequate, has important inadequacies. One is that new capital frequently eliminates jobs. Machines often substitute for high skill labor, through robots or allowing lower skill workers to use "idiot proof" or "dumbed down" machines. In turn, machines often reduce or eliminate use of lower skill labor. To be sure, servicing these machines requires relatively high skill, highly paid labor, but these workers are a small fraction of those displaced.

In advanced economies, roughly half of gross investment is replacement that is not part of net investment. Replacement investment that embodies the latest technology can lead to substantial increases in productivity even in the face of relatively anemic levels of net investment. This replacement investment is often designed to reduce use of both high and low skill labor.

High-Skill Services

In analyzing capital that replaces both high and low skill labor, note that services go into allowing this new capital to exist. The new capital derives from basic research that is then used for applied research. There is much design involved and increasing use of computer hardware and software. Some of the increased demand for high skill labor involved in the replacement of (high and low skill) labor with capital comes from the generation of the new types of capital rather than from jobs servicing the new, complex capital.

From the supply side, economists often view output as depending on inputs of labor and capital. It is fruitful to think of output as also depending on inputs of services. Some services are: accounting, legal, instructions writing, research and development, headquarters, advertising, trouble shooting, training, personnel, and many more–even advice from economists.[25] Such services are important in producing Volvos even though service providers never turn their hands to the cars. In the case of a service like WordPerfect, the tangible product is computer disks for installing the program; a tiny fraction of the work

[25] Of course, it is possible to think of all these services as depending on the use of labor and capital, but breaking out these functions separately focuses attention on the issue of services.

force makes the disks, a small portion actually writes the computer code.

As countries become richer, the demand for services rises. In the U.S., the services component of consumption is larger than the sum of the other components, durable and nondurable goods; services employ 70 percent of all working Americans and "nine tenths of all new jobs created in the 1980s went to ... white-collar workers".[26] It is not clear which EC members' future is in high-tech services, but it would be a mistake to ignore this possibility and focus solely on manufacturing, particularly lower-skilled manufacturing.[27]

In the service sector high demand for high skill workers often requires little plant relative to manufacturing, though not always.[28] Of course, these services may use a lot of equipment–for example, computers. Indeed, investment to support services is a major reason for the burst of FDI in the 1980s;[29] in the U.S., services "account for 85% of total private information-technology investment".[30] This suggests that using total amounts of FDI to judge success in attracting FDI can be misleading; the quality of FDI can be more important than its quantity. A little of the right kind of FDI can be better than a lot of the wrong kind.

It is easier for Sweden or any EC country to do well from supplying high skill services to the EC and world markets if firms can unbundle white-collar services from plant and sales locations. Often a firm does not need a plant near

---

[26] See The Economist, Aug. 24, 1991, p. 30

[27] The Economist (Aug. 10, 1991, p. 55) reports that "for the past decade Japanese manufacturers, like their rivals in America and Europe, have been shifting much of their attention away from honing their production processes to applying new information-processing technologies and competing in fast-growing service businesses....the biggest problem for Japanese companies is .... retraining spare manufacturing hands to become skilled knowledge workers." It also reports (Aug. 10, 1991, pp. 21-22) that "Hong Kong companies employed more than 2m factory workers in Guangdong; manufacturing employment in Hong Kong itself is down to around 700,000. In other words, Hong Kong is becoming a high-wage service economy, the marketing and management headquarters for manufacturing in southern China." The International Herald Tribune (Paul Blustein, "Freedom Worries Aside, Hong Kong Economy is Hot," May 26, 1992, pp. 1,4) reports that many in Hong Kong view its economic future as bright because it will serve as the commercial connection to the world of a booming South China economy; "Hong Kong's business community expects to continue this shift of low-cost labor into Guangdong long after 1997, creating higher-paying jobs for Hong Kong in the process."

[28] Particular services like telecommunications may require substantial plant.

[29] See The Economist, Aug. 24, 1991, p. 57.

[30] See The Economist, Aug. 24, 1991, p. 30.

every point of sale to final customers or distributors.[31] Often the services a firm uses need not be located near its plants.[32] Already some U.S. firms use the EC for some of their services operations for the U.S. market, though some of these are middle-tech services.[33]

Low-cost transport, air service and telecommunications greatly help unbundling high skill services from plant and sales locations. Air service is currently relatively high cost in Europe; telecommunications are high cost and inefficient in a number of EC countries.[34] These high costs and inefficiencies particularly hurt countries offering high skill services.

Globalization

"Globalization" is today's premier business buzzword. Often globalization's message is missed. For FDI, globalization means more ferocious worldwide competition. Because of this increased competition, globalization favors firms that see competition and profits as two of their major goals. In turn, globalization leads to more "invasion" of national markets and thus more FDI. This subsection discusses some general issues in globalization and then draws some conclusions for investment in a world of trading blocks.

Global Competition and Rents

Barriers of culture, language, law and regulation protect home-country firms from foreign competition. Another powerful deterrent to foreign competition is specificity of the national market. Home-country firms have the background and knowledge to deal with the market; foreign firms do not. Home-country firms and products are known in their market, with this knowledge like a stock

---

[31] Some services, such as retail banking, require locations near customers. This is an example of how some services are less amenable to exports than are goods. Many of the backoffice services provided by banks can be, and very often are, located far from the average customer.

[32] Some steel mini-mills capitalize on being near their main customers and being flexible in meeting customer needs on specifications and timing of deliveries. Mini-mills owned by a large firm need not, however, have their pro rata share of overhead services located nearby.

[33] See Wysocki (1991).

[34] Wysocki (1991) reports Ireland spent $3.5 billion on telecommunications in the 1980s, an investment that helped attract white-collar back-office jobs from abroad, including from the U.S. He notes, however, that getting a phone installed in Ireland may take three months.

of capital; foreign rivals find it expensive to build a similar stock.

Globalization is changing this, and will force even greater changes. One well-known aspect of globalization is the rise of some internationally standardized markets; autos is one example frequently discussed, computers another. This important phenomenon can be overstated. Many products cannot be internationally standardized; it will be a long time before the French eat Wonder Bread in quantity.

Another type of globalization is less noticed. Information and the ability to process it have become much cheaper, and their prices will continue to fall relative to other prices and costs; a well-known example is the decrease in the real and even nominal price of computing power.[35] Firms can now more cheaply acquire and use the information needed to invade foreign markets, and to control and manage sales and output there; these costs will continue to fall. Further, the invading firms can now more cheaply build up the consumer's stock of knowledge about its product. For many products the start-up costs and ongoing costs of dealing with foreign markets are now cheaper in real terms. To be sure, it is expensive for the firm to modify products and market approaches, and to learn to deal with the host-country government, with host-country culture, with the different attitudes, aptitudes, skills and training of host-country workers, but it is relatively cheaper than before.[36] Globalization means that the costs of handling these differences are declining over time for firms that think globally.

The global competitor acquires this knowledge and skill as an investment; the cost of the investment is declining in real terms. Once the investment is made, on economic grounds the firm competes on more or less the same terms as host-country firms;[37] a global firm committed to market competition will on average outcompete a domestic firm that has become sluggish from natural or government protection.

---

[35] The Economist (Aug. 24, 1991, p. 30) says that "between 1960 and 1990 the price of computing power in America shrank, in real terms by a factor of 6,000–or by a fairly constant (and continuing) 25-30% a year."

[36] There is an extensive literature on the degree to which countries are similar to each other and how this convergence changes over time. Some studies argue that convergence has not increased much over time. The global firm does not need convergence to make profits in foreign markets. Essentially, it needs large enough foreign markets with low enough start-up costs.

[37] This depends of course on the attitude of the host-country government. Some observers charge that the Japanese government puts many roadblocks in the way of foreign firms whose products would otherwise be well accepted by consumers and generate adequate profit margins.

The global firm also has the option of roundabout investment. Instead of simply paying to get up to speed in a given country, it can invest in the general ability to come up to speed in a range of countries. It can, for example, foster a corporate culture where dealing with a range of national markets is an important part of the firm's mission. It can become good at seeking out information about markets not just in France or Pakistan, but in foreign markets in general. It can hire permanent employees whose main task and expertise is dealing with foreign markets in a particular region or in general. In the global market place, long-run success is more likely for firms set up to learn cheaply about international opportunities and how to take advantage of them.

Globalization and the Evolution of FDI

If protection is low enough in foreign markets, a globally-oriented firm is likely to evolve from producing for a home market to exporting to FDI. If protection is high enough, a firm that develops global skills may be forced to cut out the exporting stage and go to FDI.

Global firms driven by the competition for economic rents are likely to find unit costs declining over time. One reason for falling unit costs is technological progress that competition-oriented firms tend to incorporate. Often unit costs fall relative to demand, reducing price. Eventually, the target-market unit revenues (net of transportation costs, tariffs, etc.) are above those in the global firm's base-country, making it profitable to export; the target-country producer that sits on profits needs increasing protection over time to avoid eventual entry by other firms' exports.

The exporting firm becomes used to dealing with this market (and other foreign markets). It also becomes a better global firm, that is, a firm that has relatively low costs of dealing with different markets, including markets new to the firm. Over time, the invading firm likely finds decreases in the estimated unit costs of producing in the protected market. With these estimated unit costs low enough, it makes sense to produce abroad. The firm then supplies the base country from the base-country plant, foreign markets from the foreign plant.[38] FDI is not guaranteed; there may be significant economies of scale over a wide range of output in the base country, and the firm may long be more productive

[38] This is under the assumption that both operations face increasing or constant marginal costs. With decreasing marginal costs in at least one country, one might export to the other.

in the base rather than foreign country.[39] At large enough outputs, base-country scale economies must tail off, however; and over time, the firm becomes better at dealing abroad at low costs.

High protection may keep out global competitors' exports for an extended period. Eventually the competitors may use FDI to enter the market at a large scale. Rather than local firms developing skill over a substantial period in dealing with import competition, they instead face large scale competition over a short time period; high protection can weaken protected producers and lead to the invading, global firm's success.

Globalization and Trading Blocks

The EC's single market in 1992 makes the EC more attractive for global firms than any one member's national market, save for some products in some of the largest member economies. EC firms and products that have survived because of government protection, customer knowledge of the firms and products, and the high costs of breaking into the market offer attractive targets for global firms after rents. The EC offers global firms potential rewards unmatched in the rest of the world. The EC single market is comparable in size and wealth to the U.S., but unlike the U.S. offers many targets that have been sheltered in national markets. Trade restriction, domestic content rules, etc. may force global firms to rely heavily on production in the EC rather than exports to the EC to go after the rents there. Whether the global firm uses EC production or relies on exports, the firm will have to depend on EC residents. Even a global firm good at dealing with new markets must rely on help from those who already know the governments, customer tastes, labor markets and products involved. Sometimes the global firm needs help in very narrow markets or with a particular country's market or government. Very often, though, the firm also needs generalized help with the EC as a whole; this will become more common as the single market takes hold. There is a niche for helping global firms compete in the EC. Which countries will be most active in providing these services is an open question.

There is an ongoing competition among Japan, the U.S. and Europe, particularly the EC, to supply services to global corporations. For example, an American or Japanese firm entering Europe or dealing with new areas in

[39] Productivity must of course be measured relative to factor costs. What matters is unit costs, not worker productivity or wages in isolation.

Europe must decide where to get some of the services to make this possible. If travel is cheap and fast, if telecommunications are cheap and reliable, then some service components of the operation can be located almost anywhere in the EC–or even outside the EC, in Japan or the U.S.

The global firm will play a major role in the twenty-first century. One of its key decisions is how to deal with the world's many languages. One model is that of United Nations organizations or the European Commission, with multiple official languages and an emphasis on multilingual employees. This is expensive; some of the expense is justified on grounds of member-nation pride. An alternative model is to pick a single language for most business purposes. There are strong trends in this direction–and the language is English. Suppose that twenty-first century global firms are essentially English-speaking. This suggests that Sweden, Denmark, the Netherlands, Ireland and the U.K. are major European competitors for providing English-language-based services that global companies in Europe will need.[40] The Netherlands, Denmark and the U.K. offer skills and amenities similar to Sweden's; these are competitors with which Sweden must reckon. Further, depending on the level of EC external barriers, the U.S. is also a formidable competitor in many services (for example, financial services). The question is not so much where global entrepreneurs want to live; many can live anywhere in the developed world. Top-rank middle managers, who often must live near the work force, typically have the income and tastes for amenities. If the work force is high skill, the question is whether a country offers a package of amenities affordable by its high skill population.

Adjustment of Investment to Policy Changes

There is an immense literature on determinants of FDI,[41] partly because of the vast range of the firms, and their products, engaged in FDI. Within the range

[40] In The Economist (Aug. 3, 1991. p. 43) the Netherlands Foreign Investment Agency had a full page, four color ad headlined "Holland has a 400-year head start gearing up for global strategies," and concluding with, "Where better to anchor the European portion of your company's global activities?" The U.K. counters with a full page, four color ad, "Countdown to Europe 1992," which points out that "Britain is already by far the Number One location in Europe for US companies" and urges the reader to "find out more about Britain's advantages for your Business as the base for tariff-free access to the European Single Market." (The Economist, Sept. 14, 1991, p. 61). The Economist has also carried ads that more narrowly extol England's virtues as a base. Luxembourg's full page, two color ad, "We may be small, but we don't think that way," points out that it is "Europe's 3rd largest financing center [and] its judicial, financial and information center." The ad notes that Luxembourg's "multilingual workforce is among the best educated in Europe [and] that many international companies wanting to do business in Europe come to Luxembourg." (The Economist, Sept. 21, 1991, p. 53.)

[41] See Dunning (1988) for a recent survey of the "eclectic," "internalization" theory of FDI, along with a partial bibliography on this theory and some of its rivals.

of all FDI, new manufacturing FDI projects are likely large scale and somewhat insensitive to policy changes, at least in the shorter run. FDI that expands ongoing operations and FDI for new operations differ importantly; much of new manufacturing FDI is very discrete and lumpy. Consider a firm with substantial sales and production in one country[42] thinking of possible foreign sales and production.

Start-Up Costs

All sorts of start-up costs can be important, depending on industry, firm or product. Many of these costs are lumpsum or fairly insensitive to the projected sales volume. Lump sum start-up costs, spread over the volume of trade or output over time, tend toward decreasing unit costs.[43] The firm must anticipate a fairly large volume of sales, with attractive profit margins, to justify the start-up costs. Usually, start-up costs are lower if the firm exports rather than produces and sells in the host country; further, knowledge and experience from exporting is useful (reduces the start-up costs) for later FDI. This biases the firm towards exports rather than FDI. It is frequently noted that market imperfections, particularly due to government policies such as trade barriers, may impel the firm directly to FDI rather than first exporting.

Scarce Factor

Firms can buy or hire more units of most factors–more land, financial and physical capital, skilled and unskilled labor, researchers, etc. Many firms find limits to stretching or expanding management-team talent. Starting up foreign sales, particularly foreign production and sales, requires major commitment of management-team energies and can distract from home-country operations. Some teams have excess managerial capacity; a new foreign operation will not reduce attention to ongoing operations. Many firms are not in this situation.[44]

---

[42] This need not be a "home-country" firm; it might be controlled and largely (or wholly) owned by nonresidents of the home country.

[43] These are not fixed cost in the usual theory of the firm that focuses on the short run, where some costs are fixed, versus the longer run where the fixed costs become variable. Rather, they are averaged over the output in many periods. Many discussions of FDI assume that a foreign firm's costs are higher than domestic firms' costs in every period. In contrast, in the approach here, the foreign firm pays start-up costs that may allow it thereafter to have much the same flow costs as if it were a domestic firm.

[44] In addition, a management team with current excess capacity has many opportunities–new or expanded domestic operations or a variety of foreign operations in many different countries; the decision to export to or invest in one market displaces other possible uses of the firm's excess capacity.

The attention management must devote to new FDI, if the FDI is to be successful, is often so large that the FDI must be on a substantial scale to justify the commitment. The required management commitment is partly a fixed cost, biasing the firm to large scale FDI as do start-up costs.

Economies of Scale

Economists often ignore economies of scale[45] that affect major FDI decisions. Scale economies argue for expanding home-country production to get lower unit costs. Expanded home-country production and sales squeeze profit margins. With profit margins squeezed enough, the firm may sell abroad; exports allow more home-country production, to reap economies of scale, but extra output sold abroad does not further squeeze home-country profit margins. If the firm turns to FDI, the FDI must be on a large scale to capture the scale economies available in the host country as in the home country and to make up for the lost economies of scale in home-country production, assuming that foreign production in part displaces home-country production that was going as exports.[46,47]

These considerations point towards new FDI on a substantial scale rather than starting small and growing incrementally. The important political economy result is that policies affecting new FDI have lumpy effects. For FDI already in place, if taxes go up a bit, output of the taxed good goes down a bit and plant expansions are curtailed a bit, in a continuous way; not so with major new FDI projects.

The distinction between FDI for marginal changes in operations already in place versus new operations has at least four implications for government policy. First, for a substantial impact on new manufacturing FDI, changes in government policies likely must be substantial rather than modest and at the

[45] One reason is that scale economies greatly complicate the models that economists use to think about the world.

[46] If both the home and foreign operations have decreasing costs, it will not pay to produce in both countries unless import barriers in the one country are so high as to offset production advantages in the other (Horst 1971; Caves 1982).

[47] In addition, the home-country operation likely faces lower profit margins. With foreign markets now sourced from outside the home country, the firm is likely to cut back home-country production by only some fraction of its lost foreign sales, so that home-country sales will be rising and hence price falling at the same time unit costs are rising.

margin. Second, a commitment to foreign production requires substantial time and thought, but when made will likely be at a substantial scale; thus, the elasticity of response rises with the time horizon considered. Third, with new, large FDI, the inevitable tendency is for government to cut special deals. This type of industrial policy should be resisted (see below); it discriminates among firms, with government making undiversified investments in particular industries. Fourth, for all but the largest and richest European countries, EC membership makes inward FDI more attractive by offering a market large enough to justify major FDI.

Block-Member Policies and FDI

Every country wants high-wage, clean industries, ceteris paribus. This correlation–nonpolluting, high wages–is often, though not always, observed; dirty, polluting industries often use low productivity, low wage workers.[48] In competing for clean, high-wage industries, individual block members offer different packages. For example, in competition with EC members, Sweden offers a package of environmental concerns, generous social policies, high wages, high taxes and high skill, high productivity people. The kinds of work at which highly trained Swedes are good require people who typically demand something like the life Sweden offers. Not just foreign managers want amenities; if host-country workers are highly productive, they want to spend part of their high incomes on amenities. A country must align its package with economic realities. Many attractive types of FDI fit with Sweden's general package of amenities, though efficiency and competitiveness may call for some adjustments of Sweden's package; from casual empiricism, the actions and plans of the centrist government that replaced the Social Democrats in 1991 seem to be on track in reducing marginal tax rates and government economic intervention.

Taxes and What They Buy

A key link in the package a country offers is between the amenities the taxpayer gets and the taxes she or he pays. People will pay for desired goods and services, from the private or public sector. They are reluctant to pay more than

[48] This is one part of the difficulties of German reunification. The average worker in Eastern Germany is less productive than the average Western German worker; the industries left from the communist regime are on average much more polluting than in the western part of Germany.

necessary for what they get or for goods and services not received; government waste ultimately drives away firms and people.[49] Further, though many people favor income or wealth redistribution, there are limits to what they will pay to reduce inequality of results. Governments often finance transfer payments with high marginal tax rates. High marginal tax rates by themselves are a major disincentive to work. Transfer payments in excess of what workers feel are fair are also a disincentive.[50] High tax rates to finance transfers are an invitation for the world's poor to immigrate and the country's most productive to emigrate.

Firms are willing to pay taxes to buy amenities, but not at too high a price. Further, they are concerned with how government taxing and spending programs affect employees. If government raises average tax rates, keeps marginal tax rates constant, and uses the extra revenues to finance expenditures that give the average worker good value for money, then workers will not pressure employers too much for higher wages to make up for the extra taxation. But higher expenditures not worthwhile to workers and higher marginal tax rates put unwelcome pressure on business to raise wages.

Experience suggests that efficiency in providing government services does not necessarily depend on whether the government or the private sector provides the services; instead, efficiency depends on whether there is competition in providing services. Many U.S. local and state governments have been experimenting in having services such as garbage collection, job training and even prisons provided by private firms awarded contracts through competitive processes. By and large, it appears the competition results in little change in quality but lower costs. Encouraging competition does not necessarily mean no government employees provide the services. When, for example, some garbage routes are private and other state-run, the example of the private sector holds down costs of state-run routes lest these routes be turned over to the

---

[49] Often the response to bad policy is slow and lumpy, as noted above in this section. Governments are then misled over the shorter run by finding little reaction to say higher taxes. If jobs and investment leave after several years, some argue that the taxes are "old news" and not responsible.

[50] An increase in marginal tax rates that holds constant average tax rates has a disproportionate effect on higher income people and tends to reduce their efforts and drive them out. An increase in average tax rates with marginal tax rates held constant leads to no incentive effect on the margin; the change reduces wealth to the extent the extra taxes are used to provide goods and services that the taxpayer would not otherwise demand. Overly generous transfer payments, beyond what the average taxpayer feels are justified, will drive away workers and firms even if marginal tax rates are not excessive; workers and firms tend to migrate to locations with comparable marginal but lower average tax rates.

private sector. To provide good value for money, government must take active steps to secure competition.[51]

EC membership, with mobility of capital, pressures governments not to let their tax policies get too far out of line. This pressure is not instantaneous, however. For a few years, a government can raise taxes and expenditures without firms leaving; it is not cheap to pack up and go. Further, minor policy changes may not induce much FDI response. Major, long-lasting changes cause major responses over time. Governments looking only at short-run responses can fool themselves into tax and expenditure increases that over time lead to substantial disinvestment. Further, when firms become convinced that a country's government is biased toward tax increases, they fear committing to that country even if current policies are attractive. Most FDI requires long-term commitment; firms look at long-term, not just current, policies. Put another way, instability in the "rules of the game" causes investors to build in a higher risk premium, a political risk premium, in the discount rate they use for assessing projects in the unstable country or region,[52] and thus reduces the level of investment both by domestic and foreign firms.

EC single-market regulations reduce intra-EC barriers to labor mobility; for example, professional licenses from one member country are accepted market wide. Labor mobility also makes it easier for firms to move to escape taxation that is excessive in terms of benefits or that depends on steep marginal tax rates. On the one hand, it is not wise to make too much of labor mobility; many EC members have work forces that are notoriously slow to change location, thus contributing to higher structural unemployment.[53] On the other hand, it is mobility at the margin that matters; a company does not need to move its entire labor force, but typically only a relatively few key people.

It is not possible to be as concrete about pressures in NAFTA or a Far-East trading block, because the one is not yet ratified and the other is mainly speculation currently. Nevertheless, some points are clear. There is and will

---

[51] Disciplining government provision of goods and services requires competition on both the revenue and cost sides. Government agencies selling in competitive markets face discipline on the revenue side. For competition to work fully, the agencies must not be able to finance losses through tax revenues or from inputs provided by government at below-market prices.

[52] See Oxelheim (1990).

[53] Often the innate reluctance to move is supported by unemployment and welfare benefits; it is thus difficult to sort out the degree to which labor mobility is culturally based or the result of incentives.

very likely continue to be virtually unhindered outward capital mobility from the U.S. and Canada. The same is almost completely true of inward capital mobility.[54] In the NAFTA negotiations, Mexico has reduced some of its barriers to foreign ownership of land and equity, but there remain restrictions, for example, in the petroleum industry; further, some observers worry that Mexican regulations may easily become much more stringent under future administrations. Legal labor mobility between the U.S. and Mexico is very unlikely to approach intra-EC ease; a major argument in the U.S. in favor of NAFTA is that it will increase Mexican income and growth and thus reduce incentives for Mexican immigration to the U.S.[55]

As for an East-Asian trading block, there is substantial outward capital mobility from Japan, but the tigers currently have a large variety of changing restrictions. Japan has a relatively small stock of inward FDI compared to the U.S., U.K., Germany or the EC[56], and is notoriously unfriendly towards foreign firms setting up shop in Japan. The tigers have widely varying attitudes toward inward FDI; Singapore and Hong Kong are quite open, South Korea quite difficult. Japanese firms have made major investments in the tigers starting in the 1980s, and have plans for substantially more.[57]

Labor mobility in a potential Far-East block is complex. A key given is that Japan and the Japanese are very reluctant to allow immigration. Partly this is cultural, partly economic; Japanese put great weight on their cultural homogeneity, and many believe that it is part of the explanation of why Japan has done

---

[54] In the U.S., there is some popular sentiment against allowing foreigners to hold companies that are deemed crucial to national or even economic security. Leftist politicians and analysts frequently raise such issues. Examples are Richard Gephart's 1988 campaign in the Democratic presidential primaries, and Bob Kerry's and Tom Harkin's in the 1992 primaries, and Patrick Buchanan in the 1992 Republican primaries. Some countries are circumspect about their inward FDI to the U.S.; for example Saudi Arabia as a policy does not take equity positions (though Kuwait does), and Japanese companies have begun to try to be "good citizens" in the jurisdictions where they locate.

[55] Many observers are doubtful that even a highly successful NAFTA will have any noticeable effect on Mexican immigration to the U.S. over the next decade or two.

[56] Brewer and Sweeney (1991). In 1991, Japan recaptured the lead in total measured net claims on foreigners (International Herald Tribune, 1992: "Japan's net overseas holdings...[rose] $55 billion...from $328.1 billion at the end of 1990..."). Since the claims are measured in terms of historical cost, they understate the current value of claims bought in the past that are likely to have appreciated in value over time; this can lead to serious understatement of the current value of U.S. foreign claims.

[57] Even if some of the tigers might hinder inward FDI beyond what Japanese and other firms currently plan, these firms can freely cut back on the planned investment; in this sense, there is free capital mobility in terms of reductions even if not necessarily in terms of increases.

so well economically in the post-WWII era, for example, relative to the U.S. which is racially and culturally much more heterogeneous. An alternative to allowing immigration to Japan is for Japanese firms to set up plants in East Asia to use lower-cost labor without allowing that labor into Japan; this is one common interpretation of the burst of Japanese inward FDI to the tigers.[58] The tigers have been open to immigration of Japanese and other managers, but not to immigration by low skill labor.[59] Thus, it is difficult to say what type of labor mobility might arise in a Far-East trading block, but it would very likely be substantially less than that allowed in the EC.

Predictability of Policy

Dealing with a block-member government is more attractive if there are clarity, simplicity, transparency, and stability of policies. The liberalizing countries of Eastern Europe do not have clear, stable economic policies; further, property rights and their meaning are not clear there. These lacks deter inward FDI to Eastern Europe. In U.S. experience, in many cities a firm undertaking a large development project has little assurance at the start that it will be allowed to carry out the project or what price government will demand for its permission; substantial risk is involved. This reduces the level of investment. Sweden has recently undertaken tax changes designed in part to make the country more attractive for investment. If these changes are reversed, rather than kept in place or augmented, investors will be discouraged not only by higher taxes but by the uncertainty of policy, which will lead to a political risk premium;[60] investors will think more seriously about other possible EC locations. Similarly, many observers believe that the Mexican reforms under the Salinas administration affected inward FDI in a major way only after

---

[58] Japanese firms have also set up research operations in the U.S. One of the stated goals is to have not only production in the U.S., but also creative work. In this view, the Japanese firms are allowing U.S. residents access to a wide range of jobs rather than only production. Another interpretation notes that the market for research personnel is tight in Japan; as an alternative to allowing substantial immigration of researchers to Japan, the firms can hire these workers in the U.S. Further, it is well known that a large share of U.S. schools' Ph.D:s in science and engineering is composed of students not born in the U.S.; thus, this Japanese strategy gets the advantage of researchers with very diverse cultural backgrounds without having to pay the price of diluting Japanese homogeneity.

[59] For example, British-run Hong Kong is quite strict in not allowing in Vietnamese boat people. Thailand makes it very difficult for Cambodian refugees to work in Thailand.

[60] As one measure of the effect of uncertain policies on financial markets and hence investment, Oxelheim (1990) reports that when the abolition of Swedish exchange controls was first announced, the differential between Swedish and foreign interest rates diminished by 1.5 percentage points.

several years when investors became more convinced that the reforms were likely to be long term. Thus, just as increases in taxes and expenditures will not have an immediate effect on FDI, so reductions are likely to take time to have their full impact; in both cases, the lag is due in part to the time involved in making investment decisions and in carrying them out, but also because investors look at least as much to long-term as to short-term policies.

Employment Flexibility

All firms trade off commitments to their workers versus flexibility in dealing with new developments and major disturbances. Many firms find it profitable to commit to long-term relationships with their employees. Through its commitment to workers, the firm gains an attachment and commitment from workers that it could not get otherwise, but loses flexibility. Some firms find lost flexibility too great a cost for the gains of commitment. The optimal mix of commitment versus flexibility appears to vary widely across firms and industries.

In some countries, firms and employees work out between them the balance of commitment and flexibility. A worker valuing long-term commitment and willing to commit in return searches for employment with firms that find commitment more than makes up for lost flexibility. Other firms find they can commit only to a much smaller fraction of their workers because flexibility is too important. Some EC members have moved to force firms into greater commitment by limiting their flexibility. By itself, workers of course value this increased commitment. Over time this government policy drives away businesses that must be flexible to survive in the EC and global market-places.

Flexibility is becoming more important to many firms. Markets in the 1970s and 1980s showed substantially greater volatility than in the 1950s and 1960s.[61] Likely markets will continue to be volatile in the coming decade. Firms believing they will face volatility are pushed to greater flexibility for survival.

---

[61] The volatility of real exchange rates since the current regime of managed floating began in March, 1973, has increased substantially. For example, the U.S. dollar-DM real exchange rate (using CPIs) has been as low as 60 and as high as 130 from April, 1973, to December, 1988, with the index normalized to have a mean value of 100.

The Maastricht agreement of December, 1991, adopted a memo of agreement among eleven of the 12 EC members for an EC social charter.[62] The operational meaning of the social charter is being worked out by negotiations and administrative and judicial interpretations; the process will take many years. Some observers interpret the social charter as a type of cartel agreement to keep some members from undercutting others by offering firms less stringent conditions;[63] social charter restrictions on flexibility may help those countries that already have laws limiting labor-market flexibility. Like all maneuvers by suppliers cartels, this works to the degree that firms have no choice beyond cartel members. Firms that have no choice beyond the EC will have to abide by the charter; some will be driven out of business. Many firms have a choice and will locate outside the EC. This might push the EC to protectionist policies to prevent runaway firms. The specter of trading blocs is unfavorable for the EC and the world.

A major issue in U.S. political battles over NAFTA is how close Mexico will come to U.S. standards for work conditions and for the environment. To protect their members, U.S. labor unions would like to see standards on Mexican wages, hours and other working conditions that are closer to U.S. law and the contracts unions have with firms in the U.S. Environmentalists want Mexican standards closer to the U.S.'s. They fear that Mexico's lower standards will attract firms for which it is expensive to meet U.S. pollution standards, thereby increasing world-wide pollution; further, because many of these firms are likely to be along the Mexican-U.S. border, where many U.S. firms in Mexico are now located, pollution in the U.S. would also rise.[64] It is not clear what standards the NAFTA accord will contain. On the one hand, the Bush administration has promised to be sensitive to these issues in the negotiations. On the other hand, the administration has "fast-track" authori-

---

62 The U.K. opted out of the social charter, so the agreement became a memo of agreement among the eleven rather than a part of the EC charter. During the U.K. parliamentary elections of April, 1992, it was widely thought that a Labor government would agree to the Maastricht version of the social charter. This is an example of the unstable policies that investors fear.

63 The cartel elements are of course only one part of the social charter.

64 U.S. labor unions support the environmentalists in this particular battle. One reason is that a coalition has a better chance of killing a NAFTA agreement. In addition, loose environmental standards are complimentary to low skill, low wage Mexican labor and thus contribute to NAFTA's effect of attracting union jobs to Mexico.

ty;[65] further, it knows that it has little to hope for politically from environmentalists and union leaders, and thus has the incentive to give them only enough to get the treaty ratified.

Environmental and social standards vary widely across the potential members of a Far-East trading block. Japanese politicians have become more conscious of pollution and are taking some slow actions; some observers view this trend as another reason for Japanese firms to invest in Asian countries where environmental standards are lower, and likely to remain lower, than in Japan. Much discussion in Taiwan focuses on environmental and associated infrastructure shortcomings. One of the charges against the military in Thailand is that their domination of Thai governments has led to destruction of major hardwood forests.

Restrictions on Services

Trading-block members often have differential restrictions on various types of services; these restrictions can place a country at an important, and perhaps growing, disadvantage relative to other block members. For example, Sweden is behind some EC members in some types of services, for example financial services in equities; Sweden, however, has an impressive record on futures, options and other derivatives. London and New York are closer to state of the art in equities, though even these are threatened by others and have been losing business; the Swedish options market is competitive with foreign options markets. This suggests looking carefully at regulations on services; for example, Swedish rules, regulations and taxes resulted in 60 percent of the volume in Swedish equities on the London exchange by the early 1990s.[66] Similarly, restrictions on entry for exchange membership in Mexico, and requirements to go through brokers for transactions, lead to high transactions costs for Mexican shares; transactions costs on the Tokyo exchange also seem high relative to average costs on more competitive markets. These markets are likely to lose volume over time.

[65] This means that Congress must vote up or down on the negotiated agreement, without being able to amend it. This gives the administration the first move in a game where this is likely to be a major advantage; in much legislation, Congress has the first move, sending the administration a bill that the president can either accept or veto. Of course the process is not this simple: Before submitting the bill, the administration must negotiate its contents with individuals and groups in Congress to get their support on the up-or-down vote; similarly, when Congress passes laws, it often negotiates on content to avoid a veto.

[66] Part of this resulted from a turnover tax of one percent of asset value, later raised to two percent. This tax has since been removed.

It may be too late for Sweden to make up lost ground in some types of financial transactions and compete with financial markets that are ahead. Instead, the appropriate regulatory stance is to allow firms locating in Sweden to use foreign services as cheaply in Sweden as if the firms were located in the U.K. or the U.S.

Negotiating on Large Projects

Because some new FDI is large and discrete, causes substantial effects in the region located, and can depend sensitively on government policies, firms and governments often negotiate the conditions of the investment. Sometimes the negotiations become a contest among rival governments to lure the firm; frequently a firm will try to engender such competition. Experience in U.S. cities, counties, and states shows two common mistakes in these negotiations.

First, in competition with other governments, often the government will make concessions (in the form of tax holidays, variances in zoning laws, subsidized loans, and many more) to one firm that it does not make to other firms, particularly those already located in the jurisdiction.[67] This discriminatory policy is often unwise. The government subsidizes one firm at the expense of others. It runs a type of industrial policy, betting on the favored firm with taxpayers' money. Often these bets are undiversified and thus fail to follow the major lesson of modern finance, to diversify risks.[68] Tax breaks that attract one project drive away other potential projects or firms already located in the jurisdiction.

Second, when there is no competition among jurisdictions, the government often tries to extract as much as possible from the firm. Many U.S. cities and counties follow this pattern in dealing with housing or commercial developers or providers of cable TV services. In this situation of bilateral monopoly, government may push its demands so far that the project is never undertaken. Further, governments sometimes overlook the longer-run benefits of the project that accrue to other firms, and thus underestimate the locality's losses if the project does not go forward.

---

[67] Wysocki (1991) reports that Ireland offers foreign investors "employment grants, training grants, and construction grants [that] alone often amount to several million dollars worth of incentives. On top of that Ireland promises foreigners a low, 10% tax rate until the year 2010."

[68] To be sure, residents of the jurisdiction can take into account the uncertain implications for their future taxes of the government's bets. Offsetting these effects generates transactions costs for the residents; further, it is often difficult for a taxpayer to know exactly the risks the government has undertaken and how best to offset these risks.

Concluding Remarks and Projections for the 1990s

FDI is sometimes desired by governments, sometimes feared, and sometimes simultaneously both. A government may fear foreign interests taking over vital segments of its economy, thus exposing the country to foreign influence and weakening its economic security;[69] every government also faces political pressure to protect domestic firms. At the same time, governments and voters often view FDI as a beneficial increase in the stock of capital the country has to use. Within the limits of national security and protectionist pressures, politicians want to attract more FDI.[70]

For the world as a whole and for many individual countries, investment is less than socially optimal.[71] A substantial part of this investment shortfall arises from excessive marginal tax rates at the corporate and personal level, from the double taxation of dividends in some countries, from unfavorable tax rules about the size and timing of deductions, from environmental, labor and social policies, from policy uncertainty that adds to the substantial market uncertainty firms already face, and from many other policy disincentives. One measure of the distortions in incentives is the gap between business's marginal physical productivity of capital before taxation and the net real rate of return to savers after personal taxation. In many countries, savers often receive a negative real rate of return though capital's social marginal product is large. Even countries with better incentives for capital formation are concerned about inadequate capital formation.

Governments are often concerned about inadequate investment and the resulting structural unemployment; they adopt policies that directly and indirectly, intentionally or not, affect investment. A key distinction is between investment-creating and -diverting policies. Investment-diverting policies

---

[69] See Moran (1990/91).

[70] Countries tend to have a more favorable view of FDI explicitly connected to increases in the capital stock (for example, a new foreign-owned factory) rather than purchases of already existing assets; see, for example, The Economist (Aug. 10, 1991). The capital-starved liberalizing countries of Eastern Europe are privatizing and adding new capital at slower rates than possible; one reason is their fears of "excessive" foreign ownership.

[71] It is sometimes argued that in centrally planned economies, misallocation or misuse of investment rather than an inadequate level of investment is the main problem. In market-oriented economies some observers deny that investment is too low; more commonly, however, those who defend policies that reduce investment argue that the reduction is a cost, but a cost justified by the benefits of the policies.

result in higher levels of investment or at least FDI for the country or trading block adopting the policies, but lower welfare for the adopter and for the world as a whole. Investment-creating policies result in higher investment for the world as a whole, along with higher welfare for the adopter and the world as a whole. A country's inward FDI may increase from policy changes that are investment creating or diverting; the impact on FDI is not related one-to-one to the desirability of the policies.

For all but the largest and richest countries, being a member of a trading block like the EC improves a country's outlook for FDI. Each block member must adopt a package of tax and expenditure policies that keeps it competitive with the other member countries. This does not mean that high-income, high-amenities countries must abandon amenities that make them attractive. Rather, inefficiencies in government and excesses in transfer payments must be cut. People are willing to pay for social services and the environment, but must get value for their money. To succeed in the competition for investment, a country cannot have marginal tax rates that are too high; high marginal rates will drive away firms and people who are eager to do more than average if they have the hope of reward.

Many richer countries will find their comparative advantage in services rather than some of the manufacturing industries they found important in the past. To be sure, manufacturing will remain important; the issue is whether the economy provides an adequate number of high-income jobs, not whether the jobs are in manufacturing or in services. Major changes in government policies may be necessary to attract new manufacturing FDI that tends to be large scale; minor changes will not help much. Such FDI does not react at all sensitively to small changes in policies; further, reaction may take time, both because of lags in the investment process and because of investors' uncertainties about the country's long-term policies. FDI for services may be major and face the same government-policy issues as for manufacturing; much service FDI will be much less discrete.

A country should regularly review its investment policies, including the whole constellation of policies whether or not consciously aimed at investment, to judge whether it will be or has become uncompetitive in attracting investment. A country cannot judge the success of it policies, however, by any simple measure of net investment. Investment resulting from investment-diverting rather than -creating policies is a sign of bad economic health. Outward FDI from major industries may be a sign of good health if it is replaced by investment leading to higher productivity and hence higher incomes for home country workers. The new jobs may be less capital intensive, so the capital-labor ratio may fall. Measures of productivity per worker or unit labor costs are not the key measure; rather real after-tax earnings per hour or per worker in the private sector give a better clue. Further, such measures must be adjusted for demographic changes; rather than looking at averages, a better measure may be what is happening for prime workers.

The outlook for sensible patters of worldwide investment is clouded. The Uruguay round of negotiations under the General Agreement on Tariffs and Trade may founder from inability to reach compromises on services and agricultural trade. Failure would damage the modest progress on codes for FDI. Perhaps more important, many observers argue that failure may lead to an upsurge in regional arrangements that may well do more to divert rather than create trade and investment.

The EC is making decisions that will determine whether its inward FDI is investment created or diverted. The outcome is not yet clear. Many proposed community-wide policies have the potential to be investment diverting; the market-induced competition among member governments to harmonize policies is investment creating. EC members and the world as a whole have major stakes in the EC adopting sound, investment-creating policies.

The EC is the major trade block active today; a NAFTA agreement looks likely, however, and a Far-East trading block centered around Japan is a major possibility. Similar to the analysis of the EC, the NAFTA may lead to a market that is investment-creating, as might a Far-East trading block. A major, justified fear is that the world may fall into trading blocks that are not only trade-diverting but also investment-diverting. The major hope of avoiding this outcome is that politicians in the U.S., Japan and the EC are willing to place their bets on a liberal world economic order, and that voters recognize that these are good bets.

References

Benson, B. L. and R. N. Johnson, (1986), "The Lagged Impact of State and Local Taxes on Economic Activity and Political Behavior," *Economic Inquiry 24*, July, 389-402.

Brewer, T. and R.J. Sweeney (1991), "U.S. Economic Security", Washington, D.C: School of Business Administration, Georgetown University, *Working paper*.

Caves, R. (1982), *Multinational Enterprise and Economic Analysis*, Cambridge: Cambridge University Press.

Dunning, J.H. (1988), "The Eclectic Paradigm of International Production: A Restatement and Some Possible Extensions", *Journal of International Business Studies 19,* Spring, 1-31.

The Economist, Advertisement, "Holland has 400-year head start gearing up for global strategies," (Aug. 3, 1991), 43.

The Economist, "As Close as Teeth and Lips," (Aug. 10, 1991), 21-22.

The Economist, "Fear of Foreigners: Americans hate some foreign investors but quite like others. European factory builders are more popular than Japanese acquirers," (Aug. 10, 1991), 15-16.

The Economist, "Japan Encourages its Young," (Aug. 10, 1991), 55.

The Economist, "Agricultural Subsidies: Sowing in Tears," (Aug. 10, 1991), 56-58.

The Economist, "Too many computers spoil the broth," (Aug. 24, 1991), 30.

The Economist, "Foreign Investment and the Triad," (Aug. 24, 1991), 57.

The Economist, "Countdown to Europe in 1992," (Sept. 14, 1991), 61.

The Economist, "We may be small, but we don't think that way," (Sept. 21, 1991), 53.

Grubel, H. G. (1990), "The Economic Effects of Europe 1992 on the Rest of the World: Diversion, Creation and Wealth", Canada: Simon Frazer University, *Working paper*.

Horst, T. (1971), "The Theory of the Multinational Firm: Optimal Behavior under Different Tariff and Tax Rules", *Journal of Political Economy 79,* Sept./Oct., 37-45.

International Herald Tribune, "Freedom Worries Aside, Hong Kong Economy is Hot, (May 26, 1992), 1,4.

International Herald Tribune, "World's Top Creditor Again...", (May 27, 1992), 15.

Levinson, J. (1991), "Testing The Imports-As-Market-Discipline Hypothesis", Cambridge, MA: National Bureau of Economic Research, *Working Paper* No. 3657.

Moran, T. (1990/91), "International Economics and National Security", *Foreign Affairs*, Winter, 74- 90.

Oxelheim, L. (1990), *International Financial Integration*, Heidelberg: Springer-Verlag.

Redburn, T. (1992), "What Look for the ECU? The Shine is Off Before It's Even On", *International Herald Tribune*, May 27.

Root, F. R., and A. A. Ahmed (1978), "The Influence of Policy Instruments on Manufacturing Direct Foreign Investment in Developing Countries", *Journal of International Business Studies* 9, Winter, 81-93.

Sweeney, R. J. (1992), "Some Political Economy Influences on International Investment", Washington, DC: School of Business Administration, Georgetown University, *Working paper*.

Viner, J. (1950), *The Customs Union Issue*, New York: Carnegie Endowment for International Peace.

Wysocki, B., Jr. (1991), "American Firms Send Office Work Abroad to Use Cheaper Labor." *Wall Street Journal*, Aug. 14, A1, A4.

Chapter 4
International Direct Investment Patterns

John H. Dunning

Introduction

Let me begin on an optimistic note. This last decade of the 20th century promises to offer more opportunities and challenges for cross-border direct investments and cooperative ventures than any of the others which preceded it. Indeed, the 1990s may well see the maturing of the global economy, the emergence of which began in the 1960s, faltered in the 1970s, and was resuscitated in the 1980s.

At the very heart of my optimism, rests my faith in the renaissance of the international market economy, and the positive role which both multinational enterprises (MNEs) and national Governments can play in facilitating and using this tried and tested mechanism to create sustainable and balanced economic development; and in a way which is both humanly acceptable and environmentally friendly.

My optimism is, however, qualified and guarded. There are many clouds on the economic horizon. Let me just identify three. First, the recurrent turbulence in the Middle East has forcibly reminded us how fragile and volatile our progress towards international accord is, and that how, in spite of man's ability to devise new ways of creating and sustaining material prosperity, differences in perceptions, values and ideologies can so easily tear our modern economic fabric to shreds.

Second, less dramatic, but scarcely of less long term economic significance, is the danger that the world may become divided into a number of regional fortresses; and that national protectionism, so damaging to the world economy in the 1920s and 30s will be replaced by regional protectionism in the 1990s. In particular, we all await the outcome of the current round of GATT negotiations with baited breath.

Third, I still have considerable reservations on the ability of both Governments and wealth creating institutions to wisely handle the kind of freedom and power which the unfettered market economy offers. One has to remember, as stated by Eatwell (1982), that "the market is an excellent servant, but a ruthless master". The 19th and early 20th centuries were replete with examples of the market dominating, rather than being dominated by the majority of mankind; and there was a perfectly natural reaction–particularly by those most adversely affected by its imperfections–for it to be controlled or be replaced by (what was perceived to be) a more benevolent and just system of organizing resources. But one man's gain is often another's loss; and if the losers happen also to be the wealth creators, in the end, no one is better off–although to be sure, misery is more equally shared! I just wonder whether, now the market mechanism has been given a powerful new lease of life, that we can use it with care and discrimination; and recognize that in our modern, economically interdependent, technologically complex and environmentally sensitive world, national Governments do have a critical role to play–albeit a very different one from that earlier perceived by socialist regimes. Even one of the archpriests of the free enterprise system–The World Bank –has written in its World Development Report (1991), "Governments and markets should pull together to create and sustain a 'market friendly' strategy for development".[1]

The Facts about Foreign Direct Investment and MNE Activity

The world stock of FDI top reached USD 1.5 trillion by the end of the 1980s. Since 1983, direct investment outflows have increased at the unprecedented compound annual rate of 29 percent a year, three times faster than that of the growth of exports (at 9.4 percent) and four times that of the growth of world output (7.8 percent).[2]

There can be no question that MNEs are not only assuming an increasingly important and pluralistic role in the global economy; but that, in the early 1990s, they are one of the principal engines of its growth and development. Such an engine is fuelled not just by the cross-border transfer of finance capital, technology and management capabilities, but by the way in which MNEs, by their product, marketing and sourcing strategies, influence the international division of labor; and, by their entrepreneurship, provide an impetus for the efficient restructuring of national economies. For example, MNEs not only

[1] Quoted from IMF Survey, July 29th 1991, p. 230.
[2] UNCTC (1991).

account for 80 percent of the private technological capacity in the world; they are also directly or indirectly, responsible for about the same proportion of world trade.

I would like to emphasize some recent changes in the pattern and significance of international direct investment. Table 4.1 sets out some data on the growth and geographical composition of the stock of outward direct investment. Two things are particularly worthy of note. These are, first, the growing importance of FDI in relation to GDP of almost all capital exporting countries; and particularly that of Germany, Japan and the U.K. The second is the widening participation of source countries. Most dramatically, the share of the world's international direct capital stake accounted for by the U.S. fell from 50.4 percent in 1967 to 30.5 percent in 1988; while the combined contribution of Germany and Japan rose from 4.0 percent to 18.9 percent. Data on 1989 and 90 investment flows reinforce these trends. They suggest that Japan has assumed the role of the world's leading outward direct investor, followed by the U.K. and the U.S.,[3] and that MNEs from developing countries are accounting for about 5 percent of all new FDI (compared with only 1 percent in the early 1980s).

Table 4.2 sets out the geographical distribution of the FDI stake by recipient countries. It should be noted for a variety of statistical reporting reasons, the figures on outward and inward investments are not the same. I will make just four observations. First, paralleling the data of Table 4.1, it can be seen that FDI has become a more important ingredient of GDP of most recipient countries over the past three decades. Secondly, in spite of the shift of interest by outward investors away from developing towards developed countries–and this continued in 1989 and 1990–the contribution of inward investment continues to be *relatively* more significant in developing countries. Other data suggest that in 10 developing countries, such investment now accounts for more than 10 percent of domestic gross capital formation, whereas, in the developed world, only in the U.K., the Netherlands, Greece, Spain, Australia and Belgium it is more than 5 percent.

Third, there has been a shift of interest by multinational investors within the third world. East and South Asia and mainland China have been the main gainers; and Latin America - with the exception of Mexico - the Caribbean and

[3] In 1988 and 1989, Japanese outward investments (excluding reinvested earnings) amounted to USD 78.4 billion, compared with the U.K. and U.S. (which included reinvested earnings) amounting to USD 69.0 million and USD 39.9 billion respectively.

Table 4.1. Stocks of Outward Foreign Direct Investment, by Major Home Country and Regions, 1967-1988.
Billions of US dollars

Countries/Regions	1967			1973			1980			1988		
	Value	% of total	% of GNP	Value	% of total	% of GNP	Value	% of total	% of GNP	Value	% of total	% of GNP
Developed Market Economies	109.3	97.3	4.8	205.0	97.1	5.1	535.7	97.2	6.2	1108.8	97.2	8.0
United States	56.6	50.4	7.1	101.3	48.0	7.7	220.3	40.0	8.2	345.4	30.5	7.1
United Kingdom	15.8	14.1	14.5	15.8	7.5	9.1	81.4	14.8	15.2	183.6	16.2	26.1
Japan	1.5	1.3	0.9	10.3	4.9	2.5	36.5	6.6	3.4	110.8	9.8	3.9
Germany (FDR)	3.0	2.7	1.6	11.9	5.6	3.4	43.1	7.8	5.3	103.4	9.1	8.6
Switzerland	2.5	2.2	10.0	7.1	3.4	16.2	38.5	7.0	37.9	44.1	3.9	23.9
Netherlands	11.0	9.8	33.1	15.8	7.5	25.8	41.9	7.6	24.7	77.5	6.8	34.0
Canada	3.7	3.3	5.3	7.8	3.7	6.1	21.6	3.9	8.2	50.7	4.4	11.6
France	6.0	5.3	7.0	8.8	4.2	3.8	3.8	3.8	3.2	56.2	5.0	5.9
Italy	2.1	1.9	2.8	3.2	1.5	2.4	7.0	1.3	1.8	39.9	3.5	4.8
Sweden	1.7	1.5	5.7	3.0	1.4	6.1	7.2	1.3	5.8	26.2	2.3	16.4
Other [1]	5.4	4.8	0.8	20.0	9.5	1.7	17.4	3.2	1.9	64.0	5.6	4.7
Developing Countries	3.0	2.7	0.6	6.1	2.9	0.6	15.3	2.8	0.7	31.7	2.8	1.1
Centrally Planned Economies of Europe	..	..	..	..	..	..	..	..	..	..	..	..
TOTAL	112.3	100.0	4.0	211.1	100.0	4.2	551.0	100.0	4.9	1140.5	100.0	6.7

Source: Data derived from those collected by United Nations Centre on Transnational Corporations; Dunning J.H. and J. Cantwell, *IRM Directory of Statistics of International Investment and Production*, (New York University Press); official national data and *World Development Report* (various editions).

[1] Australia, Belgium, Denmark, Finland, Greece, Ireland, New Zealand, Norway, Portugal, South Africa, Spain.

Table 4.2. Stocks of Inward Foreign Direct Investment, by Major Host Countries and Regions, 1967-1988.
Billions of US dollars

Countries/Regions	1967 Value	1967 % of total	1967 % of GNP	1973 Value	1973 % of total	1973 % of GNP	1980 Value	1980 % of total	1980 % of GNP	1988 Value	1988 % of total	1988 % of GNP
Developed Market Economies	73.2	69.4	3.2	153.7	73.9	3.8	403.4	78.5	4.7	959.5	78.7	9.6
Western Europe	31.4	29.8	4.2	73.8	35.5	5.6	186.9	36.4	4.2	444.5	36.5	8.4
U.K.	7.9	7.5	7.2	24.1	11.6	13.9	63.0	12.3	12.0	119.6	9.8	17.0
Germany	3.6	3.4	1.9	13.1	6.3	3.8	47.9	9.3	5.8	83.5	6.8	6.9
Switzerland	2.1	2.0	8.4	4.3	2.1	9.8	14.3	2.8	14.1	23.2	1.9	12.6
United States	9.9	9.4	1.2	20.6	9.9	1.6	83.0	16.2	3.2	328.9	27.0	6.8
Other [1)]	31.9	30.2	4.2	59.3	28.5	4.2	133.5	26.0	8.7	175.7	14.4	4.8
Japan	0.6	0.6	0.3	1.6	0.8	0.4	3.3	0.6	0.3	10.4	0.9	0.4
Developing Countries	32.3	30.6	6.4	54.7	26.3	5.4	110.3	21.5	5.4	259.8	21.3	9.0
Africa	5.6	5.3	9.0	10.2	4.9	8.7	13.1	2.6	4.1	30.9	2.5	9.7
Asia	8.3	7.9	3.9	15.3	7.4	3.6	34.9	6.8	5.0	114.0	9.3	8.9
Latin America and the Caribbean	18.5	17.5	15.8	28.9	13.9	12.3	62.3	12.1	8.4	114.9	9.4	14.2
Other [2)]	na	na	na	0.3	0.1	0.1	na	na	na	na	na	na
TOTAL	105.5	100.0	3.8	208.1	100.0	4.1	513.7	100.0	4.8	1219.3	100.0	7.2

Source: Data derived from those collected by United Nations Centre on Transnational Corporations; Dunning J.H. and J. Cantwell, *IRM Directory of Statistics of International Investment and Production*, (New York University Press); official national data and *World Development Report* (various editions).

[1] Other Developed market economies - Australia, Canada, Japan, New Zealand, South Africa, Subsaharan Africa, Algeria, Egypt, Tunisia, Morocco.

[2] Other Developing Countries - Fiji, Papua New Guinea, Saudi Arabia, Turkey, Yugoslavia, Kuwait, U.A.E.

most African countries, the main losers. It is also an unfortunate fact that the share of new inward investment directed towards the poorest developing countries has fallen over the last decade.

A fourth observation on Table 4.2 is the emergence of the U.S. as the leading recipient of foreign MNE activity. To give but one set of figures; in 1972, U.S. firms had nearly four times as much invested in the EC than did EC firms have invested in the U.S. Sixteen years later, EC firms had half as much again invested in the U.S. than American firms had invested in the EC. And this is in spite of the fact that, in preparation for Europe 1992, U.S. firms (like their Japanese counterparts) have considerably stepped up their pace of new investment since the mid 1980s. Indeed, plans for capital expenditure by U.S. foreign affiliates show that EC countries are expected to account for one-half of the total foreign plant and equipment expenditure of U.S. firms in 1991 and 1992, compared with 38.5 percent in 1985 and 24.2 percent in 1972.

It is, however, the Japanese firms which are stepping up their investments in the EC at the most remarkable rate. These have risen over four fold from USD 3.3 billion to USD 14.0 billion in 1989 and USD 6 billion in the first half of 1990.[4] About a fifth of all new Japanese outward investment is currently going into the EC, compared with less than 10 percent only seven years ago. All the same, the U.S. remains the most favored destination of Japanese MNEs, and over the past five years, has attracted between 40 and 50 percent of all new investment.

You will observe that these data tell us nothing about one of the most momentous developments of the last few years viz the opening up of Central and Eastern Europe to foreign direct investment. Latest figures suggest that at the middle of 1991, there were over 25,000 registered joint ventures in this part of the world, in which foreign firms were involved. However, only about 10 percent of these were active; and the total value of foreign capital so far invested in the erstwhile communist countries is probably not more than USD 9 billion, one half of which was made in 1990.[5] As of mid 1991, in spite of the serious economic difficulties in most East European countries, there are signs of a considerable speeding up of new investment, especially in Hungary and Poland; and the abortive coup in the erstwhile USSR will most certainly

---

[4] The Japanese year end for all their FDI data is March 31st. Thus the first half of 1990/1991 is April/ September 1990.

[5] Overall, the stock of FDI in Eastern and Central Europe amounted to about 0.5 percent of the total stock of FDI. In 1989 and 1990, however, flows of new investment were running at about 2 percent of the world total.

reinforce this trend. But in the foreseeable future, the most promising area of economic growth is likely to be undertaken by Western German firms, and this will not be counted as foreign investment in the statistics.

Taking the data of Tables 4.1 and 4.2 together, one of the most remarkable features of the last decade has been the growing degree of internationalization of business and the extent to which countries are engaging in two way investment. Within the Triad nations,[6] at least, patterns of the international production of firms are increasingly coming to resemble those of international trade. More and more, trade and foreign investment are complementing, rather than substituting for, each other. Increasingly, too, outward and inward investment are becoming more balanced. In 1990, of the leading industrial nations, only Japan and France had a large direct investment surplus with other countries. As of March 1990, the value of Japanese cumulative foreign direct investments were 16 times those of investment by foreign MNEs in Japan. By contrast, between them, four of the other five leading capital exporters–the U.S., U.K., Germany, and Italy–had, on average, only 20 percent more invested abroad than they had invested in them.

One final indicator of the globalization of economic activity is the fact that, on average, in 1989 the leading billion dollar industrial companies– i.e., those with global sales of more than USD 1 billion, and which account for about four fifths of all MNE activity, produced about one third of their output from outside their home countries. This proportion varied between countries. As might be expected, it was highest for MNEs from the smaller European countries, notably Belgium, Switzerland, the Netherlands, Sweden and lowest for Japanese MNEs, where, with a few exceptions, less than 10 percent of their world output was produced overseas. The fact that Japan is in an early stage of her internationalization process shows the great potential of Japanese MNE activity. To take just one example: of the goods and services produced by U.S. owned firms and bought by U.K. consumers, 85 percent are made by U.S. subsidiaries in the U.K., and balance imported from the U.S. In the case of goods produced by Japanese firms and bought by U.K. consumers, these ratios are reversed, i.e., 15 percent are manufactured by Japanese subsidiaries in the U.K. (or elsewhere in Europe) and the remainder are imported from Japan.

[6] Which consists of the EC, the U.S. and Japan.

Once one gets away from FDI statistics, the data on globalization become very unsatisfactory. Only a few countries, for example, collect information on the foreign employment of their own MNEs, or on the employment of the foreign affiliates in their midst; and even fewer give any insight into the ownership structure of their firms. We do know, however, from U.S., Japanese and U.K. data, that the number of joint ventures has been expanding more rapidly than that of 100 percent owned affiliates; and that small and medium size MNEs have recorded particularly impressive rates of growth. At the same time, as a percentage of world wide sales of MNEs, those accounted for by fully owned subsidiaries continue to rise. Partly this reflects the corporate response to regional economic integration; partly the fact that technological advances, particularly in areas like micro-electronics and biotechnology, are demanding a closer coordination of related areas of value added activity; and partly the more relaxed attitude of many host Governments to the non-residential ownership of their firms.

Closely allied to the expansion of joint ventures, has been the rapid growth of cross-border non-equity cooperative alliances of one kind or another. Such alliances, though concluded for specific reasons and limited in time, are no less a feature of globalization than is FDI. They number tens of thousands; they are most prevalent between large or medium size MNEs from the EC, U.S. and Japan, in technologically advanced or information intensive sectors; and they are concluded both between firms producing at similar stages of the value added or production chain, e.g. research agreements, and between firms producing at different stages of the value chain, e.g. between R&D. While the motives for alliances may vary, most are formed to capture the economies of scale or synergy, and to advance the competitive position of the participating firms.

Why have cooperative agreements increased so rapidly in the last five or so years? Primarily, I suggest, there are four reasons. The *first* is the steeply escalating costs of R&D and the increasing rate of technological obsolescence; the *second* is the perceived need of companies to share their core technologies to produce a new generation of products; the *third* is the intense competitive pressure to gain speedy and efficient access to new and often unfamiliar markets; and the *fourth* is the need to protect or advance ones global competitive position in a turbulent and ever changing world economic environment.

Increasingly, cross border cooperative and competitive relationships are becoming interwined; the boundaries of firms are becoming increasingly blurred; and the discrete and dyadic transactional relationships between firms and their customers, suppliers and competitors are being replaced by networks or systems of value added activities. It is indeed the belief of many IB scholars, e.g. Ghoshal and Bartlett, Hedlund and Casson[7], that the ability of firms to manage and organize a system of quite complex cross-border innovatory production, and transactional relations, both along and between value added chains, will be the main competitive advantages of MNEs in the 1990s and beyond.

This brings us neatly to the question of the organization of MNE activity. Here –again mainly in response to technological advances–not least in information and communications technology–and the changing shape of the world economy– quite revolutionary changes are afoot. From being mainly a provider of resources and capabilities to its outlying affiliates, each of which operated more or less independently of each other; and then a coordinator of the way in which resources are used within a closely knit family of affiliates; the decision taking nexus of the MNEs in the early 1990s has come to resemble the central nervous system of a much larger group of interdependent, but less formally governed activities, the purpose of each of which is primarily to advance the global competitive strategy and the core organization. However, unlike the earlier dyadic and mother/daughter relationships which existed between parent and subsidiary, the modern global corporation is better perceived as a heterarchy rather than a hierarchy. Paraphrasing the words of Hedlund and Rolander, "the organisation of the genuinely global MNE is made up of a set of reciprocally interdependent and geographically dispersed centres, held together largely by shared strategies, norms and a multilateral channelling of experiences, information and resources".[8]

This new organizational form–which Hedlund and Rolander liken to a hologram –is having enormous implications for both the structure of MNE activities, and the way in which they impinge upon nation states. To discuss this further would take us far beyond the scope of this presentation, but the point I wish to emphasize is that purely statistical measures of MNE activity, e.g. sales, assets, employment, exports and so on, may well disguise the quality and stability of the contribution of MNEs, and of how in the long run, their presence affects a particular country's economic prosperity and its relationships with the rest of the world. The whole question of the impact of inward direct investment on the upgrading of domestic technological capacity and human skills of a

---

[7] As expressed in Casson (1990) and in a volume of readings edited by Bartlett, Doz and Hedlund (1990).

[8] As quoted in Bartlett, Doz and Hedlund (1990), p. 7.

particular host country is, for example, intimately bound up with the global structure of the investing organisation; and of how the MNE sees the contribution of its foreign subsidiaries to its wider strategic objectives.

In this compressed run through of recent trends in international investment, I would like to say a final word about the changing modality by which firms are engaging in international direct investment. Traditionally, the main form of entry has been the greenfield venture; and numerically, it still remains important today. However, the most dramatic development of the last half of the 1980s has been the accelerating growth of mergers and acquisition as a means of entry into or expansion of MNE activity. This is particularly noticeable in the case of transatlantic investments, although, in the last two years, there have been sizeable M&As by Japanese firms both in the U.S. and Europe. We shall offer our reasons for this growth later in this presentation. For the moment, we would observe that of the *new* capital outflows of MNEs (as opposed to reinvested profits), it is common for four fifths or more to take the form of M&As. In 1989 and 1990, even 40 percent of the new investment by Japanese firms in the EC were of this form. By contrast, because of legal and institutional obstacles, there are very few permitted takeovers of Japanese firms by foreign investors.

The main features of the recent movements and patterns in MNE activity are put together in Figure 4.1. To conclude, it is assuming increasing importance in employment, trade and output of most nation states; and it is taking on the role of both the leading engine of economic growth and the main fashioner of the global market economy. It is also becoming more pluralistic in its origin, in its geographical distribution, and in its modality. In the last few years, FDI, as a form of international economic involvement, has been increasingly complemented by (and occasionally replaced by) a whole range of cooperative ventures. At the same time, the strategic acquisition of assets and capabilities has become an increasingly important motive for the transnationalization of firms–and particularly of the less competitive and latecomer firms on the international scene.

Finally the organisation of MNEs becoming more complex and interwoven. From behaving largely as a federation of loosely knit and foreign production units which were designed primarily to serve the parent company with natural resources or local markets with manufactured goods and services, the MNE is now increasingly assuming the role of an orchestrator of production and transactions within a cluster or network of cross-border internal and external relationships, which may not always involve equity capital, but which are

Figure 4.1. Current Trends in MNE Activity.

1. Increasing importance of MNEs in the world economy.
2. More pluralistic in origin and geographical distribution.
3. More strategic asset acquiring international direct investment.
4. The development of clusters or networks of value added activities, designed to serve the global interest of MNEs or groups of MNEs.

intended to serve its global strategic interests.

The Future Prospects

To predict the likely course of international direct investment for the rest of the 1990s, in a world whose economic and political senario is changing so rapidly, and often so unexpectedly, is a daunting task. However, without some assumptions about the course of future events–which only time will show to be justified or not–we could make no progress at all.

I propose, as shown in Figure 4.2 to make three basic assumptions about the next decade or so–which, in a sense, are also forecasts. The first is that while economic development in certain parts of the world, notably in East Asia, will proceed rapidly; the centre of economic gravity will continue to rest with the Triad nations - whose interaction with each other, with neighboring territories and with the developing world will largely determine the future pace and direction of global economic progress.

The second assumption is that technological developments will continue to shrink national boundaries, yet, at the same time, force firms both to seek foreign markets and to collaborate with each other in their value added activities.

The third assumption I shall make is that economic relationships between countries will continue to be dominated by the desire of Governments to reap the benefits of economic interdependence but, at the same time, maintain real

Figure 4.2. Assumptions about the Future.

(a) *Basic*

1. The world's centre of economic gravity to remain in the Triad.
2. Technological developments will continue to transcend and shrink national boundaries.
3. Governments will continue to play a crucial role in affecting economic relations between countries.

(b) *Subsidiary*

4. Governments in their policies towards MNEs will be increasingly influenced by their contribution to national competitiveness.
5. Extra economic (especially environmental) issues will play a more up-front role on the attitudes of the international community towards international direct investment.
6. The development of clusters or networks of value added activities, designed to serve the global interest of MNEs or groups of MNEs.

political sovereignty. On balance, I believe that the world, as a whole, is moving in the direction of a global village, but one in which national or regional cultures, ideologies and aspirations will continue to play an important role.

Added to these three basic assumptions, I shall offer two others which have special implications for MNE activity. The first is that national Governments in their policies towards both outward and inward MNE acitivty are likely to be increasingly influenced by their contribution to national competitiveness; as all the signs are that the 1990s will be a decade of intense competition between countries for the world's supply of technological, financial and human resources. Second, I shall assume that some extra-economic issues - notably the environment and national security - will play a more up-front role in the attitudes of both national Governments and the international community towards MNE activity.

It is not difficult to identify the conditions under which international direct investment flourishes. Imagine the global economy as an extension of the national state; and MNEs as an extension of national firms; then, all the conditions for national economic success–strong markets, successful macro-economic policies, a climate for entrepreneurship and innovation, effective competition and so on–apply in the international arena. However, I will, if I may, just concentrate on seven factors which I think are particularly likely to condition the growth pattern of international investment in the 1990s.

Economic Growth and Stability

The first of these is the general environment for economic growth. In the past, the growth of international direct investment has taken on a cyclical pattern. It flourished particularly in the three decades prior to the first World War; and the 25 years after the end of the Second World War; and, since the mid 1980s, it appears to be entering a new golden age. Each of these eras was (and is) characterized by a prosperous world economy, rapid technological development and a relatively free movement of assets, goods and people across national boundaries. By contrast, MNE activity stagnated (relatively speaking) in the restrictive economic and political climate of the inter war years; and in what might be termed the confrontational, or anti-MNE, period of the 1970s.

While I believe that the 1990s will see a continuation of the golden age, as I mentioned at the beginning of this presentation, there are too many clouds on the international horizon to warrant making a direct comparison with the two earlier periods of MNE growth. For all its technological and organizational advances, the world is a much more uncertain and volatile place than it was. Indeed, because of the pace of change and the increasing ease at which people, ideas and money move about, the opportunity for human beings, and particularly those whose life styles and beliefs are threatened by these events, to behave in an economically destructive way is greatly enhanced. In many ways, the world is much more on an economic knife edge that it used to be. It has the resources and capabilities to generate wealth as never before; but its institutional machinery to organize the economic restructuring demanded by technological change is often inappropriate, or outdated. In the last decade, we have already had hints of the fragility of the financial system, and almost monthly we seem to be running into new political crises, which, unless controlled, can embroil nations, which otherwise are moving closer to detente.

Like all commercial entities, MNEs dislike uncertainties; although, where the long term prospects are perceived sufficiently favorable, e.g. as in Eastern Europe, for example, they will embrace them. But as shown by the shifting geographical balance of investment in the past twenty years, MNEs have generally increased their investments in the fastest growing markets; and ones in which they believe the political and economic risks are the lowest. With a widening choice of investment outlets, they have eschewed countries like India, which impose too stringent entry demands or performance requirements, and have focused their attention to countries or regions liberalizing their markets, e.g. the EC, North America and Australia. Academic research[9] has suggested that countries which follow market oriented economic policies and which impose the fewest performance requirements on inward direct investors are those which have attracted the most additional U.S. investment in the late 70s and early 80s; and this is more than borne out by case studies of particular countries, e.g. Mexico and Chile.

The Direction of Growth; New Technologies

Second, a no less important factor influencing MNE activity in the 1990s will be the kind of economic growth likely to occur. One reason for the increasing role of international investment in the world economy has been that the sectors in which MNEs have particular competitive advantages are those which have been increasing their share of world output. Examples include petroleum, motor vehicles, electronics and telecommunications, pharmaceuticals, information technology, financial services, hotels and management consultancies. In the 1990s, these sectors are likely to be augmented or replaced by others. But perhaps more importantly, the classification of economic activity itself, is likely to require modification as technologies become more generic and multipurpose. Indeed, Van Tulden and Junne (1988) have suggested that rather than group industries by their technological inputs, it might be more appropriate to classify value added activities by the impact they make on their industrial customers. Van Tulden and Junne define core technologies as those which will lead to many products, have a strong impact on production processes, are applicable in many sectors and fashion the extent and pattern of economic progress. They identify two clusters of such core technologies of the 1990s–viz the micro-electronics or information technology cluster and the biotechnology cluster. Around these basic new technologies, new technology webs are being created. These include those comprising semi-conductors, telecommunica-

---

9 By e.g. Contractor (1990).

tions equipment, computer aided design and manufacturing equipment in the case of the micro-electronics cluster; and DNA technology, cell fusion, enzyme technology and bio process technology in the case of the bio-technology cluster.

Each of these clusters is linked with the other; and advances in one cluster often become a precondition for further progress in another. In turn, each cluster generates its own network of overlapping technologies, and is critically linked to the development of new materials. The result is a complex changing configuration of technologies which companies will have to master if they are to sustain, let alone advance their resource based advantages. While such mastery may offer valuable economies of technological scope, it also makes enormous financial demands. For the technologies we have described are costly to produce and to assimilate. They also frequently require new organizational structures. While the technologies are often environmentally friendly, and while they provide more flexibility in the production of goods and services, they also demand a sophisticated and diverse network of skills and competences–the sources of which are likely to be both industrially and geographically diversified.

All these features of technological progress point to the need for administrative systems which are either managed by and within large single firms (incidentally although there may be some hollowing out among the producers of technological systems, I am not persuaded that you can separate the management and control of software from hardware–anymore than an industrially advanced State can hope to maintain its prosperity on the basis of its services sector alone), or jointly and severally managed by consortia of firms with a network of cross-border cooperative agreements. In either event, the technological imperative would seem to point to a shift in the unique advantages of the MNE from being an owner of specific intangible assets which it utilizes in different countries, to an organizer of a system of interdependent technological inputs, which can then be used to produce a range of products. The extent of the product range will depend both on the efficiency of the MNE as an innovator and producer, and the extent to which it can exploit the geographical economies of scope, not only in R&D and production, but in sales and marketing activities as well. The full implications of the new marketing and distribution methods, arising from the micro-electronics and communications revolution, is yet to be assessed, but in service oriented sectors, e.g. banking, they are already being seen.

Kinds of Value Added Activity

I now wish to consider another quality related change in the activities of MNEs in the 1990s; and that relates to the increasing internationalization of *higher value* production.[10] I have already referred to two past golden ages of MNE activity. In the first, the growth essentially occurred in the natural resource based sectors and was largely directed to territories owned or managed by the investing countries. Most of the high value secondary processing, however, was carried out in the home countries. In the second, FDI was primarily undertaken to service local foreign markets with goods and services which, in an earlier phase of their life cycle, had been supplied by the home countries. While in the more advanced host countries, there was some innovatory activity, for the most part, this was undertaken in the home countries–although there is not quite the hard and fast dividing line between the second and the third stage as I might seem to be drawing.

The current phase of MNE expansion is very different from the other two. The more pronounced motive for FDI in the 1990s is not likely to be to acquire natural resources or to seek out markets[11]; but to restructure or rationalize existing investments to capitalize on the advantages of regional economic integration (e.g. as in EC and North America); or to acquire new technological or marketing assets in order to more effectively pursue, to maintain or advance, a global competitive position. These latter two motives for FDI imply a very different cross-border configuration of value added activities than the first two. While the former is likely to lead to more specialized and complementary, but complete, lines of activity - this is increasingly the strategy of companies like IBM, Fords and Du Pont and Philips; the latter is encouraging large MNEs to establish a substantial R&D presence in each of the main innovating regions of the world viz the EC, U.S. and Japan. In some cases, this has led to the setting up of greenfield and self contained R&D laboratories, notably in science and technology parks–often in university cities; in others it has meant the acquisition of foreign companies with innovatory facilities. Such a strategy is being pursued not only by first world MNEs but by those from the Third World, e.g. Taiwan, India and Korea, seeking to acquire an insight into the latest technological developments.

Hard and fast macro data are scant on the geographical diffusion of innovatory capacities of MNEs. We do know, however, from U.S. figures, that R&D

---

[10] Described at some length in Pearce (1990) and Casson (1991).

[11] Of course, there are exceptions, e.g. market-seeking investment is likely to grow.

expenditure both by foreign firms in the U.S., and U.S. firms abroad, is increasing faster than both the total sales of such companies and R&D undertaken by indigenous U.S. firms. International patent statistics also demonstrate that the share of new innovations originating from the foreign subsidiaries of MNEs is rising[12] ;while data on cross-border royalties and fees suggest that these are increasing relative to the foreign investment stake. Company data lend further support to the diffusion hypothesis. The Japanese MNEs, in particular, are sensitive to criticism that their foreign operations are just bridgeheads to Japanese exporters of intermediate products, and as a consequence, are accelerating the rate at which the local content of their sales in Europe and U.S. is increased; while several European MNEs, again especially from smaller nations, are now locating upwards of one third of their R&D activities abroad–B.A.T., Philips, Nestlé and SKF are examples.[13]

Service MNEs

It is not only manufacturing MNEs which are globalizing their value added activities to sustain or improve as well as to exploit their competitive or ownership specific advantages.[14] The fastest rate of growth of FDI in the 1980s actually occurred in the services sector, and especially in trade and finance. Over the period 1975-89, the stock of U.S. outward direct investment in the tertiary sector rose by 12.6 percent per annum compared with 7.4 percent in the secondary sector and 4.7 percent in the primary sector. For Japan, the corresponding percentages were 26.5 percent, 19.9 percent and 10.0 percent and for Germany, 14.0 percent, 10.7 percent and 7.6 percent (UNCTC 1992). Table 4.3 shows that services now account for one-half or more of the new outflows of FDI in the leading capital exporting countries. It is particularly high in the case of Japan, where there has been a surge of new investment in financial and insurance activities. At the end of March 1990, this sector alone accounted for just under one-half of all Japanese investment in Europe and is increasing at the rate of 35 percent per year.

Trade and finance related activities, in fact, account for the bulk of outbound service investment by MNEs, but it is also increasing rapidly in many other areas, notably management and engineering consultancy, hotels and fast food chains, and construction and related activities. The 1990s will almost certainly see a further increase in the significance of this sector–for three main reasons.

---

[12] See Cantwell and Hodson (1991) and Dunning (1992).

[13] For further details of the R&D activities of Swedish MNEs, see Håkanson and Nobel (1989).

[14] See Dunning (1988).

Table 4.3. Sectoral Composition of Outward Foreign Direct Investment of Major home Countries.
Percentage share and compound annual growth rate

Country	Period	Sectors			
		Primary	Secondary	Tertiary	Total
Canada					
Composition	1975	9	62	29	100
	1989	7	52	42	100
Growth Rate	1975-89	13	14	19	17
France [a]					
Composition	1975	22	38	40	100
	1989	13	40	47	100
Growth Rate	1975-89	23	28	29	27
Germany					
Composition	1975	5	48	47	100
	1989	3	42	56	100
Growth Rate	1975-89	8	11	14	12
Japan					
Composition	1975	28	32	40	100
	1989	7	26	67	100
Growth Rate	1975-89	10	20	27	22
Netherlands					
Composition	1975	47	39	15	100
	1989	35	24	41	100
Growth Rate	1975-89	6	5	17	12
United Kingdom					
Composition	1975	31	43	26	100
	1989	27	34	39	100
Growth Rate	1975-89	13	11	23	15
United States[b]					
Composition	1975	26	45	29	100
	1989	8	44	47	100
Growth Rate	1975-89	5	7	13	9

[a] Based on cumulative flows of direct investment from 1972.

[b] The vertically-integrated petroleum industry is included in the primary sector in 1975. In 1990, only the extractive portion of the industry is included in the primary sector, with processing included in the secondary sector and marketing and distribution in the tertiary sector.

Source: UNCTC estimates, based on UNCTC (1992).

First, services are accounting for a rising proportion of consumer spending. Second, the service intensity of manufactured goods (particularly in the core technology sectors earlier described) is increasing. Third, the liberalization of cross-border (and particularly intra-EC markets) markets, coupled with the dramatic technological advances in telecommunication facilities, is likely to lead to a substantial rise in the cross-border activities of firms.

It is, of course, one thing to forecast a change in the level or pattern of international economic activity, and quite another to argue that a rising proportion of activities will be concentrated in the hands of MNEs. In the services, as in other sectors, I would foresee pluralistic hierarchies of firms developing. At the top tier, stand the MNEs–the population of which are likely to change over time. They will continue to dominate in the internationally oriented industries, simply because technological and economic forces are continuing to favor firms which can exploit the benefits of arbitrage and risk diversification, the economies of specialization, and the economies of scope of operating in different cultures. The second tier of firms are the medium to large, but predominantly nationally oriented companies, which operate either in sectors supplying local markets or are specialist but leading subcontractors to MNEs–i.e. they comprise the inner ring of a particular global network. Often, these firms produce under licence to, or engage in cooperative ventures with, foreign MNEs. The third tier is a heterogenous group of small specialist firms - some of whom provide the seedbed for new innovations, and others are secondary subcontractors.

While I would not wish to predict the extent to which international investment might increase over the next decade, I do believe that MNE related activity–by which I mean all activity which is driven, or influenced by firms which have major international interests–is likely to become more, and substantially more, important. While I am somewhat sceptical of the recent outcome of the spate of strategic alliances now being concluded–I would contend that, alongside multinational hierarchies, which are designed to circumvent the failure of cross-border intermediate markets–cooperative ventures (which may be thought of as a kind of market internalization), in one form or another, will continue to flourish, and indeed, become both more numerous, and more diverse in their form. In brief, technological, national objectives and international political events (including the schizophrenic attitudes of Governments towards protectionism on the one hand and regional integration on the other) will continue to generate the kind of resource governance needs which MNEs, working with, rather than against, markets and working with, rather than against Governments, are best suited to provide.

FDI Led Trade and Integration

There are every signs that international investment will not only be a major engine of growth in the 1990s, but also of integration and world trade. Not only is three quarters of the world trade (outside that of China and Eastern Europe) in the hands of the MNEs, between two fifths and one-half of this amount is either internal to MNEs or between companies engaging in cross-border cooperative agreements of one kind or another. Paraphrasing the words of Dr. DeAnne Julius, Chief Economist at Shell International, "International investment is both multiplying and deepening the trade and production linkages among national markets, in the same way as that international financial integration took place from the mid 1970s to the mid 1980s"[15] Such corporate led integration is likely to have enormous implications for national Governments. In particular, I believe that just as there are currently efforts to coordinate macro-economic policies among the group of leading industrial nations, so the 1990s will force a convergence of macro-organizational and structural adjustment policies among these same nations. At the same time, that for reasons I have already suggested, I think there will be more rivalry among nation states–especially in Europe–for inward investment, as Governments seek to use the benefits of such investment to protect and advance their own competitive stake in the global economy.

MNEs and Environmental Issues

The sixth, and in many ways, the most difficult area to get to grips with is the likely course of interaction between international direct investment and - to use a phrase which is now coming into popular usage–"environmentally friendly or sustainable economic development". Along with many other actors, MNEs are likely to play a critical role in fashioning the quality of the future environment, and the health and safety of the world's population. This is chiefly because of their dominance as users of both renewable and non renewable resources, and as innovators of new production methods and products[16] , which may or may not be environmentally friendly; and because of their ability to influence the cross border dissemination of safety and health protection standards especially for high hazard products and processes. In the

---

[15] See Julius (1990).

[16] This, for example, ozone depleting chlorofluorcarbons (CFCs) are (or were) produced almost exclusively by MNEs, while they are involved in activities which generate more than half the greenhouse gases emitted by the six industrial sectors with the greatest impact on global warming (UNCTC 1991).

past, MNEs have had a mixed record on their impact on sustainable development, but there can be no doubt that they possess the resources, which, given the right signals by Governments and the international community, could be harnessed to the benefit of the environment. There is also evidence, that many of the larger international investors engaged in environmentally sensitive production are becoming increasingly aware of their responsibilities as trail blazers in promoting environmentally friendly development, and that this need not necessarily be at the expense of their more commercially oriented goals. It is very much to be hoped that the outcome of the 1992 UN Conference on Environmental Development will be used as a window of opportunity for fashioning global policies and instruments to channel and use the enormous potential that MNEs possess to further the objectives of sustainable development; and not as an arena for lambasting the commercial sector for all the adverse environmental effects it may have had on the planet's well being over the past century or more.

The Geography of MNE Activity

Seventh and finally, I would like to take a birds eye view about the geography of MNE activity over the next decade.

First, I believe the outward pattern of FDI will increasingly resemble that of trade in manufactured goods and services. This would suggest the share of the U.S. will continue to fall–and probably that of the U.K. as well. By contrast that of the larger continental European countries will increase, as will that–and most markedly so–of Japan and the first generation of the Asian tigers viz Hong Kong, Korea, Taiwan and Singapore. At the same time, the contribution of the leading investing nations may be expected to fluctuate according to the competitiveness of their firms and the strength of their domestic economies. Depending on the progress of their own industrialization, their macro-policies and their debt reducing capacities, I would also think that Brazil and Mexico could enter the league as quite important outward investors. I would expect the Nordic countries to more or less maintain their share of outward FDI–with rather more Swedish and Finnish investment being directed to the EC than in the past.

Second, the destination of FDI is very much likely to reflect the resources, capabilities and markets of the recipient nations, and the attitude of host Governments towards their nations' role in the international economy, and how they perceive inward investment contributing to that role. Relating these variables to the assumptions we made earlier about the configuration of the world economy in the 1990s, let us pinpoint each of the main likely growth areas.

* **Central and Eastern Europe.** Excluding the Eastern Lander (i.e. district) of a unified Germany, which, in any case is likely to attract an overwhelming proportion of its new investment from the Western Lander, the other parts of Central and Eastern Europe, while most certainly stepping up their capital imports in the early 1990s, are unlikely to attract really large sums until the mid 1990s. Economic recession, uncertainty about the political and social outlook for the area; and the dehabilitating economic performance of Russia are all contributing to the dampening of an earlier euphoria by foreign investors. All being well, however, and depending very much on the extent to which the West is prepared to assist Russia and the other members of the Commonwealth of Independent States in their market liberalization and industrial restructuring program, the stock of inward investment could rise to between USD 75 and USD 100 billion by the late 1990s, or between 1/4 and 1/2 of its current level in Western Europe.

* **Western Europe.** EC 1992 has already proved a major boost to inward investment and providing the targets of the European Commission are met, U.S. and Japanese FDI should continue to flow into the Community well into the 1990s. One suspects that the renewed vigour of the economic community, the reduction of intra-EC transaction costs, and the perceived need of non-EC firms to be insiders in the single market (partly for defensive and partly for aggressive reasons) will also lead to a substantial increase in both intra-EC investment and a stepping up of investment by other European, including Scandinavian investors. If Sweden, for instance, does not join the EC, there will be a marked increase in market and strategic asset seeking Swedish investment in the EC. If she does join, Swedish exports will be favored relative to Swedish MNEs investing in the internal market (Swedenborg, 1990).

* **North and Central America.** The NAFTA will stimulate more intra regional MNE activity. It is also likely to lead to some restructuring of non-American investment within the integrated region. For example, one might expect more European or Japanese companies set up plants in labor intensive sectors in Mexico to supply the U.S. market.

* **Asia.** India is the big uncertainty here, but, most certainly, it is the country which offers enormous potential to foreign investors. The easing of the regulations on inward investment announced in July 1991, and which included raising the equity limit for foreign investment in high priority joint ventures to 51 percent from 40 percent, should go some of the way in raising the flow of inward investment from a paltry USD 75 million in 1990; but much more needs to be done to inject a more market oriented and entrepreneurial culture if foreign MNEs are to have their sights tempted away from the more lucrative and less risky markets of East and South Asia. Here, I see the most rapid progress being made by the second generation of Asian tigers–notably Thailand, Indonesia–and if only it would get its political problems sorted out–the Philippines. For the first half of the 1990s, Thailand seems set to follow in the wake of the Republic of China (Taiwan) and South Korea, but because of its larger population and an industrial base and its oil revenue, Indonesia is perhaps the more promising long term prospect for foreign investors.

The outlook for FDI in the People's Republic of China, clearly rests with the future of the Chinese economic system. It is all too tempting to conclude that the events in Central and Eastern Europe will soon be repeated in China as well. But even if this were to happen in the next couple of years or so, the experience of Western firms with the first flush of liberalization would suggest they will exercise considerably more caution before making large resource commitments in a country whose infrastructure for a globally oriented market based economy is even more backward and inappropriate than that of the Soviet Union. Much, one suspects, will depend on the extent to which Taiwan, Hong Kong and the Eastern provinces of China manage to resolve their political differences, and form a new regional trading bloc.

If the future is uncertain in India, and difficult to predict in mainland China, Japan is the great enigma–even inscrutable–variable of the East. Japan, with a current GNP *per capita* 15 percent higher than Western Germany, attracts only one eighth of the latters inward FDI. Accepting all the problems of investing in Japan–many of which according to foreign firms which are operating successfully in that country–are considerably exaggerated–it is difficult to see how inward investment cannot expand–and expand markedly in the 1990s. U.S. MNEs report that they plan to increase their capital expenditures in Japan by a greater percentage amount at the beginning of the 1990s than in any other major industrial area. As Japanese consumers become more accustomed to (hopefully) better quality Western goods, then FDI is likely to follow trade in the traditional product cycle fashion.

It is however, the very unfamiliarity with the Japanese way of life and the lack of knowledge about Japanese suppliers, business practices and Government regulations, that makes foreign firms hesitant to make resource commitments until they are doubly sure of their market prospects. But as the Japanese market grows and prospers, I suspect that an increasing number of Western firms will find the costs of not engaging in FDI will be more costly than they can bear. It is also reasonable to expect that some FDI will grow out of the collaborative alliances now being forged between Western and Japanese firms. It does, however, seem unlikely that, in the foreseeable future at least, Japan will allow, or have the institutional machinery to properly deal with, acquisitions and mergers involving foreign firms. This may then well keep down the scale of foreign investment in Japan and of Japanese investment in Europe and the U.S., as well.

* **The rest of the world.** For the rest of the world, I see a patchy picture. As the African continent struggles to find its economic soul, I would anticipate some increase in some kinds of FDI in countries like Kenya, Nigeria, Zimbabwe, particularly by Third World MNEs. Indeed, it could well be that Asian FDI in sub-Saharan Africa will be one of the main forces counteracting the marginalization of this part of the world. By the end of the 1990s, South Africa too, may be attracting much more interest by foreign investors. One prediction I would like to make is that investment flows are likely to become more regionalized than in the past. Intra Triad investments are likely to dominate the activities of First World MNEs–although the European component will increasingly embrace parts of Central and East Europe and the American component, Mexico. But within the developing world, I see the fastest growth occurring in intra-regional FDI (especially in Latin America and Asia) and of Third World investment in Sub-Saharan Africa (excluding South Africa). I also foresee some smaller, and somewhat less industrialized, developed countries like New Zealand and Norway entering the international area.

Concluding Remarks

Let me conclude by underlining two recurrent themes of my presentation. The first is that the MNE is a continually evolving organizational entity, and that the typical international investor of the early 1990s is very different from that of the 1960s, who, in turn, was very different from that of the early 20th Century. My speculation about the MNE of the late 1990s is that it is likely to be the centre of governance for a network of pluralistic organizational and operating units, each of which is systematically linked to the other as part of a global heterarchy.

Secondly, all the various global scenarios I have painted rest on a mainly peaceful world and one which acknowledges the benefits of economic interdependence and international commerce. Unfortunately, neither event is guaranteed. While the outlook for harmony among the major powers is as good as it has been for a century or more, trouble which could embroil the major powers–as, for example is occurring in Yugoslavia, could flair up in various parts of Middle East Asia or Latin America–is never far away. The world is truly a tinder box of ideological uncertainties and economic unrest.

The question of economic interdependence both with the developed world and between it and the developing world is also delicately balanced. Here, the outcome of the GATT talks could determine the future course of events for at least the next decade. If international direct investment is increasingly the engine of economic growth; and entrepreneurship, technology and human skills are the fuel which makes possible that growth; it is Governments–both individually and collectively–which provide the signals which in the last resort, will determine the extent, speed, direction and quality of that growth. At the moment, the signals appear to be set to two yellows–rather than green –which suggests the track is clear ahead for a reasonable distance; yet further down the line, if the engine of growth proceeds too fast, or goes on the wrong track–be warned–the signal could be at stop.

References

Bartlett, C.A, Y. Doz, and G. Hedlund (eds.) (1990), *Managing the Global Firm*, London and New York: Routledge.

Cantwell, J. and C. Hodson (1991), "Global Research & Development and U.K. Competitiveness" in M.C. Casson, (ed.), *Global Research Strategy and International Competitiveness*, Oxford: Basil Blackwell.

Casson, M.C. (1990), *Enterprise and Competitiveness*, Oxford: Clarendon Press.

Casson, M.C. (ed.), (1991), *Global Research Strategy and International Competitiveness*, Oxford: Basil Blackwell.

Contractor, F. (1990) "Ownership Patterns of U.S. Joint Ventures Abroad and the Liberalization of Foreign Government Regulations in the 1980s: Evidence from the Benchmark Surveys", *Journal of International Business Studies*, Vol. 21, No.1, pp. 55-73.

Dunning, J.H. (1988), *Explaining International Production*, London: Unwin Hyman.

Dunning, J.H.(1991), "The Prospects for Foreign Direct Investment in Eastern Europe", *Development and International Cooperation*, Vol. VII, pp. 21-40.

Dunning, J.H. (1992), "Multinational Enterprises and the Globalization of Innovatory Capacity", in O.Granstrand, S. Sjölander, and L. Håkanson, (eds.), *Technology Management and International Business*, Chichester: John Wiley. (forthcoming).

Dunning, J.H. and R. Cantwell (1987), *IRM Directory of Statistics of International Investment and Production*, New York: University Press.

Eatwell, J. (1982), *Whatever Happened to Britain*, London: Duckworth.

Håkanson, L. and R. Nobel (1989), "Overseas Research & Development in Swedish Multinationals", *Stockholm Institute of International Business, Research Paper* 89/3.

IMF (1991), *Survey*, July 29th, Washington: IMF.

Julius D. (1990), *Global Companies and Public Policy*, London: Pinter Publishers.

McMillan, C. (1991), *Foreign Direct Investment Flows to Eastern Europe and their Implications for Developing Countries*, New York: U.N., April.

Pearce, R.D. (1990), *The Internationalization of Research & Development*, Basingstoke: Macmillan.

Swedenborg, B. (1990), "The EC and the Locational Choice of Swedish Multinational Companies", Stockholm: The Industrial Institute for Economic and Social Research, *Working paper* No. 284.

UNCTC (1991), *World Investment Report 1991*, New York.

UNCTC (1992), *World Investment Report 1992*, New York.

UN (1991), "Transnational Corporations and Issues Relating to the Environment". *Report of Secretary General* presented at 17th Session of Commission on Transnational Corporations, New York: E/C, 10/ 1991/3.

Van Tulden, R. and G. Junne (1988), *European Multinationals in Core Technologies*, Chichester: John Wiley.

World Bank (1991), *World Development Report 1991*, Washington D.C.

Chapter 5

The Instability of the International Financial System and Its Implications for Trade and Investment

Gunter Dufey

Introduction

The topic is the instability of the international financial system and its implications for trade and investment. This is a very vast and difficult subject, but recognizing its significance is important. Due to its nature, the thrust of the paper must be in identifying the relevant issues. While the literature on various aspects of the subject is extensive, the very volume attests to the fact that definite answers are few, and those that exist are contested. Nevertheless, an increase or decrease in instability represents an important strategic forecast. It affects the actions of companies as well as individuals to arrange their affairs in such a way as to minimize the effect of instability. This includes the possibility of a reduction in the scope and volume of economic activity, i.e., economic growth. The significance of these matters justifies even a degree of speculation that goes beyond conventional economic analysis.

We shall develop this topic in three steps. First, we shall explore the nature of the international financial system and the meaning of instability. Second, we will identify three major sources of change that affect the stability of the international financial system. As a final and third step, we shall review the implications of these changes with respect to trade and investment.

Instability of the International Financial System: What Does It Mean?

Before establishing performance standards for anything, including the implication of "instability," it is useful to circumscribe the nature of the beast. When it comes to the international financial system, this is not easy because it is not possible to simply use the prototype of any financial system and define it by adding the word "international." National financial systems are characterized by their respective governments. Governments, with few and insignificant exceptions, usurp the power to create money, a task executed by a central bank or similar monetary institution. The essential function of the central bank is the creation of money, hopefully at a rate that is noninflationary and not too inimical to macroeconomic stability. Together with commercial banks and similar institutions that offer the public demand deposit, the central bank performs an essential function for the economy: the payment function. Commercial banks, together with other nonbank financial intermediaries (NBFIs) also play an important role in the other essential function of any national financial system, namely, the channeling of funds from savers to those who invest in real assets. This is known as the credit function. Financial intermediaries, however, must share this function with the primary securities markets where (liquid) financial claims are issued by borrowers directly to savers, using facilitating agencies such as brokers and informal or organized securities markets.

The international financial system shares with national systems only its tasks, the payments and the credit function. The institutions are different; there is no international central bank (occasional ambitions of the IMF notwithstanding) and virtually no international financial institutions. Activities are carried out by institutions such as banks, NBFIs, and others, some of which are very active internationally, but all are based in a national financial system and regulated by the respective national government of the jurisdiction where they operate. Thus, the essence of the international financial system is really the interaction of national financial systems.

This interaction takes place through financial markets for payments (the foreign exchange market) and markets for various financial assets. It is useful in this respect to distinguish between (a) markets for intermediated credit, where claims are transferred via financial intermediaries whose assets are different from their liabilities and (b) markets for securities, where liquid claims, either equities or a wide variety of fixed income securities and derivatives (futures, options, swaps) are traded across borders. Clearly, without these international financial markets, the international (and often the national) exchange of real goods and services as well as productive assets (foreign direct investment) could hardly function. Anyone who has studied the costs and problems of conducting international trade via barter has learned this fact very quickly.

These international financial markets, however, do not operate in a vacuum. They are imbedded in what is referred to usually as international monetary arrangements. These are normally characterized by the resulting exchange rate regime: freely floating exchange rates, and managed rates, where the authorities intervene in the market by buying and selling foreign currencies for their own money in order to influence rates. Sometimes countries agree, either unilaterally or by bilateral or multilateral agreements, to manage their currencies to such an extent that rates are virtually "fixed". Such efforts, as it is well known, require a consistent implementation of monetary and economic policies that support such efforts. When governments do not have the determination or power to pursue such policies, and yet do not want to abandon exchange rate targets, they tend to get frustrated and resort to exchange and capital controls. Such controls imply that certain categories of transactions are only permitted upon specific authorization. Governments quickly learn to appreciate an interesting side effect of such policies: when foreign exchange becomes scarce as the domestic currency becomes overvalued, the authorities must resort to allocation, which is a very useful way to reward friends and punish enemies. Figure 5.1 summarizes in a schematic presentation the international financial system.

This thumbnail sketch of the international financial system serves as a reminder that a system in some form always exists. However, there are

Figure 5.1. The Firm, the Markets and the System.

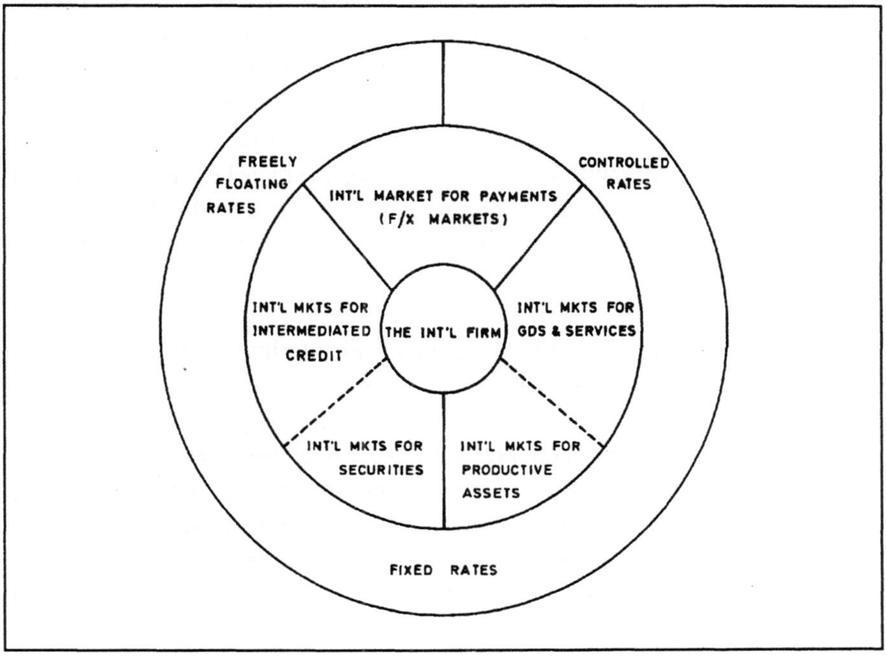

substantial differences in the degree of efficiency by which it facilitates payments and the flow of financial assets, which in turn seems to have a considerable effect on economic growth in the countries that participate in the system. The current discussion about the convertibility of the ruble associated with economic reforms in the former Soviet Union provides a textbook illustration of the issues involved.

There seems to be widespread agreement, although by no means unanimous, that the effect of market forces is more conducive to maximizing economic output with a given resource base, as compared to political/bureaucratic allocation policies.

Instability of the international system is less easy to define. The word "crisis" in this context easily flows from the journalist's pen. Since instability means many things to many people, we will arrive at a working concept by approaching it from extreme vantage points. For some, instability means the threat of system breakdown, where many transactions, both financial and real, are at risk to be interrupted because of widespread default of contractual obligations. This process can accelerate if such defaults are the result of government intervention taking the form of newly imposed controls on financial transactions (foreign exchange and capital controls) as well as on the exchange of goods and services (trade restrictions). Such an event is accompanied by a drastic reduction of trade and investment in the real sector of the economies that participate in the system. For those at the other end of the spectrum, what is involved is simply the concept of volatility of exchange rates, interest rates, and prices of financial assets in general that exceed whatever is considered "normal". The only rational definition of such a "normal" state of affairs is a magnitude of volatility with which economic agents have become accustomed to and have subsequently developed the ability to cope with. A crisis, then, may involve no more than a higher degree of volatility that will test the cohesion of the system.

Obviously, the two concepts of instability are not unrelated. Volatility of prices of financial assets can conceivably become so large as to trigger government intervention because of politically intolerable reallocation effects. However, such breakdowns of the system are more likely to come about through purely political events, including civil war or war involving major nation states that participate in the international financial system, or conceivably even natural catastrophes. Such events are essentially random, thus nonpredictable; therefore we focus here on instability in the sense of a possible increase in the volatility of rates and prices, leading to widespread destruction of the net worth of firms and financial institutions and possibly to government reactions in an attempt (not the success) of insulating a national economy from external events.

Systematic Change in the World Economy

While we cannot deal with random events that impact on the international financial system, it is possible to review some of the systematic changes that are already underway and that will continue to shape the international financial system as it evolves. Three major changes appear to be noteworthy in this respect. First, there is the continuing advance in the technology of information and data processing, leading ultimately to liberalization of cross border financial transactions and the globalization of markets. Second, there is the nature of inter-governmental coordination of regulatory structures and macroeconomic policies. Third, there is a distinctly discernable trend of regionalization, involving economic and monetary cooperation among countries, substituting for the hegemonic role of the United States in the past. We shall elaborate on these issues next.

Much has been made of the increase in the quality and the reduction in the cost of international communications. Indeed, in many countries it is easier to communicate internationally by phone, fax, or computer networks than it is to reach someone at the other end of town through an overloaded local network. This affects not only private communication, but the use of satellites and other means of mass communication spread the news, including the news that is financially relevant. To be informed today seems to require only access to a satellite dish and a TV set, although the investor still has to provide his own analysis. A parallel phenomenon is taking place in the data processing field; indeed, information technology and data processing are closely linked.

The effects of such technological advances on financial markets are manyfold. Not only have markets become more integrated, and price deviations due to differential knowledge less possible (exit the practice of triangular arbitrage in foreign exchange, discussed to such great detail in yesterday's international finance textbooks), but more importantly they have compelled countries to liberalize restrictions on international financial transactions, lest the cost of such restraints become ever more burdensome on the institutions operating within the respective government's jurisdiction. With more and more transactors having the possibility to conduct their affairs offshore and to create innovative structures that circumvent all those restrictions, which are less than all comprehensive (the "Albanian solution"), regulatory measures become ineffective even when they are enforced with diligence and complied with by the letter of the law. More and more value-creating transactions simply migrate to jurisdictions that are more hospitable to economic enterprise. This holds true not only for financial transactions in a narrow sense, but for economic transactions in general. Thus, restrictions affect a smaller and smaller part of total economic activity and become in the end self-defeating.

The considerable liberalization movement that has been observed during the late 1970s and accelerating in the 1980s in OECD countries, and even in many developing countries, is truly astounding when one takes into account the natural obstacles to such trends emanating from the bureaucracy and government for whom regulation is not only important from the standpoint of employment, but as a source of power. By the same token, established competitors are typically quite content with regulations because they have learned that such regulatory regimes also tend to keep out foreign competition. A change of heart by established competitors comes only with the recognition that the protected market becomes smaller as customers do business "offshore", and in the end reciprocity considerations compel the most entrenched competitors to become champions of liberalization, if they wish to follow their clients abroad.

All this has led to the globalization of markets, an ugly term but appropriate characterization of a phenomenon that has affected virtually all developed countries and an increasingly large part of the developing world. What it means for the international financial system is quite revolutionary. Traditionally, we have been thinking of financial markets as being defined by three interconnected dimensions, depicted in Figure 5.2, the market and its jurisdiction, the currency and interest rate structure and the institution.

The practical implications of globalization are simple. In the past, when someone wanted a deposit denominated in yen, because of the attractive currency and the interest rate structure, there was no other way than to subject oneself to the regulatory rigmarole of the Japanese authorities and to deal with the procedures and costs of Japanese financial institutions in Japan. In contrast, today one can easily maintain a yen deposit in a German bank in Singapore, achieving an optimal combination of currency and interest rate risk, political or sovereign risk, and credit risk. Thus, globalization means that the linkages

Figure 5.2. Dimensions of Globalization.

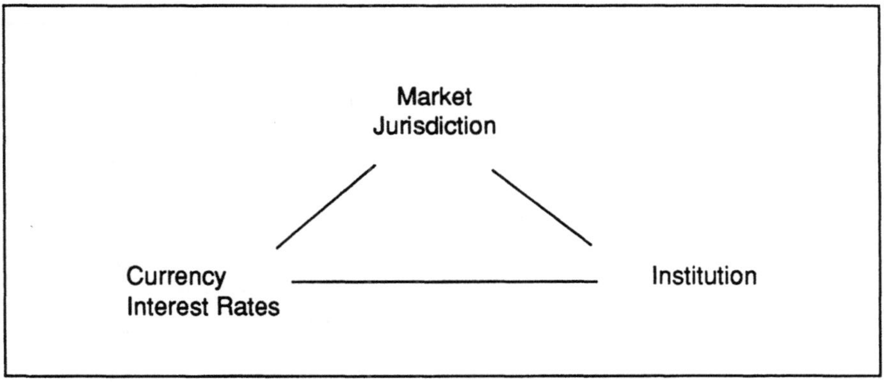

of the factors which define a financial market are dissolving. Of course, all this makes financial markets more flexible for users, but it also increases the scope for the transmission of external and internal "shocks".

This brings to the forefront the second trend which pertains to the role of government in this new world of globalized markets. The phenomena sketched out above have compelled governments to change their manner of cooperation. With hindsight, the relative stability of the international monetary system during the late 1950s and the 1960s can be largely attributed to a lower degree of international capital mobility as well as to the dominant role of the dollar around which the international monetary system was based, if not de jure, definitely de facto. Much has been written about this historical episode and its gradual demise, and the data in Table 5.1 provide some evidence of the underlying changes that caused this evolution. During those decades, differences in unilateral fiscal and monetary policies caused international payment imbalances that were small enough to be managed without sacrificing policy-making autonomy itself. As capital and the institutions that intermediated internationally became more mobile, however, the pressure on governments increased to move toward international coordination of macroeconomic and regulatory policies.

Undoubtedly, some progress toward policy coordination has been made on technical issues. The G-10 agreements reached within the forum of the Bank for International Settlements (BIS) regarding "parental responsibility," establishing primary regulatory reponsibility for a financial institution operating abroad with its home country's regulators, and the subsequent agreements regarding minimum capital standards, both with respect to size as well as to

Table 5.1. The Relative Size of the U.S. Economy.
Based on 1990 GDP, current Prices

	% of U.S. 1955	% of U.S. 1970	% of U.S. 1990
United States	100	100	100
Canada	6	9	12
Japan	6	20	50
West Germany	11	19	24
France	13	15	18
Britain	14	12	11
Italy	6	9	12
Brazil	n.a.	1	10
Soviet Union[a]	n.a.	n.a.	27

[a] GDP for the Soviet Union estimated by NMP (Net Material Production)

measurement, serve as evidence of considerable progress in that area. However, the coordination of fiscal and monetary policy was a different matter altogether.

This is a complex issue. To get some insight into this matter, it is necessary not only to deal with the intricacies of macroeconomic analysis, but one must pierce through the fog and noise of political battles. There can be little doubt that macroeconomic policy coordination among countries has been more a topic for editorials and speeches than for practice. To put it bluntly, governments tend to use the forum of major international conferences to intellectually and politically rationalize policies that they were already intent upon pursuing.[1] To conclude with this somewhat cynical observation, however, would leave the true picture unfinished. While governments pay no more than lipservice, if that much, to taking into account the situation of their trading partners, they can not escape the requirements of the international market place for financial and real assets. If the lengthy discussions on the international adjustment process under fixed vs. flexible exchange rate regimes have yielded one

[1] For an extensive review of the issues and the literature see Webb (1991).

important insight, it is the recognition that–when external financing becomes scarce–individual countries must take the necessary (and painful) measures to reign in consumption and domestic investment in order to hold them within the constraints of the productive capacity of the respective economy. And when prices and wages are inflexible downward (in real terms), the attempt to accomplish this objective leads to losses in output that will make the process even more painful. When seen in this light, the much cited "sovereignty" of national economic policy setting proves to be an illusion. (This is not to say, however, that illusions are not important!)

If one looks back at the performance of the international financial system during the past two decades that spans the "post-Bretton Woods era", it is difficult to escape the conlusion that what kept the system from developing destructive imbalances was the fact that two of the major players, Germany and Japan, consistently pursued policies that were internally stable. And it was such policies, which made it relatively easy for their trading partners to use those policies as a basis for adjustment within their own economies. Even the United States, which began the 1970s with considerable inflation, was able to put its economy through the crunch during the recessions of the late 1970s and early 1980s, which put it on a much less inflationary path–a process that has lasted through the last decade. Thus, to the extent that countries did actually adjust in response to the requirements of the system, this happened invariably due to external market pressure when capital outflows or inflows forced governments to pursue policies that were not too inconsistent with those of the governments of other leading countries.

A related issue has received considerable attention in the economics literature: the effectiveness of monetary and fiscal policy in an era of new financial instruments and increased mobility of financial and even productive capital (technology, FDI). While there are obviously new technical issues in measuring and interpreting relevant macroeconomic data (what is money?), these issues are relatively minor when compared to the difficulties of solving distributional problems as well as allocating political blame after what are invariably unpopular measures. While the technical problems may further complicate "fine tuning", governments do have the capabilities to pursue appropriate policies. What is also true is that in a world of instant communication and global markets, internally inconsistent policies result in more pronounced reactions of exchange rates, interest rates, and prices of financial assets in general, and lead times tend to become close to zero.

We would conclude at this point that the international monetary system survived the dislocations of the 1980s with relative ease, due to the fact that governments were willing to make sufficient compromises to the requirements of international markets, not because of political coordination. The effect, however, was essentially the same: major accidents were avoided. Obviously, a little bit of luck always helps and the performance of the past is no guarantee that the system will not break apart when the shocks become greater in the future.

While forced policy coordination, as we argued above, was partially driven by a more equal distribution of economic power among major industrialized countries in the world, a third development has begun to counteract that trend: increased economic and monetary regionalization. The origins of this process lie undoubtedly in Europe where, for a variety of reasons, the European Economic Community started to grow. Its magnetic effects, however, were increased with the successful introduction of its Single Market Initiative in the mid-1980s, which ultimately led to its absorption of competing structures, such as the European Free Trade Association. Most of the member countries of that entity are now at various stages of joining the EC de jure, and in the monetary field de facto by tieing the value of their currencies to the European Monetary System. The recent developments in Eastern Europe can only accelerate that process whereby it is largely irrelevant whether the EC will be deepened or widened. Economically and monetarily the newly liberalized economies of Eastern Europe cannot help but to link their economic and even political future firmly to that of the EC.

Partially as a result of the seemingly successful EC unification efforts, the creation of a North American Free Trade Association gives further impetus to the trend toward regionalization in the 1990s. While the problems looming in the future for NAFTA are manyfold, for each of the participants the lure of additional growth through liberalized trade and the free flow of capital is such that success is likely to be assured. While in the United States the reaction against the EC phenomenon is one of the driving forces, Canada is politically divided and feels economically too small to go alone. Trade theory teaches convincingly that the cost of trade restrictions tends to be larger the smaller the entity affected is relative to the total market. With respect to Mexico, finally, the joining of the NAFTA is part of a process not only of economic but political reformation that goes far beyond pure trade matters.

In the Far East, incipient efforts are underway to provide an institutional framework of a yen bloc that somehow circumvents the lingering political problems of Japan's past imperialistic role and current economic dominance. The East Asian Economic Group is clearly one institutional response to the realities where trade and investment flows between individual Pacific countries and the United States and Europe are rapidly being surpassed by links of countries in the region to the economic superpower, Japan. And while there are tremendous and well-known political aversions against Japanese dominance, the trends of trade and investments will inexorably compel closer cooperation over time.[2]

Implications for Trade and Investment

The three forces of change reviewed above are, of course, related to some extent; they tend to reinforce each other. Technology will further increase the degree of globalization of financial markets. This in turn will put further pressure on governments to adjust macroeconomic policies to external forces. And the need to adjust policies to external forces gives additional impetus for individual countries to look for a "refuge" within the appropriate regional entity. This in turn provides a rationalization for unpopular economic policy measures as well as insurance against a prolonged crisis in the international financial system since one can rely on the larger entity which (hopefully) continues to function. Regionalization, finally, provides for a shift in the adjustment mechanism by easing adjustment *within* the bloc, making more difficult adjustment *between* blocs.

This latter inference is true even if the blocs do not become inward-looking fortresses, simply because discriminatory reduction of barriers among their members will lead to trade and investment diversion. As our discussion of trends in the Pacific area showed, such diversion is already occurring by the impact of economic forces as proximity and industrial structure alone, without even the support of specific policies. We can draw from this discussion one conclusion: there will be a tendency for less volatility of asset prices, including exchange rates within each trade bloc, whereas there will be more variability with respect to third countries. Such effects are not only policy driven, but are forced by the adjustment mechanism.

---

[2] "Together Under the Sun The Yen Block", The Economist Survey, July 15, 1989, and McCracken (1990).

While one can find considerable support for this proposition in the literature on the adjustment process, the precise impact on trade and investment is considerably less certain. The basic problem is that economic entities can learn. The 1970s and 1980s have provided companies and individuals, active in international trade and investment, with considerable experience on the problem of how to cope with economic dislocations caused by exchange (and interest) rate volatility. An increasing literature on how firms can or should deal with such uncertainty is symptomatic of these efforts.[3] Both practice and theory have well advanced beyond the traditional wisdom of prescribing that each transaction be hedged with forward contracts in the foreign exchange market. Practitioners and theoreticians have brought into much sharper focus the nature of "exposures" to financial instability found in economic entities.

It is now widespread practice that people distinguish carefully between accounting exposure and the impact of unexpected exchange rate changes on the economics of entities that are involved in international trade and investment. This latter effect includes the exposure of firms that are only operating within the confines of a national market, but that confront international competition either in product or factor markets. The more recent literature begins to consider the competitive structure of markets associated with the exposure problem. People are now starting to recognize explicitly not only linear but also nonlinear and discontinuous exposure functions.[4]

By the same token, the process of financial innovation and globalization has increased the range of recognized hedging tools. Such hedging tools comprise traditional financial instruments, such as foreign currency debt denomination – directly, or indirectly through the use of forwards and futures. The inventory of these traditional tools has been broadend by a whole range of products and techniques that address the issue of managing discontinuous and nonlinear exposures, such as options and a whole range of derivative products with option character.[5] Most importantly, we begin to understand operational aspects of exposure management such as sourcing flexibility, pricing strategies, as well as market diversification. Flexible manufacturing systems, installed to adjust to the vagaries of product markets, can also be used for coping with market distortions introduced by exchange rate volatility. A schematic summary of exposure management at the level of the firm is provided in Figure 5.3.

---

[3] For example, see Oxelheim and Wihlborg (1989), and Dufey and Srinivasulu (1983).

[4] von Ungern-Sternberg and von Weizäcker (1990), and Luehrman (1990).

[5] See Smith, Jr., Smithson and Wilford (1990).

Government policymakers have become increasingly aware of the fact that one of the costs of exchange and capital controls in financial markets is based on the notion that such measures deprive economic entities within their borders of the full range of hedging tools. Thus, while the impact of instability emanating from the international financial system may (just possibly) be mitigated via controls in national markets, the cost to companies of doing business in that jurisdiction is increased as they are less able to protect themselves from the risk of financial and monetary shocks. This is definitely one of the aspects that underlies the considerable momentum toward the liberalization of international financial transactions.

Figure 5.3. Schematic Summary of the Corporate Foreign Exchange Exposure Challenge.

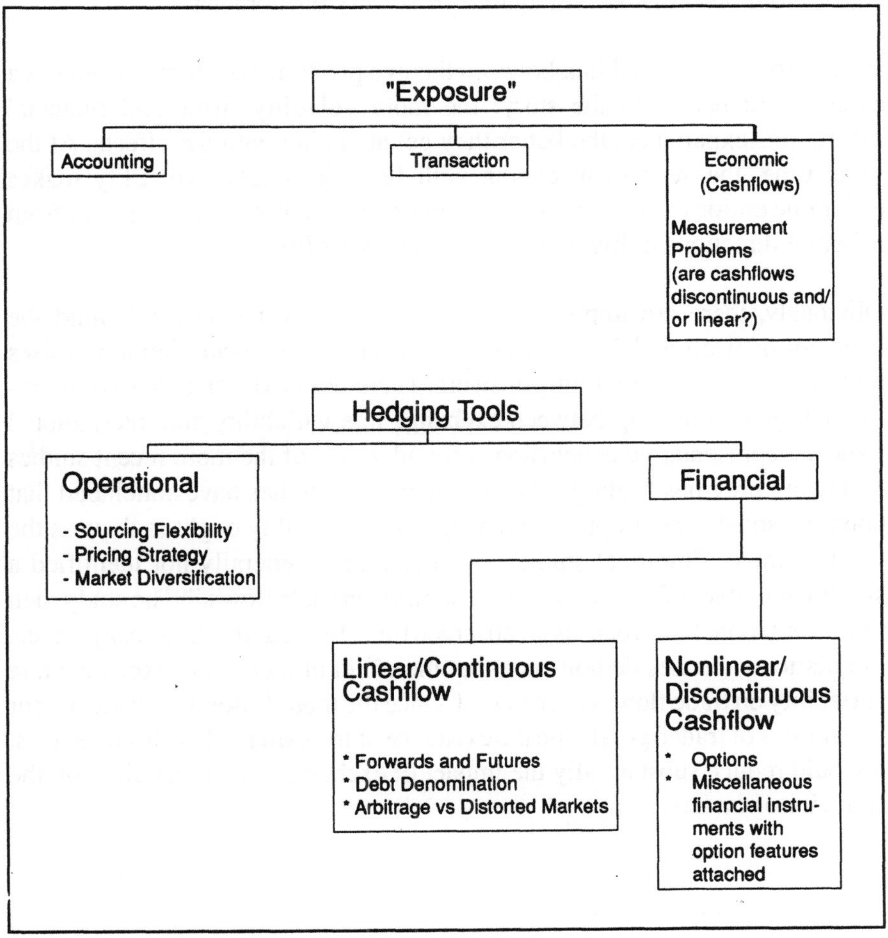

While the emphasis in both theory and practice is properly on the ability of productive enterprise to cope with exchange rate variability, it would be a mistake to omit mentioning the opportunities of international financial markets for private investors to hedge consumption risks that are caused by monetary instability.

The offshoot of the previous discussion is simply the recognition that the very trends of liberalization that cause a more unstable international financial system on the one hand will, on the other hand, allow economic entities to cope with these risks more effectively. Thus, one can view the prognosis of instability of the international financial system in terms of the outcome of a contest between changes in the environment that cause (1) more variability in financial asset prices and (2) the incentives and the opportunity for economic entities to protect themselves against these very phenomena.

Indeed, there is a causal link between the two phenomena which introduces a dynamic element into the story: the more volatility firms and financial institutions experience, the better they get at coping with the effects. At the same time, the success in coping with financial market volatility makes economic entities more complacent, setting themselves up for surprises from different directions or higher than expected volatility.

Obviously, there are important and as yet unanswered issues behind the behavior of firms and financial institutions and the relevant literature raises more questions than providing answers. There does exist an extensive literature on the relationship between exchange rate variability and international trade. A representative conclusion is found in one of the more recent studies reviewing previous findings. "Many theoretical studies have concluded that under reasonable assumptions exchange rate variability ought to depress the level of trade. Empirical studies, however, have generally not identified a significant effect of exchange rate variability on trade flows."[6] The study then provides a model that focuses on observed trade flows and real exchange rates. Simulation exercises demonstrate that the effect of increasing exchange rate variability on trade flows is very small. Once the model allows realistically for inventories of traded goods and the existence of forward markets in currencies, it would reduce substantially the impact of exchange rate uncertainty on the behavior of traders.

---

[6] See Gagnon (1989).

More importantly, if trading firms (a) have access to international capital markets, and (b) are owned by investors with diversified portfolios, and (c) the degree of risk aversion is not too large, the conclusion that the effect of exchange rate variability on trade is quite negligible is further buttressed.[7] This conclusion is received additional support in a recent paper[8] that presents a model showing that an increase in real exchange rate volatility causes firms, under certain realistic assumptions, to have an increase in expected cashflows from exporting, if they have low entry and exit costs (operational flexibility). This effect is particularly pronounced for firms that do not have a comparative advantage. Indeed, the theoretical work shows the case where firms with a comparative disadvantage enjoy increased export volume with exchange rate volatility. If such conditions hold for a sufficient number of firms, the expected volume of international trade grows together with exchange rate volatility. While such conditions may be extreme cases, they cast doubt on the conventional wisdom. For the purpose of the present paper it may suffice to note that operational flexibility is a managerial decision-variabel.

When it comes to investment, either financial or foreign direct investment (FDI), it must be recognized that it represents an alternative to trade, at least in a static sense. Firms that enjoy a competitive advantage can minimize existing or threatened trade barriers by moving some of their activities abroad. As a side effect, they tend to be somewhat more insulated from monetary instability. Of course, this is only possible if the effects of higher and/or rigid cost structures do not offset the beneficial effects of risk reduction.

In terms of trade in financial assets, financial theory has well documented the advantage of international diversification and while there are many interesting questions unanswered as to the optimal asset allocation in light of the fact that people have different consumption baskets, the general thrust of the argument for international diversification holds quite well.

Last, but not least, there is a growing awareness of the interdependency among markets for goods and services as well as for productive assets; they clearly tend to complement one another.

---

[7] A thorough review of the empirical difficulties in showing the relationship and a review of the previous literature is found in Smaghi (1990).

[8] See Franke (1991).

> "When technology shocks occur, for example, the opening of asset markets increases the gains from trade and the volume of trade in goods and services. In reciprocal fashion, the opening of goods markets increases uncertainty and aggregate output, and therefore increases the gains from the diversification of this risk on asset markets."[9]

Finally, in an environment that is characterized (a) by uncertainty in production and domestic market investment returns, and (b) by the absence of international asset markets, individuals will choose to allocate labor away from those industries that enjoy a comparative advantage in order to reduce uncertainty in generating real income. In doing so, they reduce risk, but expected income (economic growth) falls as well. This trade-off disappears when firms and individuals are able to diversify risk in international financial markets, thus minimizing the risk as well as maximizing expected income. As a result, trade in asset markets provides an alternative to reallocation decisions which permit agents more efficiently to insure against industry specific risks.

Perspectives on the 1990s

Among the trends reviewed here, it is relatively easy to speculate that progress in information and communication technology, and especially the dissemmination of these technologies, will advance at a steady pace. More difficult is to predict change with respect to regionalization and government policy in the 1990s. The linkage between the two trends may provide an opportunity for some educated guessing. The unification of Europe will, in due time, result in a reduction in the number of players necessary for obtaining agreement on trade and related matters. By the same token, experience has shown that larger entities tend to become more inward looking. The variable that will yield to the pressure of different policies is the exchange rate. From this consideration we predict greater foreign exchange rate volatility among economic blocs, as volatility within the blocs subsides. At the same time, as trade and economic exchange in general within blocs substitutes for such activities among blocs, the danger of policy-induced interruption increases as the perceived cost of such measures becomes less.

In addition, the realignment of financial markets and the arrival of new currencies or the increasing role of existing ones will cause both public and private entities to rebalance their portfolios which has inherent the potential for

[9] See Feeney (1991).

large and extended disequilibria in financial and real goods markets. All this spells more volatility. Whether this increases systemic risk depends on the susceptibility of the system, i.e. its exposure.

It is at this juncture, where the crucial, twofold role of government policy becomes apparent: Not only is it important that governments set steady parameters with respect to macroeconomic measures, but at the same time provide the proper microeconomic and regulatory framework to make firms and financial institutions safer. This requires the removal of perverse incentives to take more instead of less financial market risk, and a careful limitation of situations giving rise to moral hazard. Thus, an assessment of instability of the international financial system requires careful analysis of both the micro- and macroeconomic of the political economy.

References

Adler, M. and B. Dumas (1983),"International Portfolio Choice and Corporation Finance: A Synthesis", *Journal of Finance*, Vol. 28, 1983, pp. 925-84.

Dufey, G. and S. Srinivasulu (1983),"The Case for Corporate Management of Foreign Exchange Risk", *Financial Management*, Winter, pp. 54-62.

Economist Survey (1989), "Together Under the Sun The Yen Block", July 15.

Feeney, J. (1991), "The Interdependence of Goods Markets and Asset Markets in a Risky World", September, University of Rochester, *Working Paper*.

Flood, E. Jr. and D.R. Lessard (1986), "On the Measurement of Operating Exposure to Exchange Rates: A Conceptual Approach", *Financial Management*, Spring, pp. 25-36.

Franke, G. (1991), "Exchange Rate Volatility and International Trading Strategy", *Journal of International Money and Finance*, Vol. 10, pp. 292-307.

Gagnon, J. E. (1989),"Exchange Rate Variability and the Level of International Trade." Board of Governors of the Federal Reserve System International Finance, *Discussion Papers*, No. 369, December.

Group of Thirty (1988), *International Macroeconomic Policy Coordination*, New York.

Hamao, Y., R.W. Masulis and V. Ng (1990), "Correlations in Price Changes and Volatility Across International Stock Markets," *The Review of Financial Studies*, Vol. 3, No. 2, pp. 281-307.

Hamao, Y., R. W. Masulis and V. Ng (1991), "The Effect of the 1987 Stock Crash on International Financial Integration", in W. Ziemba, W. Bailey, and Y. Hamao (eds.), *Japanese Financial Market Research,* North-Holland. (Forthcoming).

Luehrman, T.A. (1990), "The Exchange Rate Exposure of a Global Competitor", *Journal of International Business Studies,* Vol. 21, pp. 225-240.

McCracken, P. W. (1990), "East Asian Development and U.S. Financial Issues in the 1990s", *Mimeo,* University of Michigan, October 18.

Ng, V.K., R. P. Chang and R.Y. Chou (1991), "An Examination of the Behavior of Pacific-Basin Stock Market Volatility" in S.G. Rhee and R.P. Chang (eds.), *Pacific Basin Capital Markets Research,* Vol. II, Elsevier Science Publishers B.V.

Oxelheim, L. and C. G. Wihlborg (1989), "Using Financial Instruments to Hedge Macroeconomic Exposure", *The Review of Futures Markets,* Vol. 7, Supplement, pp. 504-526.

Smaghi, L. B. (1990), *Exchange Rate Variability and Trade. Why is it so Difficult to Find Any Empirical Relationship?* Banca D'Italia, No. 145, December.

Smith, C.W. Jr., C. W. Smithson and D. S. Wilford, (1990), *Managing Financial Risk,* Harper Business, The Institutional Investor Series in Finance, Ballinger Publishing Company.

von Ungern-Sternberg, T. and C.C. von Weizsäcker (1990), "Strategic Foreign Exchange Management", *Journal of Industrial Economics,* Vol. XXXVIII, June, pp. 381-395.

Webb, M. C. (1991), "International Economic Structures, Government Interests, and International Coordination of Macroeconomic Adjustment Policies", *International Organization* , Vol. 45, No 3, Summer, pp. 309-342.

Chapter 6

The Role of Mergers and Acquisitions in Foreign Direct Investment

Ingo Walter

Introduction

Global and regional interpenetration of markets during the 1970s and 1980s led to a great deal of industrial restructuring among developed as well as developing countries. Trade liberalization under the auspices of the GATT, in particular the Kennedy and Tokyo rounds of multilateral tariff cuts and establishment of codes of conduct on non-tariff barriers, helped to remove a broad array of trade distortions applied at the customs checkpoints of the industrial countries–to a large extent on a most-favored-nation basis. At the regional level, the EC economic integration of the 1960s and 1970s and its recommitment in 1985 through Single European Act, as well as the Canada-U.S. free trade pact, contributed a further freeing-up of markets, even as complementary monetary developments based on a broad-based removal of exchange controls liberalized international payments.

All of these policy initiatives coincided with a reinforced dramatic reductions in transactions costs associated with international trade, and the continued rapid evolution of the multinational firm as a catalyst in promoting international specialization, intra-industry trade, and technology transfers. Firms in the United States, Europe and elsewhere have thus increasingly been subject to international and external competition, as their respective markets and competitors have become global. This in turn has placed a premium on the search for economies of scale and economies of scope, alongside the search for low-cost productive factors and appropriate skill levels worldwide. To a significant degree, this restructuring has occurred through domestic and cross-border mergers and acquisitions (M&A) transactions in Europe and the United States.

Historical Patterns in M&A-Activities

In order to trace the patterns of mergers and acquisitions in the latter half of the 1980s, a comprehensive global database of announced M&A transactions was assembled covering the 1985-91 period. The transactions-flow during this peak period of such activity can be examined in terms of numbers and values, industry and geographic breakdown, type of activity, hostile v.s. agreed transactions, and the use of financial advisers. This permits, for example, comparisons to be drawn between M&A patterns in different regions. It also may be used as a point of departure for a discussion about the role of M&A activities in the global industrial restructuring process to come in the 1990s.

M&A Transactions in the United States

The most active area for M&A-based corporate restructuring during 1985-91 was within the United States, where more than USD 1.3 trillion of disclosed merger and acquisition activities took place. These involved almost 9,500 transactions. The U.S. transaction volume rose dramatically in about 1981, rising in volume and numbers throughout the period to reach a peak in 1988 (the year in which the USD 25 billion RJR-Nabisco leveraged buy-out–LBO–transaction was announced). The volume of completed intra-U.S. transactions declined dramatically in 1990 and 1991–partly because of the virtual discontinuation of large junk bond and bank-financed LBOs.

The intense M&A activity in the United States during the 1980s represented the fourth merger boom of the twentieth century. During the earlier booms (1898-1904, the 1920s, and the 1960s) there had been somewhat parallel activity in the

Table 6.1. Merger Activities.
Billions USD

	1991	1990	1989	1988
U.S. Domestic Transactions	48.0	106.8	244.8	294.5
U.S. Cross-Border Transactions	16.4	71.4	77.7	68.1
Intra-European Transactions	47.9	110.0	121.8	79.0
Other Transactions Outside U.S.	35.3	94.4	81.2	45.2
Global Total	147.7	382.6	525.5	486.8
U.S. as % of Global	32.5 %	27.9 %	46.6%	60.5 %

Millions USD [c]

Year	Domestic U.S. #	Domestic U.S. $M	CROSS BORDER Buyer U.S. #	Buyer U.S. $M	Seller U.S. #	Seller U.S. $M	Total X-border #	Total X-border $M	Outside U.S. #	Outside U.S. $M	Global Total #	Global Total $M
1985	804 (868)[d]	192 863.2	25 (57)	3 854.9	76 (109)	9 999.1	101 (163)	13 854.0	143 (106)	20 721.3	1 048 (1 137)	227 438.5
1986	1 178 (1 288)	203 985.7	39 (50)	2 918.4	164 (144)	31 126.8	203 (194)	34 045.2	296 (203)	38 728.9	1 677 (1 685)	276 759.8
1987	1 311 (1 311)	205 814.3	52 (89)	8 492.5	187 (135)	36 940.3	239 (224)	45 432.8	586 (366)	86 602.5	2 136 (1 901)	337 849.6
1988	1 580 (1 249)	294 429.7	81 (127)	6 687.6	247 (175)	61 450.9	328 (302)	68 138.5	1 452 (858)	124 230.1	3 360 (2 409)	486 798.3
1989	1 872 (1 705)	244 793.3	149 (213)	25 336.3	405 (236)	52 393.2	554 (449)	77 729.5	1 832 (1 575)	203 032.9	4 258 (3 729)	525 555.7
1990	1 564 (2 332)	106 802.1	143 (237)	20 896.8	398 (325)	50 458.2	541 (562)	71 335.0	1 986 (1 565)	204 448.1	4 091 (4 549)	382 605.2
1991	1 139 (1 666)	48 032.8	133 (228)	8 268.5	212 (187)	8 152.8	345 (415)	16 421.0	1 354 (1 299)	83 237.8	2 838 (1 752)	147 691.9
TOT.	9 448 (10 429)	1 296 721.1	622 (1 001)	76 455.0	1 689 (1 311)	250 521.3	2 311 (2 309)	326 976.3	7 649 (5 972)	761 001.6	19 408 (17 162)	2 384 699.0

[a] Completed transactions include: mergers, tender-mergers, tender-offers, purchases of stakes, diverstitures, recapitalizations, exchange offers and LBOs.

[b] The volume data are classified according to the announcement of a transaction – not taking into consideration when a transaction is completed.

[c] Million dollar of purchase price – excluding fees and expenses – at current excange rates. The dollar value includes the amount paid for all common stock, common stock equivalents, preferred stock, debt, options, assets, warrants, and stake purchases made within a month of the announcement date of the transaction. Liabilities assumed are included if they are disclosed in press releases or newspaper articles.

[d] Number of completed transactions with undisclosed dollar values.

Source: Securities Data Corporation, Mergers and Transactions database

United Kingdom, indicating a certain degree of international involvement and spillover, but the absence of similar M&A transactions in continental Europe and Japan–neither of which had any history or experience with such market-driven transactions–impeded a broader spreading of M&A transactions. The U.S. merger boom of the 1980s did, however, ignite a substantial global response, one that in the United States had subsided. (See Table 6.1)

Table 6.2 shows 1985-91 completed merger and corporate restructuring transactions in the United States, transactions involving U.S. and non-U.S. corporations, transactions outside the United States, and the global volume of such transactions. The data demonstrate the extent to which M&A transactions have indeed become international. In 1985, for example, domestic U.S. transactions accounted for 85 percent of global M&A activity; by 1991 this had declined to under 33 percent.

Cross-border transactions involving U.S. companies grew rapidly during most of the period–one in which U.S. domestic M&A volume declined overall–with 77 percent (by volume) of the cross-border transactions representing sales of U.S. companies to non U.S. buyers.

M&A Transactions in Europe

Transactions entirely outside the United States grew most rapidly of all during 1985-91–from USD 20.7 billion in 1985 to USD 204.4 billion in 1990, an almost ten-fold increase during the seven-year period. Of the total sum of these transactions, USD 437 billion, or 57 percent, were intra-European. An additional USD 309 billion (about half of the remainder) involved Europe/non-Europe transactions–a significant part of which undoubtedly is also reflected in the U.S. cross-border data. Intra-European transactions increased rapidly during most of the period. Europe/non-Europe deals (in which 60 percent of the transactions by volume involved European acquisitions of non-European corporations) likewise grew substantially as shown in Table 6.3.

European corporations thus were demonstrably entering M&A transactions more aggressively, with volume growing far more rapidly than anywhere else in the world, during the 1985-91 period. This expansion was occurring simultaneously on two fronts–within Europe and in other regions of global importance to European corporations, mainly the United States.

The data suggest that an M&A boom has indeed taken hold in Europe, which appears to involve acquisitions within single European countries, between

Table 6.3. Number and Volume of Completed International Merger and Corporate Transactions [a, b], Europe, 1985-1991 [c].
Millions USD [d]

Year	Intra-Europe #	Intra-Europe $M	Cross Border: European Buyer #	European Buyer $M	European Seller #	European Seller $M	Total X-border #	Total X-border $M
1985	72 (43)[e]	10 613.7	45 (46)	6 267.4	29 (44)	2 342.3	74 (90)	8 609.7
1986	195 (101)	18 985 2	106 (66)	18 631.7	44 (36)	6 082.5	150 (102)	24 714.2
1987	416 (220)	48 965.3	132 (75)	28 161.4	63 (82)	12 314.6	195 (157)	40 476.0
1988	1091 (613)	78 996.0	209 (139)	38 389.0	133 (138)	13 566.8	342 (277)	51 995.8
1989	1359 (1 037)	121 830.3	306 (167)	40 129.7	212 (284)	25 091.8	518 (451)	65 221.5
1990	1296 (896)	109 994.7	261 (180)	47 672.6	297 (333)	50 129.7	558.0 (513)	97 802.3
1991	788 (828)	47 903.6	142 (130)	6 324.0	211 (253)	13 935.3	353.0 (383)	20 259.3
Totals	5217 (3 738)	437 288.8	1201 (803)	185 575.8	989 (1 170)	123 463.0	2190 (1 973)	309 078.8

[a] Completed transactions include: mergers, tender-mergers, tender-offers, purchases of stakes, divestitures, recapitalizations, exchange offers and LBOs.

[b] The volume data are classified according to the announcement of a transaction–not taking into consideration when a transaction is completed.

[c] The region includes East European Countries.

[d] Million dollar of purchase price–excluding fees and expenses–at current excange rates. The dollar value includes the amount paid for all common stock, common stock equivalents, preferred stock, debt, options, assets, warrants, and stake purchases made within a month of the announcement date of the transaction. Liabilities assumed are included if they are disclosed in press releases or newspaper articles.

[e] Number of completed transactions with undisclosed dollar values.

Source: Securities Data Corporation, Mergers and Transactions database

European countries, and between European and non-European companies. The development is the result of:

* an overdue need for industrial restructuring in Europe similar to that experienced in the United States

* the special motivations associated with the 1992 single market initiatives

* the availability of adequate financial resources

* the increasing liberalization of capital markets in Europe, and

* the transfer to Europe of much of the M&A knowhow that accumulated in the United States during the 1980s.

Although it is difficult to predict how long the growth in M&A volume will continue, it appears that, barring any unexpected reversal of government policies affecting market-driven transactions, or a substantial reversal of economic prospects in Europe, there remains a great deal more to be done. We will return to that issue later in this chapter.

Intra-Europe Patterns of M&A Activity

Most of the M&A activity in Europe during the period 1985-91 has involved United Kingdom corporations, which have a long history and familiarity with such transactions. French and Italian corporations have been the next most active M&A participants, followed by German corporations which–despite the size of the German economy–accounted for only 5.8 percent of intra-European transaction volume during 1985-91.

It is useful to examine European M&A patterns somewhat more closely. These can be observed by sorting transactions by the nationality of buyers and sellers for each of the years in the data series, presented in Table 6.4. The average annual rate of growth of all intra-European M&A volume was exceptionally high during most of 1985-91. As noted, U.K. activity in the European merger marketplace was by far the greatest, although British seller volume grew at an average annual rate lower than the overall intra-European growth rates. French and Italian companies, however, were acquiring other European companies (including British companies) at an even more rapid pace. Especially active on the buy-side in the intra-European market, French buyer-transactions grew at

Table 6.4. Volume of Completed Intra-European M&A Transactions by Country, 1985-1991.
Millions of USD

		Country of Seller Company					
Country of Buyer	Year	U.K.	France	Italy	Germany	Other European	TOTALS Buyer
U.K.	1985	8 363.9	0.0	0.0	0.0	12.2	8 376.1
	1986	12 401.1	23.8	0.0	1.0	70.0	12 495.9
	1987	29 859.4	124.5	125.9	216.5	520.5	30 846.8
	1988	39 537.9	1 172.8	480.8	201.6	1 012.3	42 405.4
	1989	54 204.9	1 261.3	290.2	361.9	3 125.3	59 243.6
	1990	26 905.8	2 561.0	115.1	1 109.4	4 049.3	34 740.6
	1991	13 202.4	385.5	3.9	233.2	540.7	14 365.7
	TOTAL	184 475.4	5 528.9	1 015.9	2 123.6	9 330.3	202 474.1
France	1985	0.0	10.7	0.0	0.0	0.0	10.7
	1986	5.9	222.0	520.9	0.0	32.1	780.9
	1987	316.6	1 674.4	207.3	0.0	0.0	2 198.3
	1988	3 137.0	7 355.1	35.7	310.2	1 056.2	11 894.2
	1989	5 211.9	15 145.6	602.4	1 989.7	3 331.9	26 281.5
	1990	3 149.0	9 498.8	3 380.9	502.9	4 421.7	20 953.3
	1991	509.8	3 736.0	285.0	756.0	2 193.7	7 480.5
	TOTAL	12 330.2	37 642.6	5 032.2	3 558.8	11 055.6	69 599.4
Italy	1985	16.8	0.0	165.0	0.0	0.0	181.8
	1986	0.0	0.0	1 199.4	129.0	0.0	1 328.4
	1987	0.0	20.4	7 876.3	0.0	1 050.8	8 947.5
	1988	0.0	325.0	1 314.2	429.3	887.7	2 956.2
	1989	7.9	294.4	7 007.8	63.1	0.0	7 373.2
	1990	55.4	602.8	11 801.2	500.6	482.1	13 442.1
	1991	59.1	320.1	2 344.2	356.1	76.2	3 155.7
	TOTAL	139.2	1 562.7	31 708.1	1 478.1	2 496.8	37 384.9
Germany	1985	0.0	0.0	0.0	898.5	445.0	1 343.5
	1986	425.0	0.3	887.4	980.0	0.0	2 292.7
	1987	159.6	330.6	0.0	425.6	0.0	915.8
	1988	59.2	154.0	866.1	2 227.3	39.6	3 346.2
	1989	817.8	1 341.3	37.5	2 221.3	1 475.3	5 893.2
	1990	1 269.7	2.2	53.2	2 124.5	1 304.7	4 754.3
	1991	626.1	8.7	0.0	4 411.9	1 884.9	6 931.6
	TOTAL	3 357.4	1 837.1	1 884.2	13 289.1	5 149.5	25 477.3
Other Euro-pean	1985	209.2	0.0	0.0	0.0	492.4	701.6
	1986	828.6	0.0	0.0	0.0	1 258.7	2 087.3
	1987	558.5	169.1	0.0	239.0	5 090.3	6 056.9
	1988	7 469.1	1 026.6	2 491.7	0.0	7 384.6	18 394.0
	1989	1 759.6	3 975.1	305.9	826.6	15 371.6	22 238.8
	1990	6 673.7	1 434.5	392.8	2 762.4	24 841.0	36 104.4
	1991	1 534.1	496.5	259.7	233.3	13 446.5	15 970.1
	TOTAL	19 052.8	7 103.8	3 450.1	4 061.3	71 885.1	101 553.1
TOTALS Seller	1985	8 589.9	10.7	165.0	898.5	949.6	10 613.7
	1986	13 660.6	246.1	2 607.7	1 110.0	1 360.8	18 985.2
	1987	30 894.1	2 319.0	8 209.5	881.1	6 661.6	48 965.3
	1988	50 223.2	10 035.5	5 188.5	3 168.4	10 380.4	78 996.0
	1989	62 002.1	22 017.7	8 243.8	5 462.6	23 304.1	121 030.3
	1990	38 053.6	14 099.3	15 743.2	6 999.8	35 098.8	109 994.7
	1991	15 931.5	4 946.8	2 892.8	5 990.5	18 142.0	47 903.6
	TOTAL	219 355.0	53 675.1	43 050.5	24 510.9	95 897.3	436 488.8

Source: Securities Data Corporation, Mergers and Transactions database

an unprecedented rate, and purchases by Italian companies grew equally impressively during the period.

Much less active in intra-European volume terms during the period, German companies substantially lagged British, French, and Italian acquirers. German sell-side activity grew even more slowly, as is evident in Table 6.4. It has become much easier for French and Italian companies to use the merger market for seller-initiated transactions than it has been for German companies, which have been perhaps the least accustomed to domestic M&A activity among all of the major home-countries of companies engaging in European mergers and acquisitions. Sellers from these four countries made up the bulk intra-European transaction volume during the period.

As is well known, in many continental European countries there are structural and/or regulatory barriers to takeover activity, management to take actions without shareholder approval, and restrictions on the availability of material information. These barriers are sufficient in some countries (especially Switzerland, Germany, the Netherlands and France) to preclude most hostile takeover attempts. In general, these barriers are being dismantled, although gradually. The barriers do not, of course, prevent a defender's board from finally coming to agreement with a pursuer, nor do they prevent a pursuer from going public with proposals for a friendly takeover at a fair price to shareholders, who in turn are free to exert pressure on the defenders. Even in Switzerland where shares owned by foreigners can be denied voting rights by unilateral management action, proposals direct to shareholders offering a high price for the stock of a company–subject to the condition that management register all the shares–would be taken very seriously.

M&A Activities Regions Outside the United States and Europe

The data in Tables 6.2 and 6.3 suggest that non-U.S., non-European M&A transaction volume was trivial–only USD 14.6 billion or 0.6 percent of the global 1985-91 total. It is likely that the bulk of this involves intra-Japan and developing-country foreign direct investment transactions, with a few deals involving Australia and New Zealand in the 1980s.

Similarities Between US and European Restructuring

The economics of industrial restructuring through M&A transactions are highly country- and industry-specific, especially at a time of rapid technological change and changing market characteristics, both of which affect firms' ability to exploit economies of scale and scope–with the most dramatic impact being felt among the most highly regulated sectors. Labor-intensive manufacturing activities should be subject to relocation to low-wage areas. Captital-intensive activities should see rationalization and consolidation–accompanied by both horizontal and vertical integration within and between firms in efforts to exploit available scale and scope economies. This includes elimination of duplicative production facilities. In some sectors, only the largest players will remain competitively viable. In others, there is ample room for smaller specialized or regional firms drawing on location-specific or technology-specific advantages.

If the pressures for industrial restructuring are indeed global in nature, European economic restructuring in the 1990s is not likely to be dissimilar to the restructuring that occurred in the United States in the 1980s, likewise propelled by intense international competition, with similar "global" industries most intensively involved in the progress. Since competition for the domestic market in the United States is interregional, coupled to free interregional flows of productive factors, limited government subsidization and relatively transparent and benign antitrust policy, U.S. economic restructuring to a significant extent occurred at the corporate level through M&A transactions.

There is ample evidence that the parallelism in U.S. and European restructuring has indeed been the case, and that the industries most intensively involved in restructuring in Europe have been the same ones that experienced restructuring in the United States during the 1980s.

Table 6.5 ranks 1985-1991 U.S. and European merger transaction volume by the industry of selling companies. Table 6.6 does the same for the industry of buying companies. In each table approximately 70 industries (classified by two-digit SIC codes) were designated. Table 6.7 indicates the Spearman rank correlations of U.S. and European industry involvement in M&A activity during the period. Of course, such rankings may well be affected by the absolute size of the various industries themselves, so that "larger" industries will be subject to the higher levels of M&A activity than "smaller" industries. Less strong relationships are found when the respective industries are scaled-back according to their stock market capitalizations. (See Smith and Walter 1991.)

Table 6.5. Rankings of Industry Groups of U.S. and European M&A Seller Companies by SIC Code [a, b], 1985 - 1991.
Millions USD

SELLER SIC	DESCRIPTION	U.S. TRANSACTIONS RANK.[d]	NUMBER	VALUE [c]	EUROPEAN TRANSACTIONS RANK.	NUMBER	VALUE
28	CHEMICALS & ALLIED PRODUCTS	1	519	143 943.1	5	236	25 361.0
13	OIL & GAS EXTRACTION	2	546	90 013.1	3	128	33 385.4
20	FOOD & KINDRED PRODUCTS	3	297	84 640.1	1	301	54 034.0
48	COMMUNICATIONS	4	526	84 244.3	28	78	4 317.6
36	ELECTRONIC & OTHER ELECT.EQUIP	5	572	78 849.8	7	257	22 172.3
60	DEPOSITORY INSTITUTIONS	6	808	70 830.9	2	135	36 299.6
35	INDUSTRIAL MACHINERY & EQUIP	7	634	63 400.8	14	284	13 570.3
27	PRINTING & PUBLISHING	8	310	46 886.5	11	217	16 929.3
53	GENERAL MERCHANDISE STORES	9	102	45 280.4	19	36	9 321.3
37	TRANSPORTATION EQUIPMENT	10	214	40 448.2	6	176	23 978.2
78	MOTION PICTURES	11	150	39 907.3	43	48	2 320.9
73	BUSINESS SERVICES	12	553	38 186.4	13	372	14 466.9
38	INSTRUMENTS & RELATED PROD.	13	443	36 108.1	36	112	3 485.7
21	TOBACCO PRODUCTS	14	15	35 860.4	57	4	560.7
61	NON-DEPOSITORY INSTITUTIONS	15	175	33 446.1	21	64	7 447.4
54	FOOD STORES	16	115	31 646.3	15	46	10 497.9
49	ELECTRIC GAS & SANITARY SERV.	17	237	31 258.5	12	75	16 45!7.4
70	HOTELS & OTHER LODGING PLACES	18	160	29 435.2	16	109	9 673.1
63	INSURANCE CARRIERS	19	306	29 341.9	4	97	32 300.5
32	STONE CLAY & GLASS PRODUCTS	20	138	27 057.2	22	123	6 315.7
30	RUBBER & MISC. PLASTIC PROD.	21	157	24 904.3	37	120	3 334.9
33	PRIMARY METAL INDUSTRIES	22	191	24 895.2	24	142	5 993.8
26	PAPER & ALLIED PRODUCTS	23	100	24 695.0	9	126	18 207.5
58	EATING & DRINKING PLACES	24	155	23 537.8	23	91	6 216.6
40	RAILROAD TRANSPORTATION	25	58	23 304.3	69	1	24.1
45	TRANSPORTATION BY AIR	26	133	23 034.5	34	34	3 549.7
80	HEALTH SERVICES	27	259	21 679.5	53	36	1 225.8
65	REAL ESTATE	28	185	19 342.7	8	212	18 237.8
34	FABRICATED METAL PRODUCTS	29	232	18 888.4	18	178	9 400.0
62	SECURITY & COMMODITY BROKERS	30	164	16 764.2	17	133	9 480.0
23	APPAREL & OTHER TEXTILE PROD.	31	91	16 002.4	41	69	2 664.0
10	METAL MINING	32	81	14 662.0	26	15	4 861.2
59	MISCELLANEOUS RETAIL	33	147	13 454.7	39	73	3 145.1
87	ENGINEERING & MGMT. SERVICES	34	251	12 959.0	32	213	3 856.1
22	TEXTILE MILL PRODUCTS	35	97	11 231.0	30	108	4 038.9
51	WHOLESALE TRADE-NONDURABLE	36	143	11 031.5	25	153	5 795.0
50	WHOLESALE TRADE-DURABLE	37	233	9 275.7	20	305	8 226.9
75	AUTO REPAIR SERV. & PARKING	38	34	8 860.2	49	26	1 753.9
64	INSURANCE AGENTS BROKER.& SER	39	30	7 597.7	40	46	2 734.5
67	HOLDING & OTHER INV'T. OFFICES	40	178	7 590.9	10	128	17 169.5
42	TRUCKING & WAREHOUSING	41	58	6 727.8	44	37	2 231.4
46	PIPELINES EXC.NATURAL GAS	42	25	6 616.9	71	3	22.6
29	PETROLEUM & COAL PRODUCTS	43	50	5 801.1	35	22	3 510.9
79	AMUSEMENT & RECREATION SERV.	44	75	5 363.7	31	47	3 857.2
39	MISC.MANUFACTURING INDUST.	45	103	5 115.8	52	67	1 255.4
24	LUMBER & WOOD PRODUCTS	46	60	5 113.8	45	40	2 099.0
56	APPAREL & ACCESSORY STORES	47	64	5 018.7	54	29	1 000.8
25	FURNITURE & FIXTURES	48	66	4 964.2	55	51	693.5
12	COAL MINING	49	48	4 269.5	61	14	389.1
57	FURNITURE & HOMEFURNISH.ST.	50	57	4 005.9	33	35	3 801.4
44	WATER TRANSPORTATION	51	48	3 798.7	29	57	4 182.8

Table 6.5. (Cont.)

SELLER SIC	DESCRIPTION	U.S. TRANSACTIONS RANK.[d]	NUMBER	VALUE [c]	EUROPEAN TRANSACTIONS RANK.	NUMBER	VALUE
52	BUILDING & GARDEN MATERIALS	52	32	3 541.3	56	15	677.2
14	NONMETALLIC MINERALS-EXC.FUELS	53	27	3 518.5	60	19	401.5
8	FORESTRY	54	22	2 412.2	62	4	229.3
1	AGRICULTURAL PROD. - CROPS	55	25	2 238.9	46	16	1 989.6
15	GENERAL BUILDING CONTRACTORS	56	54	1 997.3	42	93	2 573.5
2	AGRICULTURAL PROD.-LIVESTOCK	57	8	1 942.5	74	2	4.2
55	AUTO DEALERS & SERV.STATIONS	58	24	1 797.4	47	56	1 788.8
16	HEAVY CONTRUCTION-EXC.BUILDING	59	38	1 782.9	48	31	1 785.4
47	TRANSPORTATION SERVICES	60	28	1 735.7	50	39	1 689.0
31	LEATHER & LEATHER PRODUCTS	61	30	1 663.4	51	32	1 351.9
O	UNKNOWN	62	45	1 523.3	38	65	3 329.9
72	PERSONAL SERVICES	63	28	1 241.3	58	39	530.3
41	LOCAL & PASSENGER TRANSIT	64	4	514.3	68	8	49.6
89	SERVICES NEC	65	8	445.8	65	3	117.0
17	SPECIAL TRADE CONTRACTORS	66	19	445.1	27	51	4 347.9
7	AGRICULTURAL SERVICES	67	3	417.1	70	3	22.7
82	EDUCATIONAL SERVICES	68	12	397.6	63	13	171.1
83	SOCIAL SERVICES	69	9	360.1	67	3	67.1
76	MISC.REPAIR SERVICES	70	7	171.3	59	6	530.1
9	FISHING HUNTING & TRAPPING	71	1	27.0	66	4	108.8
81	LEGAL SERVICES	72	1	5.0	73	1	4.9
91	EXEC. LEGISLATIVE & GENERAL	0	0	0.0	72	1	10.2
88	PRIVATE HOUSEHOLDS	0	0	0.0	64	1	152.9

[a] Completed transactions include: mergers, tender-mergers, tender-offers, purchases of stakes, divestitures, recapitalizations, exchange offers and LBOs.

[b] The volume data are classified according to the announcement date of a transaction–not taking into consideration when a transaction is completed.

[c] Million dollars of purchase price–excluding fees and expenses–at current exchange rates.

[d] Ranking is based on total dollar value of target industry.

Source: Securities Data Corporation, Mergers and Corporate Transactions database.

Table 6.6. Rankings of Industry Groups of U.S. and European M&A Buyer Companies by SIC Code [a, b], 1985-1991.
Million USD

SELLER SIC	DESCRIPTION	U. S. TRANSACTIONS			EUROPEAN TRANSACTIONS		
		RANK.[d]	NUMBER	VALUE [c]	RANK.	NUMBER	VALUE
67	HOLDING & OTHER INV'T. OFFICES	1	2 660	357 438.0	1	792	74 311.3
28	CHEMICALS & ALLIED PRODUCTS	2	378	95 991.0	2	303	51 030.4
13	OIL & GAS EXTRACTION	3	432	80 269.3	6	145	28 695.8
48	COMMUNICATIONS	4	408	66 571.5	23	64	7 057.0
60	DEPOSITORY INSTITUTIONS	5	689	65 857.5	4	172	40 869.3
27	PRINTING & PUBLISHING	6	220	44 868.8	8	229	20 074.0
20	FOOD & KINDRED PRODUCTS	7	230	44 111.5	3	290	47 048.5
35	INDUSTRIAL MACHINERY & EQUIP.	8	391	43 413.5	16	293	10 502.8
36	ELECTRONIC & OTHER ELECT.EQUIP	9	317	39 619.2	7	279	27 300.2
21	TOBACCO PRODUCTS	10	15	38 185.7	56	5	487.3
37	TRANSPORTATION EQUIPMENT	11	140	37 923.6	9	134	16 835.1
38	INSTRUMENTS & RELATED PROD.	12	256	31 142.3	35	79	3 531.7
63	INSURANCE CARRIERS	13	273	30 072.9	5	169	32 262.1
62	SECURITY & COMMODITY BROKERS	14	315	25 682.4	10	242	15 659.7
53	GENERAL MERCHANDISE STORES	15	58	22 440.1	28	30	5 011.3
49	ELECTRIC GAS & SANITARY SERV.	16	210	21 233.6	20	64	9 384.6
61	NONDEPOSITORY INSTITUTIONS	17	141	20 415.2	36	43	3 457.8
78	MOTION PICTURES	18	107	20 162.8	33	30	4 145.4
73	BUSINESS SERVICES	19	321	19 336.6	18	230	9 887.2
40	RAILROAD TRANSPORTATION	20	37	18 414.0	66	1	78.4
45	TRANSPORTATION BY AIR	21	76	17 291.6	41	22	2 722.4
26	PAPER & ALLIED PRODUCTS	22	87	15 858.5	14	84	11 090.1
33	PRIMARY METAL INDUSTRIES	23	110	14 395.9	19	172	9 645.2
32	STONE CLAY & GLASS PRODUCTS	24	92	12 934.2	13	160	12 958.8
54	FOOD STORES	25	48	11 896.4	31	29	4 851.3
34	FABRICATED METAL PRODUCTS	26	111	11 061.4	32	122	4 613.4
10	METAL MINING	27	72	10 948.0	24	33	6 722.0
65	REAL ESTATE	28	123	10 359.9	25	138	5 485.1
70	HOTELS & OTHER LODGING PLACES	29	61	10 035.1	17	97	10 260.4
30	RUBBER & MISC. PLASTIC PROD.	30	84	9 582.3	21	100	7 292.5
80	HEALTH SERVICES	31	171	7 740.4	50	23	971.6
24	LUMBER & WOOD PRODUCTS	32	36	7 271.7	38	35	3 272.9
58	EATING & DRINKING PLACES	33	73	6 670.4	15	70	10 659.6
23	APPAREL & OTHER TEXTILE PROD.	34	45	6 026.1	34	60	3 893.7
64	INSURANCE AGENTS BROKER.& SERV	35	22	5 920.8	29	46	5 001.0
50	WHOLESALE TRADE-DURABLE	36	111	5 356.4	26	210	5 414.8
51	WHOLESALE TRADE-NONDURABLE	37	82	5 226.0	12	164	13 406.3
59	MISCELLANEOUS RETAIL	38	69	5 091.7	39	45	2 797.7
0	UNKNOWN	39	56	4 184.7	47	38	1 047.2
87	ENGINEERING & MGMT. SERVICES	40	116	3 809.2	22	226	7 062.1
15	GENERAL BUILDING CONTRACTORS	41	35	3 714.7	30	94	4 869.3
12	COAL MINING	42	35	3 373.5	46	15	1 108.3
39	MISC. MANUFACTURING INDUST.	43	52	3 272.7	59	34	333.3
29	PETROLEUM & COAL PRODUCTS	44	25	2 209.1	37	29	3 450.9
46	PIPELINES EXC. NATURAL GAS	45	20	2 198.6	0	0	0.0
22	TEXTILE MILL PRODUCTS	46	41	2 066.2	42	89	2 333.1
52	BUILDING & GARDEN MATERIALS	47	11	2 059.8	55	8	752.4
42	TRUCKING & WAREHOUSING	48	27	1 976.1	57	18	383.6
44	WATER TRANSPORTATION	49	30	1 865.7	27	62	5 360.7
75	AUTO REPAIR SERV. & PARKING	50	12	1 809.6	58	18	358.3
25	FURNITURE & FIXTURES	51	26	1 449.4	52	32	873.0

Table 6.6. (Cont.)

SELLER SIC	DESCRIPTION	U.S. TRANSACTIONS RANK.[d]	NUMBER	VALUE [c]	EUROPEAN TRANSACTIONS RANK.	NUMBER	VALUE
56	APPAREL & ACCESSORY STORES	52	25	1 384.9	44	20	1 513.9
47	TRANSPORTATION SERVICES	53	14	1 277.3	53	24	813.9
79	AMUSEMENT & RECREATION SERV.	54	26	1 218.0	49	24	1 028.1
14	NONMETALLIC MINERALS-EXC.FUELS	55	11	1 132.5	63	11	158.1
41	LOCAL & PASSENGER TRANSIT	56	6	934.5	68	1	12.1
55	AUTO DEALERS & SERV.STATIONS	57	9	774.8	61	32	264.5
72	PERSONAL SERVICES	58	18	773.2	51	62	909.7
8	FORESTRY	59	5	731.1	40	21	2 730.4
16	HEAVY CONTRUCTION-EXC.BUILD.	60	24	729.1	43	45	1 623.2
82	EDUCATIONAL SERVICES	61	14	617.4	60	8	288.2
1	AGRICULTURAL PRODUCTION-CR.	62	13	440.3	54	9	806.8
31	LEATHER & LEATHER PRODUCTS	63	9	356.3	11	33	13 673.6
83	SOCIAL SERVICES	64	9	353.4	71	1	1.3
57	FURNITURE & HOMEFURNISH.ST.	65	20	290.9	48	24	1 038.2
9	FISHING HUNTING & TRAPPING	66	3	272.1	67	2	58.4
17	SPECIAL TRADE CONTRACTORS	67	13	99.7	45	37	1 119.2
2	AGRICULTURAL PROD.-LIVESTOCK	68	2	90.5	70	1	4.1
96	ADMIN. OF ECON. PROGRAMS	69	2	70.0	0	0	0.0
86	MEMBERSHIP ORGANIZATIONS	70	3	49.9	0	0	0.0
76	MISC.REPAIR SERVICES	71	5	26.9	64	9	110.3
89	SERVICES NEC	72	3	16.8	69	2	8.1
81	LEGAL SERVICES	73	1	1.0	0	0	0.0
95	ENVIRONMENTAL HOUSING/QUALITY	74	1	1.0	0	0	0.0
94	ADMINIST. OF HUMAN RESOURCES	0	0	0.0	62	1	234.2
7	AGRICULTURAL SERVICES	0	0	0.0	65	1	90.0

[a] Completed transactions include: mergers, tender-mergers, tender-offers, purchases of stakes, divestitures, recapitalizations, exchange offers and LBOs.

[b] The volume data are classified according to the announcement date of a transaction–not taking into consideration when a transaction is completed.

[c] Million dollars of purchase price–excluding fees and expenses– at current exchange rates.

[d] Ranking is based on total dollar value of acquiring industry.

Source: Securities Data Corporation, Mergers and Corporate Transactions Database.

Table 6.7. Spearman Rank Correlation of U.S. and European Industries Participating in M&A Transactions [a], 1985-1991.

		SIC of Buyer	SIC of Seller
# of Deals	r	0.8043	0.8463
	N	(69)	(72)
	p^b	0.000	0.0000
$ Volume	r	0.7416	0.7532
	N	(69)	(72)
	p^b	0.0000	0.0000

[a] Correlations are based on the number of transactions and the dollar volume of U.S. and European Industries (2-digit SIC codes).
[b] One-tailed significance.

Source: See Table 6.5.

Minority Stakeholdings and Strategic Alliances

European companies frequently enter into strategic alliances with other companies in an effort to secure many of the benefits of an acquisition without incurring all of the costs, financial and otherwise. Such alliances have been seen as character in European companies, reflecting cultural patterns with a strong traditional base as well as the fact that those controlling a substantial minority investment often may be able to control the company itself. In such cases the level of investment needed to achieve effective control of the business and assets of a company may be comparatively small.

In the United States, on the other hand, and in the United Kingdom to a somewhat lesser extent, minority interests can be difficult to manage. If a company has a minority interests outstanding, such shareholders may institute litigation to ensure that their rights are not infringed, or that the value of their investments are not diminished by actions taken by controlling stockholders. Minority shareholders have for many years received the protection of the courts from inappropriate loss of rights or values. For example, multiple-plaintiff (class action) suits are permitted in the United States, which means that the slightest perceived irregularity will almost assuredly provoke a lawsuit against controlling shareholders. For this reason, few controlling shareholders in the United States wish to leave minority interests outstanding for any length of time.

In the United States also, many companies have experienced joint shareholding arrangements with partners which were unwound after a few years. Either the two parties did not share the same expectations, or shoulder the burdens of the venture equally, or business or personnel changes took place that altered the importance of the venture in one or both parties' minds. Very few partnership arrangements of this sort last very long, but for many individuals contemplating new challenges, it is tempting to think that one can face those challenges best with a like-minded partner.

Table 6.8. Partial Ownership Positions as a Percentage of All Completed U.S. and European M&A Transactions [a,b] ,1985-1990.
In percentage terms [c]

	U.S. SELLER [d]	EUROPEAN SELLER [e]		INTRA-EUROP. DEALS [f]	
YEAR		UNITED KINGDOM	REST OF EUROPE	UNITED KINGDOM	REST OF EUROPE
1985	5.82%	15.49%	22.41%	5.60%	23.02%
1986	14.59%	9.77%	43.23%	6.27%	36.83%
1987	12.65%	40.71%	4.89%	31.81%	3.36%
1988	9.58%	27.28%	35.70%	13.59%	28.55%
1989	20.91%	26.87%	33.12%	30.02%	28.08%
1990	13.39%	21.33%	22.12%	17.45 %	17.11 %
AVERAGE 1985-90	12.82%	23.8%	26.91%	17.46%	22.82%

[a] Partial ownership positions involve open or privately negotiated stake purchases of stock or assets.
[b] Data include only completed transactions. Data are classified according to the announcement date of a transaction–not taking into consideration when a transaction is completed.
[c] Percentage values denote the fraction of total transaction volume which involves partial stakes.
[d] Completed partial stakes as a percentage of total dollar volume of completed M&A transactions in which the seller is a U.S. company.
[e] Completed partial stakes as a percentage of total dollar volume of completed M&A transactions in which the seller is a European company–i.e. when the seller is a U.K. company or when the seller is a European company different from the U.K.
[f] Completed partial stakes as a percentage of total dollar volume of completed M&A transactions in which the buyer and the seller are European companies.

Source: Securities Data Corporation, Mergers and Corporate Transactions database.

Table 6.8 shows completed partial ownership positions as a percentage of all attempted U.S. and European M&A transactions. As expected, the incidence of these transactions is relatively small in the United States, where they accounted for about 13 percent of all transactions since 1985.

In Europe, the use of partial ownership positions differs significantly between the U.K. and continental European transactions. The incidence of stakeholdings in the United Kingdom has been larger than in the United States, depending on whether the acqurirers of U.K. companies were more easily persuaded that partial ownership was the right way to take over a British company than were European acquirers, although there are insufficient data to allow more than speculation on this point.

With respect to continental Europe as compared to the United States, a much higher incidence of partial ownership is also inevident . The incidence was 21 percent of all seller transactions for the 1985-91 period. It may be, however, that the rate of partial ownership transactions in the rest of Europe has begun to decline, particularly as difficult managerial lessons are learned from experience in stakeholdings. Note also the higher share of partial acquisitions in continental than U.K. intra-European transactions.

Hostile Transactions and the Market for Corporate Control

M&A activity can be broken down into unopposed (friendly) and opposed (hostile) transactions. In the former case, the boards of two firms exercising their fiduciary roles find it in the mutual interest of their respective shareholders to engage in a full legal merger (e.g., through an exchange of shares), a full takeover of the shares of one firm by the other, or the unilateral or reciprocal acquisition of equity stakes. In the "opposed" case the board of the target firm rejects the transaction, which is nevertheless attempted (successfully or unsuccessfully) by the other firm on a hostile basis. The economic fundamentals of the latter, in terms of their impact on the shareholders of both firms, is the focus of the market for corporate control.

Since the values concerned inevitably are *ex ante,* the argumentation is by definition normative in nature. Management of the predator firm will tend to point to the static and dynamic gains it expects to achieve–usually related to reduced transactions costs, scale and scope economies in production, distribution, R&D, etc.–as well as market-share advantages, as reflected in the premium it is willing to pay for the target's shares relative to the market price.

Management of the target firm will tend to refute these advantages, or will point to a series of steps it is intending to take designed to bring about the same gains without sacrificing the firm's independence–e.g., rationalizing production and distribution, share repurchases and increased leverage in the firm's capital structure, non-strategic dispositions, and the like. To the extent that it can defeat the predator by non-market devices, management entrenchment practice may succeed in thwarting the interests of the shareholders of both firms. Typical non-market techniques include restriction of shareholder rights anchored in company bylaws and appeals for external intervention on antitrust or other regulatory grounds. It may also appeal to shareholders directly in a proxy battle–arguing for example that long-term shareholder interests are better served by continued independence despite the foregone control premium. Or it may engage in greenmail, in which case there is a transfer of the control premiumholders of the target firm.

The economic impact of hostile transactions has been extensively discussed in the literature, and remains highly controversial. (See e.g. Walter and Smith, 1991). The debate generally pits the "Anglo-Saxon" view that an active market for corporate control provides that best possible check on management performance and safeguard of shareholder interests against the "continental" view that large blocks of shares and voting rights in the hands of interested parties (including banks and governmental agencies) provides a more efficient information conduit and a more effective corporate control structure that facilitates greater stability and sounder long-term corporate strategic development. Consequently, hostile transactions are often viewed as an unwelcome creation of overly aggressive Anglo-Saxon bankers and enterpreneurs, and have little role to play in continental Europe.

Unlike the tradition of public ownership in the United States and the United Kingdom, shareholding patterns in continental Europe are often quite different. Many enterprises, including some very large ones, are not organized as publicly-owned limited liability corporations. A recent study for the EC Commission shows, for example, that only 54 percent of the top 400 EC companies are quoted, versus 99 percent in the United States. (Booz Allen Acquisition Services, 1990). Out of the top 100 domestic companies, 67 are quoted in the U.K., 56 in France, 45 in Germany and less than a third in all other EC countries. Furthermore, in the three largest EC economies, only a relatively minor share of the domestic GNP can actually be "accessed through public takeovers".

Given such factors, many of the continental European countries lack a tradition of, or substantial experience with, market-driven internal (i.e., domestic) M&A activity. Only a comparatively small percentage of enterprises in continental European countries have so far participated in such transactions. As more of them do participate, and the benefits of doing so become more visible (such as utilizing an efficient market for corporate control to dispose of shares in family owned or closely-held businesses that have limited liquidity), participation in M&A activity should continue to increase and with it will come a rise in unwanted takeover attempts. There are at least two reasons why continental European companies are becoming more willing to resort to hostile bidding techniques, despite their traditional reluctance to do so.

First, many larger European companies have either participated in (or observed closely) takeover activity in the United States or the United Kingdom and have become sufficiently familiar with takeover practices to consider importing them back to their home countries. And second, capital market activity in Europe has increased substantially in volume and sophistication, so that funds are available to entrepreneurs seeking to launch takeovers, and institutional investors have come to understand the pros and cons of takeovers better and to behave more objectively than they did in the past.

The greatest progress in breaking through takeover barriers have been achieved in France, Italy and Spain where, as noted earlier, aggregate growth in M&A activity has been the highest in all of Europe. As Table 6.9 shows, the preponderance of hostile deals, flourished in the United States and the United Kingdom (domestic transactions), is evident. They accounted for an average of 5.6 percent and 21.4 percent to total attempted transactions by volume, respectively, during the 1985-91 period. This was a time when hostile bids were relatively easy to arrange and finance, and were therefore in especially active use in these two countries particularly for larger sized transactions. In the case of both the United States and the United Kingdom, however, after 1988 the level of hostile activity declined considerably.

American companies, although rarely employing hostile bids when acquiring firms abroad, were frequently targets of hostile bids from non-U.S. companies, especially British companies. The U.K. experience was also different in cross-border transactions, whether U.K. companies were acquirers or targets. Continental European companies experienced a much lower incidence of hostile activity, averaging 2.9 percent of all intra-European transactions.

Table 6.9. Unsolicited or Hostile Offers as a Percentage of All Completed U.S. and European M&A Transactions [a, b], 1985-1991.
In percentage terms [c]

YEAR	UNITED STATES U.S. DOMESTIC [d]	CROSS-BORDER [e] U.S. BUYER	CROSS-BORDER [e] U.S. SELLER	INTRA-EUROPEAN TRANSACTIONS UNITED KINGDOM U.K. DOMESTIC [f]	REST OF EUROPE [g] U.K. BUYER	REST OF EUROPE [g] U.K. SELLER	REST OF EUROPE [h]
1985	9.98%	0.00%	16.17 %	71.80 %	0.00%	0.00%	4.89%
1986	5.82%	0.00%	15.78%	7.62 %	0.00%	20.79%	0.00%
1987	3.51%	2.12%	9.86 %	22.27%	0.00%	0.00%	0.00%
1988	21.62%	2.03%	29.91%	17.23%	7.66%	60.66%	4.31%
1989	3.80 %	0.00%	2.89 %	13.75%	0.00%	0.00%	11.14%
1990	0.00 %	0.00%	0.00%	14.72%	0.00%	0.00%	0.27%
1991	0.00%	0.00%	0.00%	2.67%	0.00%	0.00%	0.00%
AVERAGE 1985-91	5.63%	0.59%	10.66%	21.44%	1.09%	11.64%	2.94%

[a] Hostile offers are defined as those transactions in which the acquiring company proceeds with its offer against the wishes of the target company's management.

[b] Data include only completed transactions. Data are classified according to the announcement date of a transaction–not taking into consideration when a transaction is completed.

[c] Percentage values denote the fraction of total transaction volume which involves hostile offers.

d Completed hostile deals as a percentage of total dollar volume of completed M&A transactions in which both buyer and seller are U.S. companies.

[e] Completed hostile deals as a percentage of total dollar volume of completed M&A transactions in which either the buyer or the seller is a U.S. company and the counterpart is a non-U.S. company.

[f] Completed hostile deals as a percentage of total dollar volume of completed M&A transactions in which both buyer and seller are U.K. companies.

[g] Completed hostile deals as a percentage of total dollar volume of completed M&A transactions in which either the buyer or the seller is a U.K. company and the counterpart is a Continental European company.

[h] Completed hostile deals as a percentage of total dollar volume of completed M&A transactions in which both buyer and seller are Continental European companies.

Source: Securities Data Corporation Mergers and Corporate Transactions database.

Leveraged Buy-Out Transactions

Besides unwanted takeover attempts between corporations, another indicator of an active market for corporate control is the volume of leveraged equity transactions, including management buy-outs and buy-ins of external investors who perceive a significant control premium in relation to the "passive" market valution of the firm.

Table 6.10. Leveraged Buyouts as a Percentage of All Completed U.S. and European M&A Transactions[a, b], 1985- 1991.
In percentage terms[c]

YEAR	U. S.[d] SELLER	EUROPEAN SELLER[e]		INTRA-EUROPEAN DEALS[f]	
		UNITED KINGDOM	REST OF EUROPE	UNITED KINGDOM	REST OF EUROPE
1985	13.52%	5.61%	0.00%	0.97%	0.00%
1986	16.44%	2.37%	1.04%	3.69%	0.00%
1987	17.33%	5.36%	0.62%	6.92%	0.65%
1988	25.82%	6.77%	3.62%	9.67%	3.21%
1989	11.10%	9.76%	2.47%	13.97%	2.37%
1990	6.63%	1.32%	0.15%	2.66%	1.67%
1991	4.50%	5.00%	0.05%	4.23%	6.49%
AVERAGE 1985-91	13.62%	5.17%	1.14%	6.02%	2.06%

[a] Leveraged buyout (LBO) is defined as a transaction in which an investor group, investor, or investment/LBO firm acquires a company, taking on an extraordinary amount of debt, with plans to repay the debt with funds generated from the company or with revenue earned by selling off the newly acquired company's assets. An acquisition is considered an LBO if the investor group includes management or if newspaper articles or press release describe the transaction as a buyout.

[b] Data include only completed transactions. Data are classified according to the announcement date of a transaction–not taking into consideration when a transaction is completed.

[c] Percentage values denote the fraction of total transaction volume which involves LBOs.

[d] Completed LBOs as a percentage of total dollar volume of completed M&A transactions in which the seller is a U.S. company.

[e] Completed LBOs as a percentage of total dollar volume of completed M&A transactions in which the seller is a European company–i.e., when the seller is a U.K. company or when the seller is a European company different from the U.K.

[f] Completed LBOs as a percentage of total dollar volume of completed M&A transactions in which the buyer and the seller are European companies.

Source: Securities Data Corporation, Mergers and Corporate Transactions database.

Table 6.11. U.S. and European Corporate Use of Financial Advisers as a Percentage of All Completed Merger and Acquisition Transactions [a], 1985-1991.

In percentage terms [b]

Year	Adviser to Buyer Frequency [c]					Adviser to Seller Frequency [d]				
		European Seller		Intra-European Deals			European Seller		Intra-European Deals	
	U.S. Seller	United Kingdom	Rest of Europe	United Kingdom	Rest of Europe	U.S. Seller	United Kingdom	Rest of Europe	United Kingdom	Rest of Europe
1985	17.27%	36.58%	100.00%	33.39%	89.41%	18.56%	12.87%	0.00%	3.84%	0.00%
1986	15.73%	54.90%	97.38%	39.80%	78.55%	31.20%	10.47%	2.62%	10.67%	0.88%
1987	12.36%	50.28%	56.13%	41.85%	42.35%	33.71%	16.96%	5.49%	17.96%	3.55%
1988	18.12%	40.09%	65.83%	33.99%	44.71%	23.01%	9.08%	19.20%	10.47%	8.41%
1989	19.07%	39.99%	67.92%	40.07%	57.90%	27.27%	15.90%	24.08%	15.88%	17.15%
1990	5.89%	46.85%	7.50%	26.69%	10.58%	32.89%	4.41%	2.30%	6.20%	1.32%
1991	4.03%	46.30%	6.84%	19.43%	12.38%	36.27%	2.89%	1.30%	4.64%	1.36%
AVERAGE 1985-91	13.20%	45.00%	57.37%	33.60%	47.98%	28.99%	10.37%	7.86%	9.951%	4.67%

[a] Data include only completed transactions. Data are classified according to the announcement date of a transaction — not taking into consideration when a transaction is completed.

[b] Percentage values denote the fraction of the total number of transactions that involves the presence of financial advisers.

[c] Presence of financial advisers to the buying company as a percentage of the total number of attempted M&A transactions.

[d] Presence of financial advisers to the selling company as a percentage of the total number of attempted M&A transactions.

Table 6.10 draws a comparison for LBO penetration in the United States, the United Kingdom and continental Europe. The U.S. level of activity peaked in 1988. United Kingdom and the rest of Europe have experienced significant increases in LBOs, which reached a peak slightly later. The significance of Table 6.10 is in the fact that LBOs are occurring in continental Europe at all. Even such a complex free-market device as the LBO can be put to use in continental Europe once the financing is available and investors understand its uses and drawbacks.

Use of Financial Advisers

A hallmark of an active market for corporate control and economic restructuring is the use of financial advisers for buyers and sellers of companies. On the sell-side, advisers can use their expertise and broad contacts to canvass the market for the highest available price and to help assure the shareholders in the assets to be sold that they have received fair value. On the buy-side, advisers can help identify targets that are undervalued or that provide a useful strategic fit for the acquiring company and that a fair price is paid. They can also help with the financing of the acquisition, including arranging bridge financing, mezzanine financing, debt and equity new issues, and occasionally putting their own capital at risk in getting the transaction done.

Table 6.11 compares the use of financial advisers in M&A transactions by companies from the United States, the United Kingdom and the rest of Europe.

Concluding Remarks on M&A Activities in the 1990s

Based on the foregoing discussion, we can draw the following inferences for the 1990s:

First, the decline in M&A activity in the United States is being replaced by a merger volume expansion in Europe that is generally regarded as beneficial to industrial corporations (both those owned by the private sector and those still owned by governments) seeking restructuring for the purpose of enhancing their competitive performance in what are now global industries, and by investors seeking liquidity and greater value-realization of longstanding holdings. Some disruption of established relationships can be seen to result from increased M&A activity, but there is little evidence to date of either public or institutional resistance to the level of activity attained, nor of extreme behavior on the part of the principals engaged in restructuring that might attract increased regulation in the future. At the same time, there is a growing recognition that clear rules of procedure, and suitable powers of enforcement must be put into place in order to prevent possible abuses.

Second, the user-benefits of a global or European market for corporate control are considerable. In many parts of continental Europe, businesses are owned by individuals, proprietorships, partnerships, or closely held corporations. Such owners have lacked liquidity in their holdings and thus have been restricted in distributing wealth to successive generations of their families, or in being able to sell out at the end of their active years. In the past, such owners have had to accept low prices for their businesses in a sale to a competitor, to a bank, or to the market in a limited "going-public" transaction. More recently, as a result of privatization issues, increasing deregulation, growing trading volumes and enhanced liquidity–in part due to investments from the United States and Japan–European equity markets have become much more active, efficient (in the sense of competing-away corporate control premiums) and transparent. With this has come the possibility of selling businesses at prices attuned to the public equity markets plus, as has long been the practice in the United States and the United Kingdom a substantial control premium. Thus the market for corporate control has attracted numerous owners of businesses seeking buyers. There is reason to believe that once this pattern of transactions has become established in Europe, as it has in the United States and the United Kingdom, it will become a permanently operating market.

Third, buyers too have become important users of the market, especially those larger European and Japanese corporations looking for strategic additions to their businesses in the large U.S. market, in anticipation of the 1992 liberalizations in Europe, or for other reasons. Many continental European and Japanese buyers have gained substantial experience in acquiring companies in the United States and in the United Kingdom, and have become comfortable operating in other countries. Moreover, many have found a growing number of experienced advisers to assist them in affecting complicated transactions, and a substantial access to needed capital. Successful buyers attract other companies from their industries as emulators.

Fourth, both buyers and sellers are benefitting from better understanding of company valuations, financing techniques, and the opportunity to dispose of businesses that no longer fit strategic objectives. Much greater financial flexibility has been developed. Sellers of businesses, in particular, have benefitted from tactics designed to utilize auction processes in order to increase selling prices. Buyers have benefitted from the increasing opportunity to make offers directly to shareholders, even if such offers are opposed by the board of directors of the companies concerned.

Finally, the extraordinary volume of transactions after 1985, relative to prior levels of activity, indicates that the market for corporate control has begun to generate its own attention, attract infrastructure to support future growth, players of all sorts (advisers, bankers, strategic consultants, lawyers, etc.) who will attempt to stimulate transactions, as well as a new breed of financial entrepreneurs who can be expected to create and exploit profit opportunities from the scene.

These factors, taken together, suggest the development of a significant momentum in the merger market in the 1990s, especially in Europe. This expansion is likely to continue until such time as a substantial proportion of large businesses, especially those intending to operate on regional or global bases, have been restructured and corporate control values have found equilibrium levels. Liquefying the market for corporate control is likely to be of lasting benefit for the efficiency and growth of the European regional economy.

References

Booz Allen Acquisition Services (1990), *Study on Obstacles to Takeover Bids in the European Community*, Paris: Booz Allen.

Commission of the European Communities (1989), "Horizontal Mergers and Competition in the European Community", *European Economy*, No. 40, May, Luxembourg: Office des Publications des Communautes Europeennes.

Fleuriet, M. (1989), "Mergers and Acquisitions: The French Experience", Paris: Chase Manhattan S.A. *Mimeo.*

Rybczynski, T. (1989), "Corporate Restructuring", *National Westminster Bank Review*, August.

Sleuwaegen, L. and H. Yamawaki (1988), "The Formation of the European Common Market and Changes in Market Structure and Performance", *European Economic Review*, No. 32.

Smith R.C. and I. Walter (1991), "Economic Restructuring in Europe and the Market for Corporate Control", *Journal of International Securities Markets*, January.

Walter, I. and R. C. Smith, (1989), *Investment Banking in Europe: Restructuring for the 1990s,* Oxford: Basil Blackwell.

Chapter 7

Foreign Direct Investment in Emerging Market Countries

Thomas L. Brewer

Introduction

The purpose of this chapter is to suggest plausible patterns and trends in foreign direct investment flows to "emerging economies" during the remainder of the 1990s.[1] As a basis for developing the forecasts, the chapter examines data on FDI flows during previous decades, especially during the 1980s. Most of the analysis is in terms of aggregate national-level FDI flows, but there is also some industry-level data. The analysis does not develop a formal econometric forecasting model, though it does utilize the results of previous theoretical and empirical studies of the determinants of FDI. The analysis includes economic and political determinants of FDI–at both the macro-level and micro-level. The analytic approach is thus interdisciplinary and multi-level.

The chapter uses the term, "emerging economies," in a comprehensive sense to refer to the developing countries of Asia, Latin America, Africa and the Middle East, as well as the countries of Eastern Europe and the former republics of the Soviet Union. All of the non-industrial countries, i.e. non-OECD countries, are included. The term thus includes the newly industrializing economies (NIEs) of Asia and Latin America, but the term is not restricted to such countries. Most data sets on FDI still exclude the economies of Eastern Europe and the former Soviet Union. Thus, although at a conceptual level most of the discussion implicitly includes those countries, they are generally omitted from the tables.

---

[1] Some portions of this chapter draw upon a study (Brewer 1991), which was originally conducted for the World Bank; however, the data, interpretations, and conclusions have been used selectively, and they have been updated and extended in several respects. As a result, almost all of the material in the chapter is new. The chapter also draws upon work in progress on a book-length manuscript tentatively titled "International Direct Investment: Global Firms, National Governments, and International Regimes". The analysis of regional patterns and trends is developed further in a paper in progress, "The Regionalization of Foreign Direct Investment: Implications for FDI Theory, Business Strategy, and Business-Government Relations." Some of the ideas concerning the effects of government policies are developed more extensively in two articles (Brewer, forthcoming-a; forthcoming-b).

Unless otherwise indicated, the data on FDI flows refer to net inflows associated with inbound FDI projects in emerging economies. Since there is relatively little outbound FDI from most emerging economies, the distinction between inflows and outflows associated with inbound FDI, on the one hand, and outflows and inflows associated with outbound FDI, on the other hand, does not usually entail a significant statistical difference; the newly industrializing economies of Asia, however, are an exception, as discussed in more detail below.[2]

Table 7.1. Average Annual FDI Inflows.[a]
Percent of Gross Domestic Capital Formation

	1980-82	1985-87
Developing Countries [b]	6.0	6.1
Latin America and Caribbean	6.0	5.0
Brazil	4.6	2.1
Mexico	4.3	4.6
Asia and Pacific	5.9	6.8
India	0.1	0.2
Indonesia	11.1	14.4
Korea, Republic of	0.5	1.4
Singapore	23.4	25.5
Africa	6.1	9.0
Nigeria	0.4	12.1
Developed Market Economy Countries [c]	2.9	3.4
Germany (FRG)	0.3	0.6
France	1.8	2.7
Japan	0.1	0.1
United Kingdom	8.2	8.8
United States	3.5	4.5

[a] Net inflows associated with inbound FDI projects.
[b] Does not include former centrally planned economies of Eastern Europe or the CIS or other republics of the former Soviet Union.
[c] Includes Saudi Arabia in the original source.

Source: UNCTC (1991), p 7-8, Table 2.

[2] In conceptual terms, in theoretical terms, and in managerial terms, the distinction between gross and net flows, the distinction between inflows and outflows, and the distinction between flows associated with inbound and outbound FDI are of course crucial; however, they are often overlooked in theoretical, empirical and public policy studies of FDI. The distinctions among the various types of "flows" (equity, reinvested earnings, long-term debt, and short-term debt) involved in FDI projects are also often ignored. See Brewer (Forthcoming-b) for further discussion of this point.

In simple aggregate terms, inbound FDI is relatively more important to emerging economies than it is to developed market economies–as measured by the ratio of FDI inflows to gross domestic capital formation. As Table 7.1 suggests, the ratio for the emerging market economies has been roughly twice that of the developed market economies. Within each of those two disparate groups of countries, of course, there are also large variations. Among the developed market economies, the large ratio for the U.K. and small ratio for Japan are well known. Among the emerging market economies, there is even greater variability–with India at the low end (0.1 - 0.2 percent) and Singapore at the high end (23.4 - 25.5 percent).

In specific industries in individual host countries, the importance of FDI is particularly striking. Thus, in the manufacturing sector, the importance of inbound FDI in the electrical, chemical and motor vehicle industries in key economies of Asia and Latin America is evident in Table 7.2.

Table 7.2. Importance of FDI In Manufacturing In Selected Host Economies.
Percent [d]

	Electrical	Chemical	Motor Vehicle	Total Manu.
Argentina [a]	83.5	61.4	100.0	na
Brazil [b]	50.9	38.9	80.6	34.2
Philippines [b]	66.1	60.6	21.9	40.8
Thailand [c]	89.4	72.0	59.8	74.8

[a] 1988, [b] 1987, [c] 1986,
[d] Percent of Total Sales in Host Economy by Local Affiliates of Foreign Parent Firms

Source: UNCTC (1991), p. 99-100.

In order to understand these and other patterns and trends in FDI and in order to assess the extent to which they may persist or change during the remainder of the 1990s, it is useful to summarize the theoretical and empirical studies of the determinants of FDI.[3] After a review of those studies, the chapter analyzes data on previous FDI, and then it discusses forecast data.

[3] A wide-ranging survey of the literature on the determinants of FDI was published recently by the United Nations Centre on Transnational Corporations (UNCTC 1992a). The UNCTC was previously an autonomous unit within the UN system; it has since become the Transnational Corporations and Management Division in the Department of Economic and Social Development. Also see Lizondo (1991) for a recent review of FDI theory.

Determinants of FDI

There are three different types of FDI projects in terms of the strategic objectives of firms: "market-seeking" projects that provide access to the host country market (and often neighboring markets as well); "efficiency-seeking" projects that provide low cost production, with export to the home country and/or other countries; and "resource-seeking" projects that provide access to raw materials. Although some FDI projects include elements of more than one of these strategic objectives, most projects are focussed on only one.

The type of project, as well as industry sector, affects the relative explanatory power of the variables posited by the theories below. For manufacturing projects that are based on a market-seeking strategy, the size of the host country market is obviously the principal concern. Thus, GNP and GNP growth rates, for instance, are important determinants. On the other hand, for manufacturing projects that are based on an efficiency-seeking strategy, the effects of host country economic conditions on the firms' production costs and competitiveness in foreign markets are a central concern for investors. Thus, inflation rates, foreign exchange rates, wage rates, savings rates and investment rates are important. In recent years such cost considerations have become particularly important as firms have restructured and further diversified and integrated their production operations internationally in response to competitive pressures.

In service industries, many FDI projects are undertaken by banks and other firms that follow their home country corporate clients into emerging economies, and in that sense they are market-seeking projects. Thus, direct investments in financial services, accounting services, and consulting services are often undertaken so that firms can better serve their corporate customers as the latter undertake their own FDI projects. To the extent that the business of the corporate clients of the service industries depends on host country economic conditions, then of course the service corporations' interests are also dependent (indirectly) on those same conditions. In addition–and of increasing importance–many service sector FDI projects serve the local host country market so that host country economic conditions are more directly relevant.

For resource-seeking investments in the primary sector (in agriculture as well as minerals), the host country endowment in the relevant natural resource is the most important feature attracting investors. In addition, world commodity prices are obviously important determinants, particularly since resource-seeking FDI projects are typically oriented to export for world markets rather than for the domestic host country market.

The explanatory and predictive power of these and other determinants of FDI thus varies across types of projects and industry sectors. In order to gain a more extensive appreciation of the factors affecting FDI, however, it is helpful to review the economic and political variables that have been found to be related to FDI. The limitations of space preclude an exhaustive consideration of such variables, but it is possible to highlight some key factors at both the macro and micro levels of economic and political analysis.

Microeconomic Determinants

There are two closely related micro-economic explanations of FDI that form the core of currently accepted FDI theory–one based on industry structure and the other based on transaction costs (Dunning and Rugman 1985; Horaguchi and Toyne 1990). According to the first, firms in oligopolistic industries have economies of scale and other characteristics that give them market power and enable them to overcome the disadvantages of being foreign and thus compete with local competitors in host countries (Hymer 1976). According to the second, firms undertake FDI because transaction costs associated with trade and licensing make them inefficient alternatives compared with FDI (Dunning 1980; 1981; 1988a; 1988b; Rugman 1980a; 1980b; 1981; 1986; Casson 1981; Hennart 1982; Teece 1985). FDI thus represents an internalization of transactions within the firm so that hierarchically-administered international transactions within the firm replace market-based transactions.

The absence of strong local competitors in most emerging economies (and the concomitant market power of large parent multinational firms from industrial countries) has made it relatively easy for firms to undertake economically viable FDI projects in emerging economies in the past. In addition, the import substitution development strategies and protectionist trade policies of host countries made FDI an efficient alternative to trade as a strategic alternative for firms wanting access to the local markets. Although both types of market imperfections (resulting from industry structure and from barriers to market-based transactions) may be declining, it is not yet clear how much of an impact such changes will have on FDI flows to emerging economies.

Dunning's expansion of internalization theory to embrace an "eclectic" approach incorporates macro-level economic variables (and political variables) as well. The "location advantages" of particular foreign countries make FDI in them preferable to FDI in other potential host countries and to domestic investment in the home country, and those location advantages depend on macro-economic and political conditions.

Macroeconomic Determinants

There have been numerous attempts to explain FDI with macroeconomic models.[4] Pfefferman and Madarassy (1992: 5-6) have summarized the macroeconomic variables that affect FDI projects in developing countries, based on studies of U.S. firms' investments. They conclude that "... market size is one of the most important considerations in making investment location decisions"–for three reasons: the "larger potential for local sales", the "greater profitability of local sales than export sales", and the "relatively diverse resources which make local sourcing more feasible". In empirical studies of FDI in emerging economies, national economic size is therefore often included as one of the determinants of FDI flows (Contractor 1991; Kobrin 1976).[5] It is not at all surprising that economically large countries such as Argentina, Brazil and Mexico are consistently among the major recipient emerging economies. Economic conditions in *neighboring* countries can also be important - as the experience of Southeast Asia demonstrates.

As for the effects of costs, Pfefferman and Madarassy (1992: 5) note that relative costs continue to be important; however, direct labor costs in particular are less important than they formerly were, while white collar and supervisory labor costs have been rising. Consequently, "it [is] increasingly attractive for multinational corporations to invest in countries which offer a well-educated pool of labor. More generally, companies focus increasingly on competence,

---

[4] Some of the early theorizing about FDI treated it as an international transfer of financial capital, and it was consequently assumed to be responsive to cross-national differentials in the rates of return on capital. However, the empirical evidence did not provide strong support for the theory. Nor could the theory account for the phenomenon of FDI flows in both directions for a given country. Another theory has viewed FDI as a way for firms to diversify their risk geographically. Although this theory could account for the phenomenon of simultaneous FDI inflows and outflows for countries, it could not explain large variations across industries in the tendency to undertake FDI. Furthermore, it was inconsistent with the assumption that investors could themselves diversify their stock portfolios internationally.

[5] In a study of FDI in industrial economies, Julius (1990) reports a strong and statistically significant relationship between real FDI growth and real GNP growth in the G-5 countries over the 25 year period (1964-1989). A simple bi-variate regression analysis yielded a regression coefficient = 3.44, with an $R^2 = 0.53$ and a t-statistic = 5.23.

education and high skills."[6] Not surprisingly, the major recipients of FDI, especially in manufacturing, among the emerging economies also tend to be countries with relatively high literacy rates and skill levels in the work force.

Both theory and evidence suggest that FDI is also responsive to *exchange rates*. There have been several different approaches to the role of exchange rates in FDI (Aliber 1970; 1971; Froot and Stein 1989; Caves 1988), but the common hypothesis among them is that FDI flows into countries with low real currency values, and it flows out of countries with high real currency values. Thus, prolonged deviations from purchasing power parity tend to prompt FDI flows. On the other hand, to the extent that currencies are allowed to float and reflect cross-national differences in inflation rates and thus maintain relatively stable real exchange rates, they should have a neutral effect on FDI.[7] Since developing countries have tended to maintain over-valued currencies in the past, their exchange rate policies probably discouraged some inbound foreign investment -whether for the domestic market or for exports. On the other hand, the recent liberalizations of exchange rate regimes in many emerging economies should make exchange rates less of a deterrent.[8]

---

[6] Pfefferman and Madarassy (1992) note the role of other variables as well: "Potential investors also look at levels of foreign investment in place as a very important indicator of the quality of the business climate. Where others are operating successfully, would-be investors are reassured. Furthermore, as more firms invest in a country, synergies develop as foreign firms become each other's suppliers, and such demand can help to develop specialized inputs, such as trained labor, marketing and distribution channels...." "It is not surprising, therefore, that the stock of existing FDI in a given country is often a good predictor of future FDI inflows." "Another essential motivating factor is the quality of infrastructure. The relative ease of doing business depends greatly on the availability and efficiency of transport, communications and energy. More broadly, the degree of industrialization attained in the host country is an important determinant of FDI location, especially for the more technical industries such as electronics."

[7] FDI is sometimes viewed as a constituent of the balance of payments adjustment process–that is, a capital account response to a current account deficit/surplus. Countries with current account deficits are accordingly expected to experience net FDI inflows, while countries with current account surpluses are expected to experience net FDI outflows. Note that it is the overall net FDI flows that are of interest here–that is, net outflows net of net inflows. International direct investment in this view is thus one of several types of capital flows–along with private portfolio investments, private bank credits, official lending by governments and international organisations, and other long-term and short-term capital flows that finance current account deficits. In terms of balance of payments accounting, such a view of FDI is straightforward and unexceptionable. However, in cause and effect terms the existence of such a relationship is questionable on both theoretical and empirical grounds.

[8] The upward revaluations of some emerging economy currencies under pressure from the governments of their industrial country export markets are of course counter examples, but such cases are relatively small in number compared with the number of emerging economy currencies that have been devalued in real terms in recent years.

Macro-Political Determinants

Investors' costs and revenues also depend on political conditions, including political stability and a variety of host and home government policies.

The effects of political instability on FDI are apparent in two ways. First, and most importantly, there are potential host countries whose histories have been marked by chronic political instability, which has deterred many investors from undertaking projects. Second, even brief periods of governmental instability can cause interruptions in FDI flows as investors wait for a return to normalcy in the political system.

Several studies have tried to determine empirically the role of instability in investors' decisions about FDI projects. The studies have generally been of two types–those based on executives' answers to survey questions and those based on events and FDI data. The studies based on surveys consistently found that executives considered host country instability to be a major deterrent in FDI project location decisions (Frank 1980, 111-112; Green 1972; Root 1968); since most of these studies were conducted more than a decade ago, it is possible that there is now less skittishness among investors on this score.

Studies of the actual record of country instability and FDI flows have yielded mixed results; some have found significant effects of political instability on FDI flows while others have not. In one of the most comprehensive and recent studies, Nigh (1985) analyzed foreign direct investments in manufacturing in 24 countries, including 11 developing countries, during 1954-1975 by multinational corporations based in the United States. He found that for the developing countries in particular FDI flows were related to internal conflicts such as riots and civil war. Whether investors from other industrial countries are as averse to political instability is unclear.

Sometimes, of course, political instability leads to instability in specific government policies that directly affect FDI projects. There is evidence, however, that host country political instability may not actually be as problematic as many investors believe. A study of governmental instability in developing countries found it to be only weakly related to instability in their restrictions on international funds transfers associated with FDI projects, and less so than among developed countries (Brewer 1983). The relationship of expropriation to government instability is also not consistent (Kobrin 1984); moreover, expropriation has declined considerably since the mid-1970s (Minor

1988). Other empirical studies (Brewer, 1985; Yu 1987) have analyzed the relationship between governmental regime instability and macro-economic policy instability, and compared developing countries and industrial countries in terms of policy stability. Those studies have found weak and statistically insignificant relationships between governmental regime instability and policy instability among developing countries; they have also found as much or more policy instability in industrial countries as in developing countries.

In any case, however, perceptions of political instability are likely to continue to affect investors' inclinations about undertaking FDI projects in particular countries or regions. Whereas the emergence of democracy in Argentina and Brazil, for instance, and the relative quiescence in the political systems of many countries in other regions should encourage investors, the continuation of ethnically-based conflicts in Eastern Europe and the republics of the former Soviet Union will surely deter many investors from undertaking projects in those areas for several more years.

Host country FDI policies can obviously provide important deterrents or incentives to prospective investors. During the past decade there was a pronounced shift in host country FDI policies among emerging economies–toward more hospitable, less restrictive policies. The changes in Eastern Europe and the republics of the former Soviet Union have been especially dramatic and are of course still in the process of being implemented. The governments of major emerging economies in other parts of the world have also undertaken significant FDI policy liberalization programmes–Mexico and India, for instance.

The extent of this shift in host country FDI policies has been recently documented by a UNCTC study (1992b) of policy changes in 26 developing countries over the 1977-1987 period, and the results of that study are summarized in Table 7.3. In terms of the overall indicators of policy changes and in terms of six of the seven categories of particular types of policy changes, there was a clear tendency toward liberalization. (The only exception was that developing countries not included in the newly industrializing category were slightly more inclined to adopt more restrictive performance requirements such as export and domestic content targets.) Studies by Brewer (1991) and by

Becsky, Young and Ordu (1991) also found widespread evidence of the trend toward liberalization in host country FDI policies.[9]

Table 7.3. Host Government Policy Changes.
Mean Policy Changes per Country [a]

	NIEs [b]		Other Developing Countries [c]	
	-	+	-	+
Ownership	0.20	1.40	0.33	0.81
Taxation	0.40	1.40	0.43	1.43
Convertibility	0	0.80	0.33	0.81
Price Controls	0.40	0.60	0.33	0.76
Performance Mandates	0	0.20	0.29	0.05
Sectoral Restrictions	0.40	1.00	0.10	0.76
Misc. Procedural	0.60	0.80	0.43	1.00
All Changes	2.00	6.20	2.24	5.62

[a] - (minus) indicates change that was less favorable to investors; + (plus) indicates change that was more favorable to investors.
[b] Brazil, Korea, Malaysia, Mexico, Singapore.
[c] Argentina, Bahamas, Chile, China, Colombia, Ecuador, Egypt, Indonesia, Jamaica, Kenya, Morocco, Nigeria, Pakistan, Panama, Peru, Philippines, Saudi Arabia, Thailand, Turkey, Venezuela.

Source: UNCTC (1992b), p. 16, Table 7.

In addition, the widespread privatization and debt-equity swap programs adopted in many emerging economies over the past decade have of course created new opportunities for FDI.

There are also numerous and diverse types of other host government policies, in addition to FDI policies, that affect FDI flows. They include monetary and fiscal policies, capital controls, transfer pricing regulations, anti-trust (i.e. competition) policy, labor relations policies, intellectual property rights enforcement, and many others. Even though each country's policy profile in

[9] The effects of *regional* development schemes that include FDI policies have not been subjected to thorough analysis. On *a priori* grounds, it is clear that such schemes can both increase and decrease foreign direct investment; for they can lead to increased FDI among the countries within the region while discouraging inbound FDI from countries outside the region. Thus, just as regional trade arrangements can have trade-creating and/or trade-diverting effects, regional FDI arrangements can have FDI-creating and/or FDI-diverting effects. Regional development arrangements can, therefore, simultaneously reduce intra-regional market imperfections, which increase intra-regional FDI, and increase market imperfections vis-á-vis countries that are outside the region, which reduces inbound FDI from those countries. See Brewer (Forthcoming-b) for further analysis of these issues.

these areas is clearly unique and subject to significant change over time, it is apparent that there has been a world-wide (albeit uneven) pattern of macro-economic policy liberalization that makes those economies' investment climates more attractive to would-be foreign investors.

FDI flows to emerging economies are sometimes facilitated or constrained by the policies of home governments as well. In the past, capital controls in some countries have restrained outbound FDI that might have gone to emerging economies, but such controls on outbound FDI are now largely gone, at least among the industrial countries. On the other hand, those countries do have in place programs of political risk insurance that are intended to encourage FDI in emerging economies; moreover, the Multilateral Investment Guarantee Agency (MIGA) in the World Bank group provides additional programs of this nature. The available evidence indicates that these programs do in fact have a positive effect on many specific FDI projects in rather direct ways. For instance, a study of the "additionality" of the programs of the US Overseas Private Investment Corporation (OPIC) concluded that 25 percent to 82 percent of the investments covered by OPIC would not have been undertaken without that coverage (Arthur Young 1982).

These and other related programs affect the perspectives and policies of both investors and host governments in other respects. As far as host governments are concerned, the programs of the international institutions in particular include the provision of policy reform assistance–for instance through the Foreign Investment Advisory Service (FIAS), which is jointly sponsored by MIGA and IFC. Although the national government programs are not likely to shrink or grow dramatically over the next several years, the multilateral programs are likely to have an increasing impact. In addition, the increased funding of the IFC and other international financial institutions, particularly for their activities in Eastern Europe, should have a further facilitative impact on FDI flows.

Micro-Political Determinants

One of the most important consequences of the activities of these multilateral programmes (and of their home national government counterparts) is that they help to create FDI "issue networks" through which firms, governmental agencies, and other organizations with an interest in FDI in emerging economies participate.[10] Such networks facilitate the flow of information among participants in the FDI process and thus make it easier for potential investors to gather and assess the large quantities and diverse types of information that are needed in the FDI project decision process.

On the basis of its experiences in Southeast Asia and Central Europe in a programme designed to explore the potential for the further development of the motor vehicle industry, for instance, the International Finance Corporation (1992) concluded that:

> "...the creation of dense networks for dialogue is essential (for the development of a motor vehicle industry, including increased FDI). Nowhere in (Central Europe) are there the industry and trade associations which play such a vital role elsewhere. Recent efforts in Indonesia, for instance, have begun to show the value of bringing together firms, particularly in the (automotive) component field, so that they can share knowledge of markets and customers, develop group training programmes, and be in a position to dialogue with the government."

Although the current state of development and the future prospects of FDI "networks" involving host governments, firms and other organizations are uneven across emerging economies, such networks will continue to expand; and as they do, they will increase the aggregate levels of FDI flows as well as shape the features of individual projects.

Of course, firms and host governments not only exchange information through dialogue; they commonly negotiate the initial terms of FDI entry as well as a variety of operational issues on an intermittent basis. Consequently, there is a vast literature on FDI in emerging economies concerning the bargaining relations between investing firms and host governments. One strand of this literature concerns the "obsolescing bargain" explanation of expropriation (Bergsten, Horst and Moran, 1978: 130-140; Vernon, 1971: 46-59). In addition, there are a large number of case studies, and more theoretically-oriented studies as well, that have analyzed the issues and behavior in such bargaining processes (e.g. Weiss 1990).

---

[10] The concept of "transorganizational strategic networks" involving multinational firms, and host and home governments, is developed in a preliminary fashion in Brewer (1992b). These and other relations between firms and governments in their interactions over FDI-related issues vary systematically across "issue-areas" (Brewer, 1992a).

A variety of considerations suggest that the bargaining position of developing countries is generally strengthening in relation to foreign direct investors. They include the rapidly growing markets of emerging economies, the strategic drive of multinational firms to seek low cost production sites to counter increasing competitive pressure in many industries, and the enhanced technological and administrative capabilities of host economies. Although such trends can certainly affect the terms of entry and the features of individual FDI projects, it seems unlikely that they will have much effect on the overall levels of FDI.

Previous Patterns and Trends

Because the determinants of FDI vary in their explanatory and predictive power across types of FDI projects and across industry sectors, it is difficult to develop precise explanations or make precise forecasts on the basis of FDI data that are aggregated across industries and types of projects and as many as 150 countries. It would be premature to suggest that there is a mathematical model with such explanatory or predictive power. However, we can document some of the basic patterns and trends, and develop plausible explanations and predictions based on them.

Global Totals

During the 1950s and until the mid 1960s, net FDI flows to emerging economies remained at low levels of approximately USD 2 billion or less per year in current dollar terms. Beginning in the late 1960s, annual net flows increased–a trend that generally persisted during the decade of the 1970s. As Table 7.4 indicates, in constant dollar terms, net annual inflows of FDI into those countries by 1979 were at nearly twice the level of 1970. These increased annual flows were responses to the combination of economic growth and industrialization in several large emerging economies, more hospitable host country policies in some cases, and more flexible policies on the part of investors about the terms of entry.

There was a period of decline from 1981 to 1986, as the recession in the industrial countries reduced demand for exports from FDI projects in emerging economies and as the deepening debt crisis dampened investors' interest in the local economies' markets for their products. In the late 1980s and early 1990s, however, there were substantial increases to the recent levels of approximately USD 25 billion (Table 7.4, and World Bank 1992a).

Table 7.4. FDI Inflows in Emerging and Developed Market Economies at Constant Prices, 1970-1989.
Constant 1989, Billions of US Dollars [a]

Year	Emerging Economies	Developed Economies	World Total
1970	7.2	34.5	41.7
1971	8.9	31.9	40.8
1972	5.1	32.8	37.9
1973	13.2	37.9	51.1
1974	8.9	41.7	50.6
1975	11.9	34.9	46.8
1976	7.7	28.1	35.7
1977	10.4	36.6	47.0
1978	10.6	41.7	52.3
1979	13.6	46.4	60.0
1980	11.5	50.6	62.1
1981	18.3	64.3	82.6
1982	16.2	54.9	71.7
1983	12.7	52.8	65.5
1984	13.2	60.4	73.6
1985	15.9	49.6	65.5
1986	12.7	75.8	88.5
1987	16.7	101.7	118.4
1988	21.3	121.3	142.6
1989	25.0	162.7	187.7

[a] The price deflator used to compute the constant price data series is the World Bank's MUV (Manufactures Unit Value) Index, which is based on the U.S. dollar value of manufactured goods exported from the G-5 countries (France, Germany, Japan, U.K., U.S.), weighted by their exports to developing countries (1980 = 100).

Source: Bachman (1991), p. 40, Table 6.

Sectoral Composition

There has been a long-term shift in the sectoral composition of FDI (Brewer 1991; OECD 1987; UNCTC 1991). In the 1950s, it was predominantly in the primary sector. Over time, the manufacturing sector became increasingly important, initially in resource-based industries, and more recently in light manufacturing. Moreover, there has been a shift within the manufacturing sector from an earlier emphasis on import substitution market-seeking projects that produced for large and rapidly industrializing markets to a more recent emphasis on efficiency-seeking projects that produce for export. There has also been a long-term increase in the proportion of FDI in the services sector in emerging economies–a trend that was highly intensified in the 1980s. However, much of this has been in financial services in particular, and especially in offshore centers.

Regional Distribution

Over the two-decade period from the beginning of the 1970s to the end of the 1980s, there were significant shifts in the regional distribution of FDI flows in emerging economies. The changing regional distributions of FDI flows are indicated in Table 7.5; and the regional distributions of stocks are in Table 7.6. At the beginning of the 1970s, Latin American countries were the recipients of over half of all FDI going to emerging economies (59 percent in1970); by the end of the 1980s, the emerging economies of Asia were the recipients of over half (53 percent in 1989). The increases in FDI in Southeast Asia in

Table 7.5. FDI Inflows in Developing Countries by Region at Constant Prices, 1970-1989.
Constant 1989, Billions of U.S. Dollars [a]

Year	Afr.	Asia	Eur [b]	L.A./Car.	M.E./N.Afr. [c]
1970	0.4	1.3	0.4	4.3	0.9
1971	1.3	1.7	0.4	5.5	-
1972	-	2.1	0.4	3.0	-0.4
1973	1.7	2.1	0.4	6.8	2.1
1974	1.4	2.8	0.2	4.0	0.5
1975	2.1	3.0	0.4	6.8	-0.4
1976	1.7	2.5	-	3.4	-
1977	1.5	2.7	0.2	6.0	-
1978	1.5	2.3	0.1	6.7	-
1979	1.6	2.8	0.1	7.5	1.6
1980	-	3.4	0.1	8.1	-0.1
1981	1.3	5.1	0.4	10.6	0.9
1982	1.3	5.6	0.1	8.4	0.8
1983	1.2	5.6	0.2	4.9	0.8
1984	0.7	6.0	0.2	4.5	1.8
1985	1.3	6.1	0.1	6.5	2.4
1986	0.5	6.3	0.3	4.1	1.5
1987	1.3	8.1	0.2	6.0	1.1
1988	0.7	10.5	0.4	8.0	1.7
1989	2.4	13.3	1.0	6.2	2.0

[a] The price deflator used to compute the constant price data series is the World Bank's MUV (Manufactures Unit Value) Index, which is based on the U.S. dollar value of manufactured goods exported from the G-5 countries (France, Germany, Japan, U.K., U.S.), weighted by their exports to developing countries (1980 = 100).
[b] Excludes Greece, includes Turkey.
[c] Excludes Saudi Arabia (which is classified as an industrial country in the original data set).

Source: Bachman (1991), p. 40, Table 6.

Table 7.6. FDI Stocks in Emerging Economies by Region.

	Constant 1988 USD Billions [a]		Percent of World Total	
	1967	1988	1967	1988
Africa	23	31	5	3
Asia	22	103	5	8
L.A./Car.	78	115	18	9
Middle East	14	11	3	1
Emerging Economies Sub-total	137	260	31	21
Developed Market Economies Sub-total 1	309	960	69	79
World Total	445	1219	100	100

[a] The price deflator used to compute the constant price data series is the World Bank's MUV (Manufactures Unit Value) Index, which is based on the U.S. dollar value of manufactured goods exported from the G-5 countries (France, Germany, Japan, U.K., U.S.), weighted by their exports to developing countries (1980=100).

Source: Bachman (1991), p. 40, Table 6.

particular, including intra-regional FDI among those countries, have been striking (Table 7.7).

Sub-Saharan Africa has traditionally experienced relatively low levels of FDI; its share was approximately 5 percent of total FDI flows to developing countries in 1970 and 10 percent in 1989. Meanwhile the share going to North Africa and the Middle East also remained at modest levels: 12 percent in 1970 and 8 percent in 1989.

Major Recipient Countries

Despite these changing patterns in the regional distribution of FDI in emerging economies, it has been highly concentrated in a relatively small number of individual countries. A few economically large and/or upper middle income countries in Asia and Latin America have consistently been among the principal recipient countries. The ten developing countries hosting the greatest amount of FDI were recipients of 72.0 percent of all FDI inflows to developing countries during 1980-84 and 64.4 percent during 1985-89 (Table 7.8).

Table 7.7. Foreign Direct Investment Flows in Selected Asian Countries.
Millions of US Dollars

Country	1985	1990
China	1659	3489
NIEs		
Korea	234	715
Singapore	1047	4808
Southeast Asia		
Indonesia	310	964
Malaysia	695	2902
Philippines	12	530
Thailand	163	2376
South Asia		
Bangladesh	2[a]	3
India[b]	160	263
Pakistan	131	249
Sri Lanka	26	31
Pacific Islands		
Fiji	22	66
Papua N. G.	83	203[c]
Soloman Is.	1	13
Vanuatu	5	13
Totals	4548	16412

[a] 1986
[b] Net, i.e. inbound less outbound
[c] 1989

Source: Asian Development Bank (1992), reported in *IMF Survey*, 21, 11 (May 25, 1992), p. 172.

Source Countries

There has also been a high degree of concentration in FDI flows in terms of source countries. Three countries–the United States, the United Kingdom, and Japan–accounted for 72 percent of total FDI flows to developing countries over the 1980-89 period (Finance and Development 1992). By 1989, FDI flows to developing countries from firms based in Japan exceeded those from firms based in the United States, and this increased outflow from Japan represents one of the most important changes in the basic patterns of FDI flows to emerging economies in recent years.

Another important trend in the past decade has been an increase in FDI flows *from* emerging economies as source countries. Malaysia, Singapore and Hong Kong are unusual among developing countries in the extent to which they are both recipients of and sources of FDI among emerging economies, reflecting the relatively intense activity in intra-regional FDI in Southeast Asia. Malaysia is especially prominent for the high proportion of its FDI that has come from other developing countries. In 1989, of the USD 3.2 billion total FDI inflows to Malaysia, USD 1.3 billion was from other emerging economies in Asia (Asian Development Bank, 1991). A recent report (Asian Development Bank 1992) observes that

> "the most significant aspect of foreign direct investment in Asia in recent years was the extremely rapid increase in intraregional investment....The NIEs [newly industrializing economies] have ... emerged as major investors in the region, almost at par with Japan."

Table 7.8 Major Recipients of FDI among Emerging Economies.
Average Annual FDI Inflows.

Country	Billions of U.S. Dollars		Percent of Global Total	
	1980-84	1985-89	1980-84	1985-89
Argentina	0.4	0.7	0.9	0.6
Brazil	2.1	1.6	4.2	1.3
China	0.5	2.5	1.1	2.1
Colombia	0.4	0.6	0.8	0.5
Egypt	0.6	1.2	1.1	1.0
Hong Kong	0.7	1.7	1.4	1.4
Malaysia	1.1	0.8	2.3	0.7
Mexico	1.5	2.0	3.0	1.7
Singapore	1.4	2.5	2.8	2.1
Thailand	0.3	0.7	0.6	0.6

Source: UNCTC (1991), p. 11, Table 4.

Future Patterns and Trends

Global Totals

One of the most important determinants of aggregate levels of future FDI flows world-wide will continue to be the growth rates in the economies of both the industrial and developing countries, and this will be true for FDI in agriculture, minerals, manufacturing and services. As Table 7.9 indicates, the real growth rate in GDP in the major industrial countries is expected to be about the same for the decade of the 1990s as it was for the 1980s–that is slightly more than 2 1/2 percent per year. Such growth rates in industrial countries could by themselves be expected to lead to only modest increases in FDI in emerging economies, particularly of course in projects for export to the industrial countries. However, in Table 7.9, there is a much higher growth rate of nearly 5 percent predicted for the 1990s for the emerging economies themselves–which is high in relation to both the industrial countries' growth rates and to the developing countries' own growth rates of the 1980s. Thus, market-seeking FDI projects in emerging economies can be expected to increase substantially during the 1990s. As a result of these and other factors, total annual flows in constant 1990 USD of 35-40 billion are plausible by the end of the decade.

Regional Trends

The forecast of a resumption of strong growth in Latin America and the Middle East, and the continuation of very high growth rates in East Asia and South Asia are especially noteworthy (Table 7.9). Otherwise, expectations for moderate rates for Africa and quite modest rates for Eastern Europe are also evident. Even allowing for substantial margins of error in these forecasts, it seems likely that growth rates in the 1990s will be marked by large regional variations among the emerging economies, with high rates in Asia and low rates in Eastern Europe, and with Latin America, the Middle East, and Africa in the middle. FDI flows can be expected to mirror these regional patterns as investors undertake market-seeking projects to serve the growing markets.

The rapid increases in FDI in East and Southeast Asia can therefore be expected to continue - to serve local domestic markets and to serve export markets in other Asian economies as well as North America and Europe.

The resumption of higher levels of FDI in Latin America in 1991-92 is probably a harbinger of continuing increases for that part of the world for the next several years. The projected real GDP growth rate of 4.2 percent per year for the 1990-2000 period, compared with 1.6 percent for the 1980-1990 period, implies much higher levels of FDI flows for those countries during the 1990s than there were during the 1980s.

Table 7.9. Actual and Forecasted Real Changes In GDP.
Percent Average Annual Change

	Actual 1980-1990	Forecasted 1990-2000
All Developing Countries	3.2	4.9
East Asia	7.9	7.1
South Asia	5.4	5 0
Latin America	1.6	4.2
Middle East & N. Africa	0.5	4.5
Africa (Sub-Saharan)	2.1	3.5
Eastern Europe	1.4	1.9
G-7 Industrial Countries	2.8	2.6

Source: World Bank (1992), p. 10,12, Tables 1.6, 1.7.

Despite widespread interest in potential FDI projects in Eastern Europe, the actual levels have remained low, and they are likely to remain low for several years. On the positive side, there are the privatization programmes of the governments that have attracted investors in existing facilities, the favorable prospects for projects that can export to the expanding EC and other West European countries, and the combination of high skill levels and low wages among workers. However, the investment climate remains highly uncertain because of the ethnic conflicts and the uncertain pace of the liberalization process. Whether the lending and policy reform programmes of the IMF and other international financial institutions can lead to significant changes in policies and overcome prospective investors' apprehensions obviously remains to be seen. The role of multilateral and national political risk insurance programmes may be especially important in this regard. In addition, the absence of business-government networks is a serious obstacle.

Table 7.10. Actual and Forecasted Demand for Motor Vehicles.
Millions of Vehicles

	1988			2000		
	Cars	Commercial [a]	Total	Cars	Commercial [a]	Total
Developing Countries	3	2	5	11	5	16
Eastern Europe	2	1	3	4	3	7
OECD Countries	30	11	41	34	12	45

[a] Trucks and busses

Source: Consultants for Trade and Industry (1989).

Manufacturing

The growth rates in markets will of course vary across industries and products. For the motor vehicle industry, for instance, forecast data for passenger cars and commercial vehicles (i.e. trucks and busses) are presented in Table 7.10. In terms of the absolute numbers of vehicles as well as the percentage change, the increases in the emerging markets of the third world are expected to be greater than the increases in the industrial countries of the first world.

Of course, not all of the vehicles sold in the emerging markets will be produced in FDI facilities in those countries. However, there is evidence of increasing FDI in emerging economies in the motor vehicle industry–for sales within the host countries as well as for export to industrial countries. The FDI facilities in Mexico owned by Chrysler, Ford, General Motors, Nissan, and Volkswagen are illustrative (UNCTC, 1991). The internationally integrated production process of Toyota that includes facilities in Indonesia, Malaysia, Philippines and Thailand is also illustrative (Far Eastern Economic Review 1989; reported in UNCTC 1991).

Primary Sector

FDI in the primary sector in emerging economies obviously depends on (highly cyclical) commodity prices–as well as GNP growth rates in the industrial countries. In Table 7.11, the contrast between the generally declining real prices in primary commodities during the 1980s and the expected increases of the 1990s are apparent. This suggests moderate growth in FDI in the primary sector during the balance of the 1990s. On the other hand, the

Table 7.11. Actual and Forecasted Real Changes in Commodity Prices.
Average Annual Percent Change [a]

	Actual 1980-1990	Forecast for 1990-2000
Petroleum	-6.6	0.2
Non-Petroleum	-5.1	0.5
Agriculture	-6.4	1.1
Food	-6.6	1.3
Raw Materials	-5.6	0.6
Timber	-2.5	1.7
Metals and Minerals	-2.8	-0.9

[a] Based on M W deflator.

Source: World Bank (1992), p. 10, Table 1-5.

projected continuation of sluggish growth in the major industrial economies (the G-7 countries indicated in Table 7.9 above) is likely to mitigate the effects of the commodity price increases. The net impact on primary sector FDI in emerging economies is therefore likely to be only slightly higher rates of FDI flows in the 1990s compared with the 1980s.

Services

Continuing restrictive host government policies in the services industries may limit FDI growth in this sector. Except for the large increases in banking services in a few offshore centers, FDI in the services sectors of emerging economies has not yet increased much, nor it is likely to do so in the future, unless there is substantial policy liberalization.

Conclusion

For the next decade, the vast bulk of the world's FDI will certainly continue to come from industrial countries, and it will just as certainly continue to flow to those countries; the "triad" countries will thus continue to be dominant as both source and recipient countries of FDI. However, the substantial and increasing amounts of FDI that do occur in emerging economies will nevertheless continue to have global significance in both economic and political terms.

The increasing economic importance will be especially true in industries, such as the motor vehicle industry, that are undergoing major restructuring; but it will extend to a variety of manufacturing industries as well as the traditionally important mining and agricultural sectors. The "triad" economies will be increasingly dependent on FDI in emerging economies.

There are also significant political implications of these projected patterns and trends. In particular, in the next round of international trade negotiations–within the GATT framework, or otherwise–FDI issues are likely to be central items on the agenda. The consideration of trade-related investment measures (TRIMs) during the Uruguay Round is a harbinger of the increasing attention that FDI issues are likely to receive in subsequent negotiations. The periodic calls for the expansion of the GATT and/or creation of a new international framework concerning FDI are thus likely to become more frequent and more salient. Economic diplomacy therefore appears to be entering a new era of sustained efforts to develop a more extensive international regime concerning FDI. In that era, it is inevitable that FDI in emerging economies will be an important political as well as economic fact.

References

Aliber, R. Z. (1970), "A Theory of Foreign Direct Investment." in Charles P. Kindleberger (ed.) *The International Corporation,* Cambridge, MA: MIT Press.

Arthur Young and Company (1982), *A Study of the Additionality of OPIC Assistance to U.S. Private Direct Investment in Developing Countries,* Washington, DC.

Asian Development Bank (1991), *Asian Development Outlook,* 1991, Manila.

Asian Development Bank (1992), *Asian Development Outlook,* 1992, Manila.

Bachman, H. B. (1991), *Industrialized Countries' Policies Affecting Foreign Direct Investment in Developing Countries - Volume I: Main Report,* Washington, DC: The World Bank - The Multilateral Investment Guarantee Agency.

Becsky, G., H. L. Young, and A. Ordu (1991), *Foreign Direct Investment in Selected Developing Countries in the Last Two Decades.* Washington, DC: The World Bank.

Bergsten, C. F., T. Horst, and T. Moran (1978), *American Multinationals and American Interests,* Washington, DC: The Brookings Institution.

Brewer, T. L. (1983), "The Instability of Governments and the Instability of Controls on Funds Transfers by Multinational Corporations", *Journal of International Business Studies,* 14, 3: 147-157.

Brewer, T. L. (ed.) (1985), *Political Risks in International Business: New Directions for Research. Management and Public Policy*, New York: Praeger Publishers.

Brewer, T. L. (1991), *Foreign Direct Investment in Developing Countries: Patterns. Policies and Prospects*, Washington, DC: The World Bank.

Brewer, T. L. (1992a), "An Issue-Area Approach to the Analysis of MNE Government Relations", *Journal of International Business Studies*, 23, 2: 295-309.

Brewer, T. L. (1992b), "MNE-Government Relations: Strategic Networks and Foreign Direct Investment in the United States in the Automotive Industry", *The International Executive*, 34, 2: 113-129.

Brewer, T. L. (Forthcoming-a), "The Effects of Government Policies on Foreign Direct Investment as a Strategic Choice of Firms: An Expansion of Internalization Theory", *International Trade Journal*.

Brewer, T. L. (Forthcoming-b), "Government Policies, Market Imperfections, and Foreign Direct Investment", *Journal of International Business Studies*.

Brewer, T. L. (In progress-a), "The Regionalization of Foreign Direct Investment: Implications for FDI Theory, Business Strategy, and Business-Government Relations."

Brewer, T. L. (In progress-b), "International Direct Investment: Global Firms. National Governments and International Regimes".

Casson, M. (1987), *The Firm and the Market*, Cambridge, MA: MIT Press.

Caves, R. E. (1988), *Exchange Rate Movements and Foreign Direct Investment in the United States*, Harvard Institute of Economic Research, Discussion Papers Series, No. 1383.

Consultants from Trade and Industry (1989), "European Industry's Investment Outlook in LDSs", June 1989 in Yannis Karmokolias, *Automotive Industry Trends and Prospects for Investment in Developing Countries*. Washington DC: The World Bank-International Finance Corporation, 1990.

Contractor, F. (1991), "Government Policies Toward Foreign Investment: An Empirical Investigation of the Link Between National Policies and FDI Flows", Paper prepared for the annual meeting of the Academy of International Business, Miami.

Dunning, J. H. (1988a), *Explaining International Production*, London: Allen and Unwin.

Dunning, J. H. (1988b), "The Eclectic Paradigm of International Production: A Restatement and Some Possible Extensions", *Journal of International Business Studies*, 19: 1-31.

Dunning, J. H. (1981), *International Production and the Multinational Enterprise*, London: Allen and Unwin.

Dunning, J. H.(1980), "Toward an Eclectic Theory of International Production", *Journal of International Business Studies,* 11:9-31.

Dunning, J. H., and A. M. Rugman (1985), "The Influence of Hymer's Dissertation on the Theory of Foreign Direct Investment", *American Economic Review*, Papers and Proceedings, 75: 228-232.

Finance and Development (1992), "Recent Trends in FDI for the Developing World", *Finance and Development*, 29, 1: 50-51.

Frank, I. (1980), *Foreign Enterprise in Developing Countries*, Baltimore, MD: Johns Hopkins University Press.

Froot, K. A., and J. C. Stein (1989), "Exchange Rates and Foreign Direct Investment: An Imperfect Capital Markets Approach", *NBER Working Paper* No. 2914, Cambridge, MA: National Bureau of Economic Research.

Green, R. (1972), *Political Instability as a Determinant of U.S.Foreign Investment,* Austin: University of Texas.

Hennart, J.-F. (1982), *A Theory of Multinational Enterprise,* Ann Arbor, Michigan: University of Michigan Press.

Horaguchi, H., and B. Toyne (1990), "Setting the Record Straight: Hymer, Internalization Theory and Transaction Cost Economics", *Journal of International Business Studies,* 20: 487-94.

Hymer, S. H. (1976), *The International Operations of National.Firms: A Study of Direct Foreign Investment,* Cambridge, MA: MIT Press. Originally, Ph.D. dissertation, MIT, 1960.

International Finance Corporation (1992), "A Report on the Automotive Industry", Workshop for Central and Eastern Europe Held in Budapest, Hungary, November 1991. Washington, DC: IFC.

Julius, D. (1990), *Global Companies and Public Policy,* New York: The Council on Foreign Relations.

Kobrin, S. J. (1976), "The Environmental Determinants of Foreign Direct Investment", *Journal of International Business Studies*, 7: 29-42.

Kobrin, S. J. (1984), "Expropriation as an Attempt to Control Foreign Firms in LDCs." *International Studies Quarterly*, 28, 3: 348-357.

Lizondo, J. S. (1991), "Foreign Direct Investment." in *Determinants and Systemic Consequences of International Capital Flows*. A Study by the Research Department of the International Monetary Fund, Occasional Paper No. 77, Washington, DC: International Monetary Fund.

Minor, M. (1988), "LDCs, TNCs and Expropriation in the 1980s", *CTC Reports,* 25: 53-55.

Nigh, D. (1985), "The Effect of Political Events on United States Direct Foreign Investment", *Journal of International Business Studies,* 16, 1: 1-17.

Organization for Economic Cooperation and Development.(1987), *International Investment and Multinational Enterprises,* Paris: Organization for Economic Cooperation and Development.

Pfefferman, G. P. and A. Madarassy (1992), "Trends in Private Investment in Developing Countries", 1992 edition, International Finance Corporation, *Discussion Paper,* No. 14, Washington, DC: The World Bank/IFC.

Root F. R. (1968), "Attitudes of American Executives Toward Foreign Governments and Investment Opportunities", *Economic and Business Bulletin,* 2:1-9.

Rugman, A. M. (1986), "New Theories of the Multinational Enterprise: An Assessment of Internalization Theory", *Bulletin of Economic Research,* 38: 101-118.

Rugman, A. M. (1981), *Inside the Multinationals: The Economics of Internal Markets,* New York: Columbia University Press.

Rugman, A. M. (1980a), "A New Theory of the Multinational Enterprise: Internationalization Versus Internalization", *Columbia Journal of World Business,* 15: 23-29.

Rugman, A. M. (1980b), "Internalization as a General Theory of Foreign Direct Investment: A Re-appraisal of the Literature", *Weltwirtschaftliches Archiv,* 116: 365-379.

Teece, D. (1985), "Multinational Enterprise, Internal Governance, and Industrial Organization", *American Economic Review, Papers and Proceedings,* 75: 233-238.

United Nations Centre on Transnational Corporations [UNCTC] (1991), *World Investment Directory,* New York: United Nations.

United Nations Centre on Transnational Corporations (1992a), *The Determinants of Foreign Direct Investment: A Survey of the Evidence,* New York: United Nations.

United Nations Centre on Transnational Corporations (1992b), *Government Policies and Foreign Direct Investment,* UNCTC Current Studies, Series A, No. 17, New York: United Nations.

United Nations Centre on Transnational Corporations (1992c), *World Investment Directory, 1992: Volume 1: Asia and the Pacific,* New York: United Nations.

Vernon, R. (1971), *Sovereignty at Bay,* New York: Basic Books.

Weiss, E. (1990), "The Long Path to the IBM-Mexico Agreement: An Analysis of the Microcomputer Investment Negotiations, 1983-86", *Journal of International Business Studies,* 21: 565-96.

World Bank (1992a), *Financial Flows to Developing Countries: Current Developments,* March, Washington D.C.

World Bank (1992b), *Global Economic Prospects and the Developing Countries.* Washington, DC.

Yu, C. (1987), "A Reconsideration of Measures of Instability", *Journal of Comparative Economics,* 11: 116-119.

Chapter 8
The Role of Japanese Foreign Direct Investment[1]

Thomas Andersson

Introduction

Business operations have generally become more internationalized in recent decades. There has also been a widening of the national origin of so-called multinational enterprises, which own and control productive assets in more than one country. Such firms used to emanate almost entirely from Western Europe and North America. The dominance of westerners is now being challenged particularly by the rise of Japanese multinationals, which rapidly expand their activities in all major markets. Their efforts are not reciprocated by western firms, and the Japanese home market remains relatively untouched by foreign-based corporations. In fact, the Japanese are becoming dominant in East Asia as a whole, which is the fastest growing region in the world.

It is tricky to evaluate the prospects for Japanese direct investment for a number of reasons. First, the internationalization of Japanese industry is a fairly recent phenomenon, and the data remain limited and unsatisfactory data. Second, the geographical pattern of Japanese direct investment differs from that which originates in western countries. Third, the competitiveness of Japanese industry is related to the special features of the Japanese home market, which has implications for its internationalization. Fourth, the asymmetries which characterize the Japanese trade and investment flows are becoming a delicate matter from a political viewpoint. The international interactions of Japanese firms, at home and abroad, now seem interrelated with the development of the entire system of trade.

In order to assess the role of Japanese direct investment in the 1990s, this chapter surveys its driving forces in the past, and discusses factors which will influence its future development. This is not only a matter of macroeconomic

[1] Financial support from the Swedish Research Council for the Humanities and Social Sciences is gratefully acknowledged.

developments, but also of business management, and even the adaptability of the Japanese society. We start by reviewing the Japanese success story and some of its global impacts. Thereafter, we trace the internationalization of Japanese firms over time.

The Japanese Success Story

Any international comparison of income, trade, technological progress or investment immediately discloses the economic rise of East Asia. The Pacific Basin has overtaken the Atlantic Basin as the core of world economic relations, and the Asian Pacific has acquired a greater income than the United States or Europe (Andersson and Burenstam Linder 1991). The prime engine of growth in East Asia is, of course, Japan. Table 8.1 shows that her share of total OECD income has doubled between 1970 and 1990. Compared to the U.S. or OECD Europe, it has increased from about a fifth of their size to about half.

Table 8.1. GDP Ratios 1970-1990.

Ratios	1970	1980	1985	1990
Japan/OECD	9.5	13.8	15.1	18.1
Japan/U.S.	20.0	40.2	33.5	54.5
Japan/OECD Europe	25.4	29.7	45.0	42.1

Source: IMF (1992), OECD (1992).

Some view Japan's success as an outcome of public planning and guidance, particularly by the Ministry of International Trade and Industry (MITI). Although MITI played a major role in the past and still does in some respects, its role is often exaggerated. Rather, the bonds between MITI and private firms reflect more fundamental characteristics of Japan. These also show up in the functioning of the factor markets. Lifetime employment, seniority wages and firm-specific unions account for stable working conditions and low mobility, which used to be viewed as an obstacle to development. In finance, "main banks" serve as the core of industrial groups, keiretsu, supporting long-term projects and acting as lenders of last resort in times of crisis. Cross-owning of equity protects against outsiders, and hostile takeovers are uncommon. Firms are not viewed as "owned" by shareholders, but rather belong to all those which are tied to them for the long term: workers, suppliers, creditors, clients, etc. From a traditional western view, this sets the stage for a strange kind of capitalism.

The Japanese success story cannot be understood without consideration to business management and organisation, and particularly how information is processed, disseminated and utilized. Information processing and operational activities are closely connected in Japan. There is a good deal of horizontal coordination, and strategic decisions are generally not imposed by top management on the basis of centralized information. Decisions require consensus, and responsibilities are to a great extent delegated to the operational level. Western companies, in contrast, rely on centralized decision making, orders are channeled hierarchically "top-down", accounting for many organizational layers and high costs for supervision (cf. Aoki 1988 and 1991).

The differences between Japan and other countries should not be overstated. Far from all Japanese firms practice lifetime employment or main-bank arrangements. Cross-owning of shares exists in western economies as well. Nevertheless, the Japanese economy as a whole forms a special set-up. Japanese organisation and management practices are adapted to the stable and long-term relations that characterize the Japanese society in general. This will be further discussed below.

In East Asia, Japan's development is followed most closely by the Asian Newly Industrialized Economies (ANIEs), i.e. the People's Republic of Korea, Taiwan, Hong Kong and Singapore. Three of the ASEAN4[2] –Malaysia, Thailand and Indonesia–also perform well, especially in exports. The governments play an active role, except for Hong Kong. In Korea and Taiwan (like in Japan), there has been an intervention with private ownership through land reform.[3] Throughout, governments secure macroeconomic stability, while prices are less distorted than in other developing countries. Still, private initiatives are the major engines of growth. Incentives for industrial performance supplement moderate protectionism and selective export promotion.

---

[2] Of the members in the Association of South East Asian Nations (ASEAN), the concept ASEAN4 leaves out Singapore, which is counted among the ANIEs, and the small sultanate Brunei.

[3] Land reform helped to create a class of independent farmers which supported the governments and accounted for social stability. Incidentally, land reform was possible due to the breakdown of the old power structures by intervention from outside.

Table 8.2. Distribution of Exports and Imports between Regions.

Exports by destination, 1980, 1985 and 1990 (percent).

Importer / Exporter	USA	JAPAN	EC	ANIEs	ASEAN4	YEARS
USA		9.4	26.7	6.8	2.8	<-1980
		10.3	22.4	7.7	2.1	<-1985
		12.3	24.9	10.4	2.7	<-1990
JAPAN	24.5		14.0	14.9	7.0	<-1980
	37.6		11.9	12.8	4.2	<-1985
	31.7		18.8	19.8	7.7	<-1990
EC	5.6	1.0	55.7	1.2	0.7	<-1980
	10.1	1.2	54.5	1.6	0.7	<-1985
	7.0	2.1	60.4	2.1	0.9	<-1990
ANIEs	24.8	10.1	16.4	9.2	10.7	<-1980
	42.1	11.2	12.4	10.2	8.6	<-1985
	29.7	12.2	16.6	12.9	9.5	<-1990
ASEAN4	18.8	34.5	13.6	18.0	3.1	<-1980
	19.8	31.0	11.8	20.0	4.5	<-1985
	19.3	24.4	15.8	21.4	4.2	<-1990

Imports by destination, 1980, 1985 and 1990 (percent).

Exporter / Importer	USA	JAPAN	EC	ANIEs	ASEAN4	YEARS
USA		12.8	15.6	7.1	2.6	<-1980
		20.8	20.3	11.9	3.2	<-1985
		18.0	18.5	12.2	3.6	<-1990
JAPAN	17.4		5.9	5.2	14.0	<-1980
	20.0		7.2	7.6	12.9	<-1985
	22.5		15.0	11.1	10.4	<-1990
EC	8.6	2.5	49.4	1.7	1.0	<-1980
	8.0	3.4	52.9	1.8	1.1	<-1985
	7.4	4.3	57.9	2.6	1.1	<-1990
ANIEs	17.6	23.4	9.8	7.1	11.0	<-1980
	17.2	22.8	10.6	8.9	9.6	<-1985
	17.1	22.9	11.7	12.2	7.9	<-1990
ASEAN4	16.2	24.2	13.5	13.6	4.0	<-1980
	16.1	23.3	14.5	16.5	6.0	<-1985
	12.9	25.9	15.0	19.1	3.9	<-1990

Source: MITI (1992).

Global Impacts

The rise of Japan, and East Asia as a whole, has exerted a global impact in many respects. Both the United States and most European countries have experienced steadily widening trade deficits with Japan for two decades. Some key relations are given in Table 8.2, which shows the weight of trading partners relative to total exports and imports.[4] Of total U.S. exports, 12.3 per cent went to Japan in 1990, up from 9.4 per cent in 1980. The EC and the U.S. are the largest targets of their respective exports. The U.S. is also the greatest market for exports from Japan and the ANIEs, while both Japan and the ANIEs obtain a greater share of ASEAN4 exports. The share of exports going to the U.S. decreased in the late 1980s, however, while the EC grew in importance. The EC's share of Japanese imports also increased conspicuously, although at a low level. Except for this, the expansion of the ANIEs' share of imports within the East Asian region is most noteworthy. The share of imports provided by Japan and ASEAN4 were rather unchanged in the late 1980s.

The Japanese financial institutions became major actors in the eurodollar markets in the 1970s. Low capital standards and dividend pressure made it possible for them to focus on size and market share, and interest rate regulations at home allowed them to arbitrage on price or with respect to risk (Dufey 1990). They were further supported by high savings at home, the current account surplus and the appreciation of the yen from 1985. Borrowing short term and lending long term, the Japanese banks shifted from a position behind the American banks in 1983–measured in international assets–to about three times their size in 1990. At the beginning of the 1990s, falling prices on previously overvalued equity and real estate caused trouble at home. They are also hampered by the capital requirements levied by the Bank of International Settlements (BIS). It remains to be seen whether the difficulties are temporary or represent a more permanent change in the prospects of Japanese financial institutions.

The Japanese success in trade and portfolio investment at first seemed unmatched in direct investment. Until the late 1970s, it made up only about 1 percent of total fixed capital formation, compared to 3 percent in Germany or 4.5 percent in the U.S. Direct investment constitutes not primarily a transfer of capital, but of firm-specific factors related to technology and skills in

---

[4] It should be noted that comparisons between the EC and the U.S. are distorted by the elimination of trade between the American states, while that between the member countries in the EC is included.

organisation, management, distribution and so forth (Dunning 1977; Caves 1982). A bundle of factors is provided which remains under the control of the investor, who also retains the risk of failure. Direct investment requires that it is better to transfer a firm's specific assets to another location than to keep them at home and trade with other firms through arm's length contracts. There must also be locational factors which make internalization of the assets in the specific host country desirable. The special features of the Japanese home market, which is the basis for the Japanese business organisation and style of management, used to be viewed as an obstacle to operations abroad.

Expansion in East Asia

Motivated by the desire to reduce risks by acquiring control of raw materials, Japanese companies started to invest in Southeast Asia at an early stage. This contributed to fueling the military aggression of the Japanese in the first part of this century, which lies outside the range of this study.

Like other peoples, the Japanese consequently started operations abroad in the neighboring countries which are the closest both in terms of geographical and cultural distance. In contrast to the other major home countries of multinational firms, however, Japan is located in Asia. As its direct investment started to grow for real in the 1970s and 1980s, it still had to compete with the already established industrial powers. The Europeans had been large in natural resources and trade since the days of colonization, especially in Indonesia, Malaysia and Singapore. The Americans had dominated since the Second World War, focusing on the same countries, as well as on the Philippines and Taiwan.

By 1979, the Japanese presence could match that of the other industrial countries in most of East and Southeast Asia. The third column in Table 8.3 compares the share of Japanese direct investment with the total stock in each major host country. The exact percentages should not be taken too seriously, since data on total and Japanese investment are not available from the same source.[5] In particular, total investments are underestimated, as certain flows are not included. One example is U.S. investment in petroleum in Indonesia, and another is Chinese capital flowing particularly to Hong Kong and Singapore. The broad trends of Japanese direct investment, and its varying degrees of

[5] In general, data on direct investment are highly uncertain, and vary between sources.

significance, are still clear from Table 8.3. In South Asia, on the other hand, there was no Japanese direct investment.

In the 1980s, there was a drastic increase in Japanese direct investment in East Asia. Between 1979 and 1989, the stock relative to GDP at least doubled in three of the ANIEs and in all four countries of ASEAN. The largest changes took place in Thailand (from 1.2 to 5.1 per cent), Hong Kong (4.2 to 17.3 percent), Singapore (7.6 to 22.2 percent) and Malaysia (2.4 to 6.7 percent). Advanced sectors were now becoming important destinations. The absolute flows were still larger in sectors based on low technology and low skill-intensity, but the relative increase was greater in advanced sectors in the 1980s (Andersson and Burenstam Linder 1991).

Table 8.3. Total and Japanese Direct Investment in Selected Asian Countries.

Host Countries	Total direct investment	Japanese direct investment			
	Stock in percent of GDP 1979	Stock in percent of GDP 1979	Percent of total stock in 1979	Stock in percent of GDP 1989	Percent increase in Japanese direct investment/ GDP 1979-89
East Asia					
ANIEs					
Korea	2.8	1.8	64	2.1	17
Taiwan	n.a.	0.8	n.a.	1.8	125
Singapore	24.9	7.6	31	22.2	192
Hong Kong	11.1	4.2	38	17.3	348
ASEAN					
Malaysia	17.0	2.4	14	6.7	179
Thailand	1.7	1.2	71	5.1	325
Philippines	6.0	1.6	27	3.2	100
Indonesia	8.3	5.4	65	11.8	118
China	0.0	0.0	-	0.6	-
South Asia					
Bangladesh	0.1	0.0	0	0	0
India	1.9	0.0	0	0	0
Pakistan	3.8	0.0	0	0	0
Sri Lanka	3.1	0.0	0	0	0

Source: Calculations on the basis of The World Bank (1990), The Asian Development Bank (1990), UNCTC (1983) and The Ministry of Finance (1991).

Foreign investment may not be the primary factor behind growth in East Asia. Japan itself, like Korea, used to be restrictive against foreign investors. Given adequate domestic policies, however, external capital appears to have made a positive contribution in several countries. Of the total capital inflows, neither development assistance nor borrowing has been exceptionally extensive. There has been considerably more emphasis on direct investment than in other developing countries, however. According to Naya (1990), direct investment has contributed to the growth of exports, but the policies of the host countries have been crucial for this impact. Balassa (1991) argues for positive effects on investment efficiency, income and savings as well.

With the product-cycle theory, Vernon (1966) highlighted that direct investment channels factors of production within firms. New goods are developed in industrial centres, and transferred to countries with lower labor costs when technologies have become standardized. Japanese researchers have argued for a special Japanese product life cycle (Ozawa 1979; Kojima and Ozawa 1984). Japanese firms transform western technologies to a format which effectively exploits the working conditions in developing countries. This way, Japanese firms would have stepped up the international division of labor. The concept of "the Flying Wild Geese" is a popular methaphor for the development process resulting from the mobility and flexibility of private business in the East Asian region. Growth has been spread by the systematic exploitation of differences in factor costs as well as natural resources. Following the "leading goose" in a wide formation, the individual countries move up the industrial ladder after each other, chasing those ahead as changing factor price relations alter comparative advantages (cf. Shinohara 1972).

The ultimate effects of direct investment depend on how the factors transferred abroad interact with the productive apparatus of the host country. The host country generally gains due to investors' inability to capture all rents that arise from their activities, which spill over to domestic agents through wages, taxes, sharper competition, etc. There may also be negative effects, especially when direct investment is motivated by barriers to trade, such as the establishment of monopolies, suppression of domestic entrepreneurs, and an anti-competitive bias of technology. Losses may also stem from the depletion of natural resources or negative external effects on the environment. It is well known, for example, that direct investment may be welfare-reducing given distortive incentives. Such incentives may stem from politically motivated objectives on the part of the host country regime, which do not reflect the welfare of the population.

The economic dominance of Japan also creates a fear of dependency in East Asia, and resentment of the cultural influence it may inflict. According to some, Japanese direct investment brings economic and political suppression, and depletes the resource basis of poor Asian countries (cf. Nester, 1990). For example, Japanese companies demanding logs for construction at home are leading the way towards a swift destruction of the native forests in Southeast Asia. After the Philippines have been entirely deforested, and exports have plummeted, the focus is now on the eastern states of Malaysia. In Sarawak, where the indigenous peoples have resisted in vain, as much as 500,000 hectares may now be logged annually (Kumazaki, 1992). If that is correct, practically all virgin forest will be gone by the mid 1990s. Precious commercial as well as non-commercial values are squandered for all future. The producer countries obtain only a fraction of the gains from the exploitation, which is much less than what could be achieved through the build-up of local processing industry (ITTO, 1991).

The local authorities bear the final responsibility for such mismanagement of resources, since they arrange with the short-term concessions which deprive foreign and domestic firms of the incentives to care for long-term management. Still, it will eventually damage the interests of the Japanese themselves, as countries experience the disappearance of rich resources. Okita (1990) has suggested that Japan should adopt a leading role in promoting environmentally sound development in poorer countries.

Irrespective of their impacts on the host economies, Japanese companies have managed to exploit business opportunities in East Asia, cutting their costs for labor and raw materials. By moving the source of exports from Japan to other Asian countries, they may also have mildered the demand for protectionism in western countries. The fear that Japan would become "deindustrialized" due to the emigration of industries to countries with lower production costs, is now more or less gone. It has become evident that crucial, advanced activities do not leave Japan (cf. Shinohara, 1989). By expanding operations throughout East Asia, Japanese companies have grown stronger and acquired more international experience, and in this way they have paved the way for continued internationalization.

The Internationalization of the 1980s

The total flow of Japanese direct investment has expanded dramatically in the last decade. In 1989, the share relative to total domestic capital formation surpassed 6 percent in Japan–more than for any other major country.

Why did Japanese firms go abroad in the 1980s? The explanation is partly to be found in general changes in business conditions. Technological progress in communication, information processing, financial systems and transportation has upgraded the organizational and managerial capabilities of enterprises. As national barriers have become less important, it has become more difficult to sustain competitiveness on the basis of operations in a single nation, or even a single region. Because Japanese firms used to lie behind in internationalization, the changing circumstances have forced them to quickly expand their international operations in order to catch up. In addition, there have been other factors which are specific for the Japanese case. Changes within Japan itself, or in Japan's relations with other countries, can be regarded as "push" factors. The following partly interrelated developments belong in this category:

* *Financial deregulation and integration.* The overhaul of Japan's foreign exchange law in 1980, and liberalization in general, has enabled Japanese financial institutions to expand activities worldwide, including the undertaking and servicing of direct investment. Financial deregulation in the United States and the United Kingdom, and the Euro-currency and Euro-bond markets also provided opportunities for Japanese financial institutions to absorb short-term borrowing and convert it into long-term lending and investment. Most went into U.S. securities in the early 1980s, while direct investment became particularly attractive towards the end of the decade.

* *Current account surpluses*, especially after 1983, have spurred capital outflows. The need to reduce the political strains, mainly with the U.S., has induced direct investment for production in importing countries or exports from third countries, such as the ANIEs.

* *Currency alignments.* An appreciating yen vis-à-vis the dollar has favored production by Japanese companies abroad from 1985 onwards.

* *Rising costs* of labor, land and other inputs in Japan. Robotization and upgrading of technology have limited the impact, but it has become relatively more favorable to move especially labor-intensive production to countries with lower costs.

In addition to these factors, there has been a series of shifts in the source of competitiveness for Japanese industry. Abegglan and Stalk (1985) mention the following industrial stages: low wages, high-volume large-scale facilities, focused production, and high flexibility. These shifts, together with an increased ability to adapt management practices and the organisation in general, have made the Japanese more capable to operate in more advanced economies, including the U.S. and Europe as well as Asia.

Thus, the composition of Japanese direct investment changed markedly in the 1980s, both in terms of sectors and regions. The sectorial focus has moved from mining, natural-resource related investment and manufacturing, towards finance, real estate, transportation, commerce and services. The geographical orientation has shifted away from developing to developed countries. East Asia, which consists of newly industrialized rather than traditional developing economies, represents the only major destination in the Third World. Again, investment in research and development, and the enhancement of crucial information networks, remain concentrated in Japan. Local assembly and the support of sales in foreign markets have become highly efficient, however. Foreign subsidiaries have relied on complete control by the parent company, and have generally had a high import propensity.

Figure 8.1 compares the flows of Japanese and U.S. direct investment to the most important regions in 1985 and 1990. The Japanese flow was smaller than the U.S. flow in the mid 1980s. By 1990, the U.S. was far behind. As seen from the stock data in Figure 8.2, the Japanese investments were much more diversified geographically. Only in Western Europe was the U.S. ahead of Japan. Of course, this was also true for some other regions which are not considered here, such as Latin America.

Figure 8.1. Flows of Japanese and U.S. Foreign Direct Investment in 1985 and 1990.
Billions of U.S. Dollars

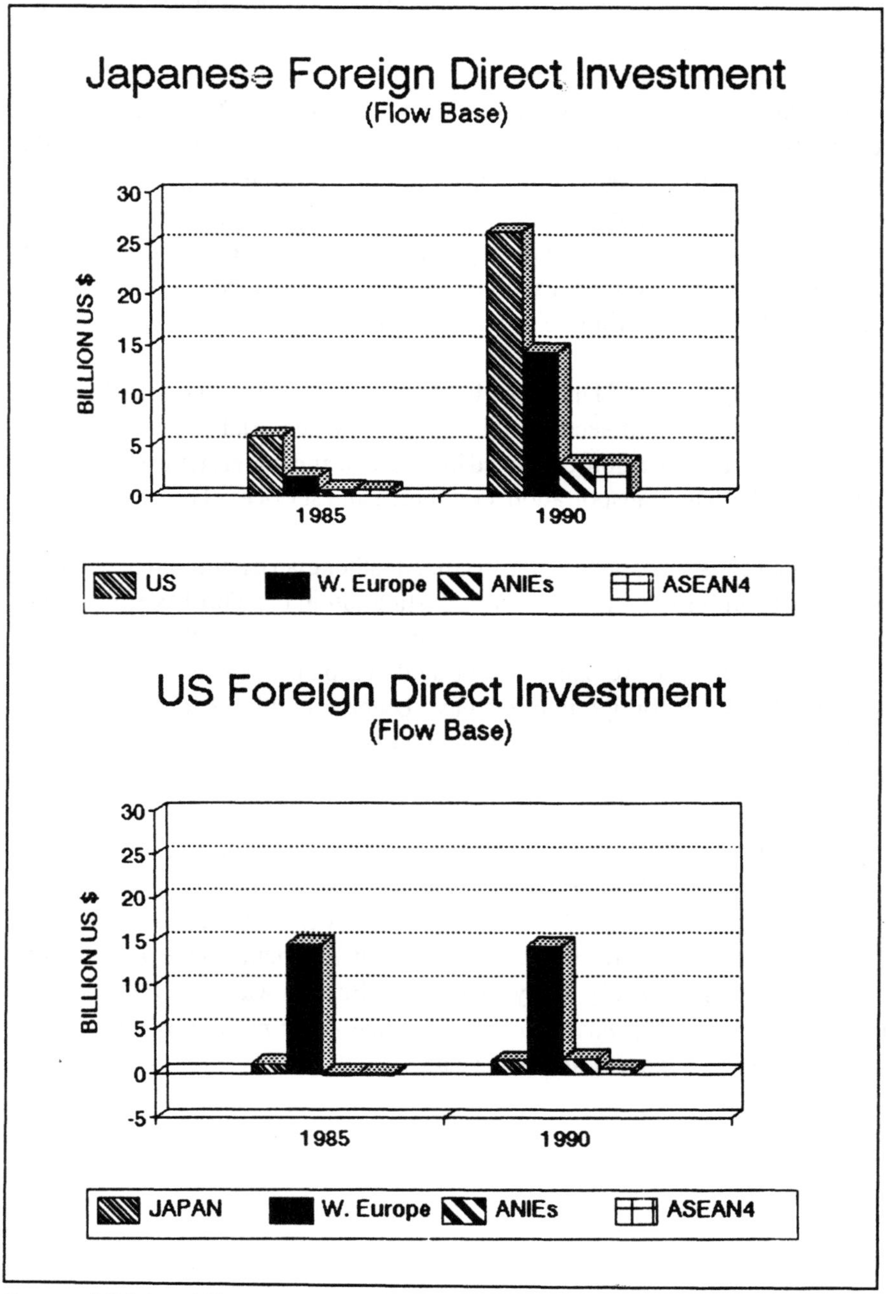

Source: Ministry of Finance (1991) and U.S. Department of Commerce (1987 and 1992).

Figure 8.2. Stocks of Japanese and U.S. Foreign Direct Investment in1990.
Billions of U.S. Dollars

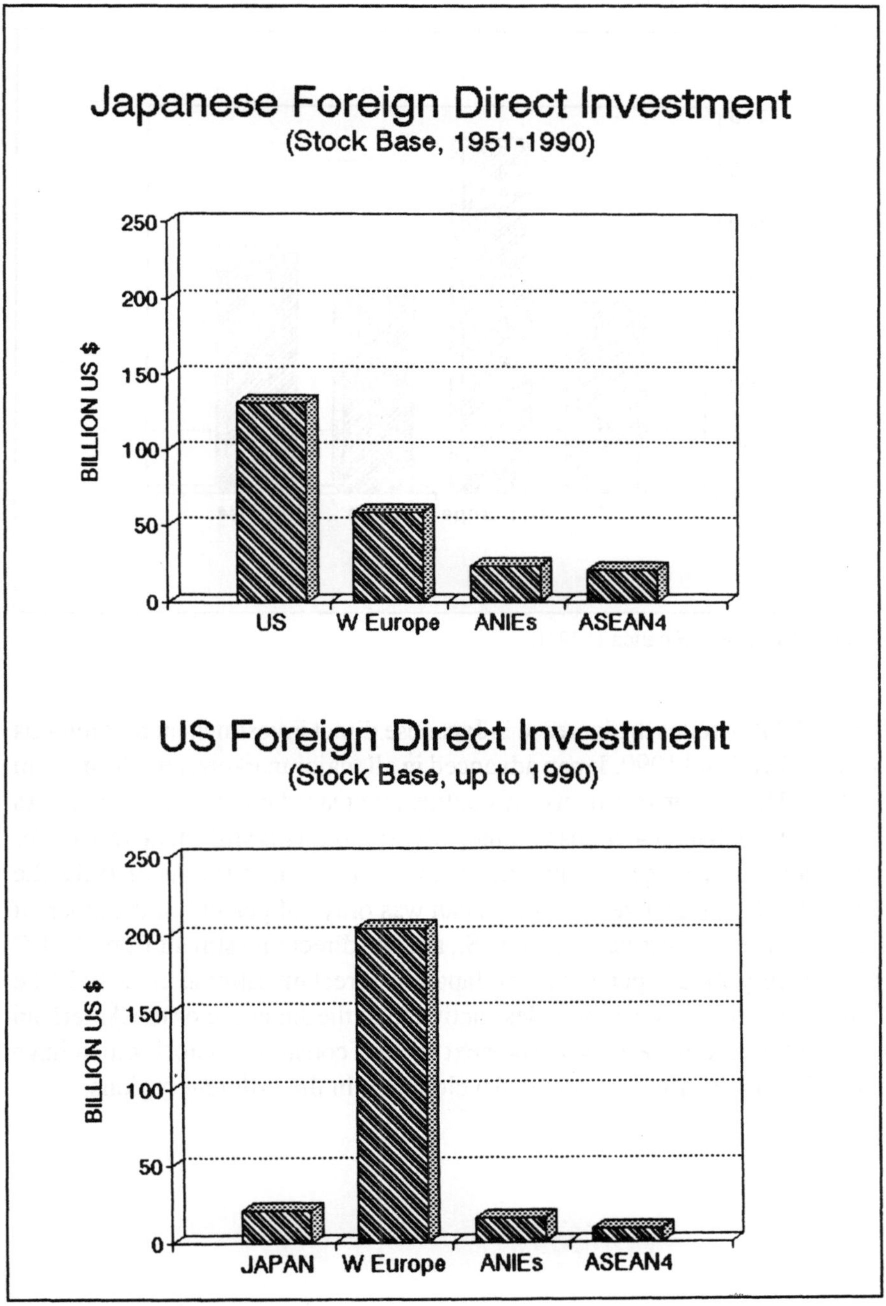

Source: Ministry of Finance (1991) and U.S. Department of Commerce (1987 and 1992).

Figure 8.3. Increase in Japanese Foreign Direct Investment, Flow base 1985-1990.
In Percent

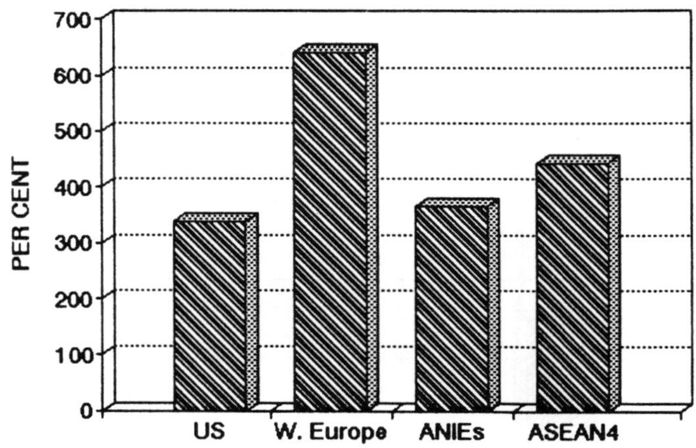

Source: Ministry of Finance (1991).

Figure 8.3 illustrates the increase in Japanese direct investment across regions between 1985 and 1990. Japan advanced in all major markets, and the most in the E.C. The U.S. investments, by contrast, increased much less in Japan. As discussed in Chapter 4 of this volume, this asymmetry is still characteristic for the Japanese exchange with practically all western countries. As of 1989, the stock of U.S. direct investment in Japan was only 7.4 percent of the stock of Japanese direct investment in the U.S., and the direct investment from the EC in Japan only about 6 percent of the Japanese direct investment in the EC. The European firms are also much less active than the Japanese or the American firms in the rest of East Asia. The next section considers factors which have exerted a major influence on the development in the different regions.

Regional Factors

Why have Japanese firms invested in specific regions in the 1980s? Most of the "pull" factors in East Asia have already been mentioned. They can be summed up as follows:

* Favorable *macroeconomic conditions,* including high growth and moderate inflation.

* Sound *economic policies,* particularly open trade regimes and low taxes. In parts of ASEAN, trade barriers have also attracted import-substituting direct investment.

* The ANIES and ASEAN-countries have had their *currencies* more or less pegged to the dollar, which made operations in these countries more attractive for Japanese firms when the yen appreciated in the mid 1980s.

* *Political stability,* including a high priority for economic development at the national level.

* *Institutional and cultural conditions,* creating a work-ethic which could readily be taken advantage of by the Japanese.

In the United States, the overvalued dollar might have been expected to discourage direct investment in the early 1980s. However, "pull" factors have turned out to be considerably more powerful. One was the spurt of consumption coupled with the need of Japanese sellers to establish a local presence in order to serve consumers effectively. Another was that the twin deficits tapped the U.S. economy of financial resources, which made investment projects lucrative in spite of the high dollar. In fact, it was the Japanese capital which enabled the dollar to remain strong and interest rates to remain moderate in the U.S. Since the late 1980s, however, the growing Japanese presence has increasingly turned into a source of political friction. The American public has not appreciated the sell-out of domestic trade marks, and prefers to put the blame on Japanese buyers rather than on U.S. polices and priorities.

Following the ending of the "Cold War", many Japanese fear that they will be the target of the 1990s for Americans in search of foreign scapegoats for domestic problems. This may turn into a major "push" effect away from the U.S. So far, Japanese firms have responded by "blending" the nationality of their products. More input is acquired locally, alliances are formed with domestic firms, and the interests of local communities are carefully assessed. To give one example, many Japanese cars made by Japanese-owned manufacturers are now more "American" in terms of content than many cars made by American-owned manufacturers. Japanese subsidiaries are actually among the largest U.S. exporters to Japan. Nevertheless, Japanese firms have generally a higher import propensity than the average firm in the U.S., and tensions remain. Comparing the investment flows in both directions, Encarnation (1992) points out that Japanese parent companies tend to exert more control. American parent companies hold smaller positions in their Japanese subsidiaries, which contributes to less imports.

Europe has evolved as a major alternative destination for Japanese investors. This applies particularly to the European Community, which contains the largest markets. The sectorial distribution of the Japanese investments in European countries are in Table 8.4 given for the cumulative flow 1951-1989. Of the total Japanese direct investment in Europe between 1951 and 1989, more than two-thirds occurred in the last three years. As can be seen, Japanese firms are widely spread across countries and sectors. As in Southeast Asia, there is a clear connection between activities and locations. For example, Britain, Luxembourg and the Netherlands attracted a relatively large amount in banking and insurance, Germany in commerce and manufacturing, and France in real estate and manufacturing. Within manufacturing, France has relatively most investment in machinery and food, and Germany in chemicals and electrical machinery. On the whole, Britain remains the dominant destination both in manufacturing and non-manufacturing. JETRO (1990) reports that the distribution system, infrastructure, quality of labor and language are the most important locational factors for Japanese firms in Europe. In Spain and Portugal, Japanese firms are attracted by low labor costs.

The attractiveness of the markets in the EC grows with the establishment of the Single Market, by which the EC is scrapping all internal barriers to flows of capital, labor, goods and services. Through advantages to scale and, particularly, stiffer competition, the aim is to strengthen the competitiveness of European firms. At the same time, it becomes less complicated for foreign firms to operate in Europe. JETRO (1990) reports that the size of a country's domestic market is now a relatively unimportant locational factor for Japanese direct investment in the EC. Broadly speaking, half the output is sold on the home country's market, and the other half in the rest of the EC. Exports back home are rare.

Table 8.4: Sectoral Distribution of Japanese Direct Investment in Selected European Countries, 1951-1989 (Cumulative) .
In percent. The total is given in billion USD.

	England	France	Germany	Netherlands	Luxembourg
Manufacturing					
Food	0.6	4.6	0.2	0.4	0.0
Chemicals	0.6	1.3	10.9	2.7	0.0
Machinery	3.2	8.0	4.0	2.5	0.3
Elec. mach.	4.9	4.1	9.9	4.8	0.0
Transp. mach.	2.9	1.8	0.7	1.5	0.0
Manufac. total	14.4	29.3	28.9	15.0	0.4
Commerce	7.8	21.1	39.6	12.0	0.0
Bank & Insurance	52.3	10.0	13.2	50.4	96.3
Service	2.7	10.2	2.3	9.9	0.3
Real Estate	10.7	16.8	0.6	11.9	0.4
Total (bill. USD)	15.8	2.9	3.4	10.1	5.4
Share*	35.1	6.4	7.7	22.4	12.0

* In percent of all Japanese direct investment in Europe.

Source: Ministry of Finance (1990).

Another factor which spurs direct investment is uncertainty regarding the external policy of the EC. The worries of a "Fortress Europe" are amplified by the frequent use of non-tariff barriers to imports, such as anti-dumping proceedings and voluntary export restraints. It is clear that such measures are used against competitive foreign firms when there are well-organized Community-firms whose interests are threatened (Messerlin 1989). In the event of higher external barriers, it becomes even more important for firms based in other countries to be present in the EC and establish themselves as insiders. Responding to the "invasion" of Japanese firms, some EC countries have adopted "local content rules", which require that a certain share of total input is provided by domestic firms. The aim appears sometimes to be a greater dispersion of rents locally, and sometimes a weakened effectiveness for the Japanese investors.

On the whole, however, the member countries of the EC are welcoming foreign direct investment. As pointed out in Chapter 3, they bargain to obtain investment, and offer investment incentives. This can be expected to continue, and even increase if the Community adopts external barriers which make Japanese goods scarce, and even more demanded by consumers. At the same time, those countries which do not obtain investment turn hostile towards it. Compare with the struggle between Britain on the one hand, and France and Italy on the other, concerning the rights of Japanese auto-manufacturers in Europe. Like in the U.S., Japanese firms are spurred to build alliances with locals to secure market access.

In finance and insurance, Japanese direct investment originally served domestic industrial partners abroad (Coulbeck 1984). Small and medium-sized manufacturing firms are now following their larger core firms into the European Community, which further raises the motivation of Japanese banks to have a strong presence. Except for integration of normal funding activities and improved fund management, operations in Europe involve multi-currency transactions and exploitation of differences in national tax rates. There is also a considerable element of control consolidation. In addition to these factors, American and Japanese banks have increased their number of subsidiaries due to the Second Banking Directive, which took effect January 1, 1993.[6] In this field, however, the importance of customized relations makes it necessary to build alliances with incumbent institutions in order to reach the bulk of the market. This has turned out to be difficult, and Japanese banks are not expected to expand further in Europe in the near future (Shigehara 1990; Feldman 1990).

The prospects of a Monetary Union in the EC may create new attractions in Europe, since this would do away with the separate transaction costs between European currencies. It is still too early to judge the importance of this factor, however. Considerable impediments need to be removed before a monetary union can be established. Hardly any of the member countries fulfill the conditions for joining it, set up by themselves. A fundamental question, still unanswered, is under what circumstances the heterogeneous European Community constitutes an optimal currency area. If a common currency would be adopted too early, it might cause further instability and lead to protectionist policies for purposes of adjustment.

---

[6] After this date, foreign banks are able to open new subsidiaries only if the laws of their home countries meet the "reciprocity requirement" that is stated by the Second Banking Directive.

In the rest of Europe, the Japanese investment has been modest so far. Certain countries are now actively seeking to attract it. Too small domestic markets will probably prevent most countries in Western Europe from obtaining any major investments as long as they remain outside the EC. There are some exceptions. In Sweden and Switzerland, the prevalence of technologically advanced and internationally experienced domestic corporations may attract activities which benefit from technological spillovers. Sweden enjoys an additional advantage in its relatively low costs for qualified labor, but suffers from an adverse geographic location. The East European countries enjoy low costs but the political situation is still highly uncertain, and the domestic markets are small. Japanese investors are most interested in those which are located close to the EC and have a good chance to acquire access to the Single Market. The main countries in this category are probably Poland and Hungary, and perhaps what will be left of the former Czechoslovakia.

International Interactions

As seen above, there have been many simultaneous developments spurring Japanese firms to go abroad in the 1980s. Some have pushed activities out of Japan, others have pulled them into certain regions. Step by step, the traditionally perceived barriers to operations abroad seem to have been overcome. But does this mean that the Japanese expansion abroad will continue? As stated above, the efficiency of Japanese firms partly build on the special characteristics of their home market. Before predicting the role of Japanese direct investment in the 1990s, we need to further consider the international interactions of the Japanese.

The Japanese spurt in exports and investments overseas can be well explained by traditional economic factors, such as terms of trade changes, savings behaviour, etc. The reason for the limited Japanese imports and inward investments is less well understood (Saxonhouse and Stern 1989; Krugman 1987). The price of western goods tends to be high in Japan, while volume is small. Still, studies have mostly found normal responses among Japanese consumers to changes in the price of western goods (Lawrence 1987). Thus, western goods seem to face invisible barriers to entry which cause a mark-up on prices.

It has already been noted that Japan is characterized by "closer" interactions between economic counterparts than is common in the West. Japan has less developed external markets, but emphasizes structures and incentives within existing configurations. Enterprises are able to rely more on subcontractors, distributors and other partner firms, externalizing any activities which are not immediately relevant for the essence of their organisations (Clark et al. 1987; Asanuma 1988). Asanuma (1989) and others have demonstrated benefits in terms of risk-diversification, complementarity of assets and enhancement of human skills from such interconnected relationships. Western firms, by contrast, seek to handle risk-sharing, moral hazard and adverse selection through internalization in the form of vertical integration.

The differences also show up in the organisation of research and development (R&D). Similar to multinational firms based in other countries, such as most American, German, British or Swedish ones, the Japanese concentrate R&D in their home country. Freeman (1987) speaks of the national system of innovation as the network of private and public institutions which foster and diffuse technologies. Imai (1990) demonstrates how the Japanese system emphasizes learning through close interactions between the producers of new technology and those who are concerned with processing and marketing. Innovations occur because different activities overlap, and an extensive sharing of information within the system takes place. In electrical engineering, Wakasugi (1992) concludes that Japanese technological progress stems from the close coordination of R&D departments with other divisions.

Imai (1991) notes that the Japanese system of overlapping may cause difficulties for international interactions. Partnerships with westerners, who do not apply such overlapping, become asymmetric. The speed of the diffusion of knowledge is greater on the Japanese side, where overlapping with other units is a critical element. The western side finds that Japanese partners do not adhere to their alliances, and mutual trust is difficult to establish. Hamel et al. (1986) conclude that the Japanese enjoy an advantage in partnerships with westerners. To the extent that this creates a barrier for interactions between the Japanese and westerners, it appears to work differently in Japan and in the West.

Looking at inter-company relations, Japanese firms in Japan can be said to focus on complementarity with particular partner firms, while western firms in the West enhance efficiency irrespectively of their partner firms. Given that Japan and the West can be characterized as two separate equilibria in this sense, one can argue for an asymmetry in the behavior of western firms in Japan and Japanese firm in the West (Andersson 1992a,b). Japanese firms are motivated to adapt to western business practices in the West, but western firms in Japan experience a dynamic inconsistency in their optimal plans. Ex ante the formation of a partnership, western firms prefer the Japanese way. Ex post, however, they prefer the western way, thereby enhancing their own capabilities and avoiding that investment is sunk in the Japanese market. In case future behavior cannot be committed, Japanese firms will then join partnerships with westerners at home only when they can control volumes, prices and information flows. The Japanese are able to enter the West, but western firms have trouble in Japan, and the prices of western goods remain high.

Based on a study of 700 firms, Odaka (1990) verified significant differences in the behaviour of Japanese and foreign-owned firms in Japan. For example, Japanese-owned firms base promotion relatively more on long careers within the company, use introductory training for newly employed and replacement as a method of lay-off rather than firing workers. In the West, however Japanese firms do adjust a good deal of their behavior; they carry out takeovers, lay off workers, and accept ordinary unions (albeit reluctantly). In other respects, however, they retain crucial elements of their organisation, increasing productivity and/or causing problems with local counterparts. For example, typical Japanese management practices have been found to function well among blue-collar workers in European countries, while offices have suffered from lack of communication, which has led to high turnover of employees (Trevor 1989; Yasui et.al 1989).

That Japanese firms are able to adjust to "western" standards in the West does not mean that they give up relations with Japanese partners there. We have already noted that both financial institutions and small- and medium-sized Japanese firms follow their industrial relatives to foreign markets. The small Japanese firms are more internationalized than corresponding firms in other countries.[7]

Predictions for the 1990s

It is time to sum up some predictions for the years ahead. We have seen that Japanese direct investment has emerged on a grand scale only lately. The primary motivation has changed from access to raw materials and low wages, to supporting progress in the world's largest and richest markets. Japanese direct investment had to be large in the late 1980s, because the Japanese firms

---

[7] For a comparision of the Japanese and Swedish experience in this respect, see Fredriksson (1992).

lagged behind in internationalization. As they are now on par with other investors, or even ahead of them, one can expect that the Japanese multinationals will be less aggressive abroad in the 1990s.

The economic debacle that Japan faces at home since the beginning of the 1990s may raise similar expectations. In retrospect, Japanese equity was grossly overvalued in the late 1980s. After several years of restraint by the Bank of Japan, the stock exchange is still contracting, real estate has lost value and the financial muscles are weakening in many institutions. Economic growth has slowed and some funds have been brought back home to support faltering accounts. Although many crashes may be expected down the road, it is unlikely that the Japanese expansion abroad will be more than temporarily restrained by these events, however. Domestic consumption has gone down, signaling an adjustment on the part of Japanese consumers to a permanently lower level of income. Meanwhile, Japanese exports continue to grow, as does the current account surplus.

On the other hand, there are serious structural problems in the Japanese economy which may show up in the longer run. The aging population may reduce savings, and new generations of Japanese consumers may be more inclined to spend than current ones. Such changes should not be taken for granted. Japan is becoming aware of its low population growth, and of the obvious connection with the obstacles for women to combine family life with a rewarding career. Although a great deal remains to be done, steps are being taken to improve the professional options for women. This may help to restore the birthrate, as well as expand and improve the work force. When it comes to consumption, long-term planning is deeply rooted in Japanese minds, and it may take a long time for a more spending-oriented attitude to break through.

It should consequently not surprise if the Japanese will, in fact, be able to handle domestic problems such as those mentioned above. With an upper hand in worker motivation and organizational capabilities, Japanese firms will continue to upgrade their technological capabilities, and the demand for their products will grow accordingly. With operations abroad supporting sales, we should expect Japanese direct investment to become increasingly important in the 1990s. In the United States, the flow is still likely to stagnate, as Japanese firms are already well established, and a continued expansion may fuel increased tension. On the other hand, Japanese firms will improve their adaptation to local requirements, and export more back to Japan.

This suggests that the Japanese multinationals will increase their presence particularly in Europe and the rest of East Asia, which represent the largest other markets in the world. In Europe, tensions with local authorities can be expected. As already discussed, it is unlikely that Japanese firms will suffer major blows from such battles. The Europeans are struggling with each other to keep their integration process going, and Japanese investment projects, with the employment opportunities and tax revenue they bring, will be lucrative prizes for individual countries and regions. If Europe becomes more protectionist, the great losers will be developing countries which cannot jump across trade barriers, rather than the Japanese. This is not to say that the Japanese will continue to invest heavily in all sectors. They are already well established in finance and insurance, where continued expansion is regarded as difficult.

What remains problematic is the limited success of western firms in the large Japanese home market. Krugman (1984) argues that this enables high profits for Japanese firms at home, allowing them to dump their output in foreign markets.[8] Meanwhile, growing trade deficits are used as an excuse for protectionist measures both in the U.S. and the EC. Voluntary export restraints and antidumping proceedings are not only costly for western consumers, but they also postpone structural change and lock resources into inefficient operations. The damage is particularly serious in intermediate goods, such as electronics and electrical parts and components. As western firms are lured into believing that they can forego the effort of competing with the Japanese on a truly global scale, the Japanese also strengthen their grip on East Asia, which is the most rapidly developing region in the world. By retaining their dominance in Japan, and achieving it in East Asia, Japanese companies become even more formidable competitors.

The crucial question concerns whether foreign firms will become more successful in Japan. The declining price level in Japan currently provides foreign firms with a golden opportunity to enter. Previous restrictions limiting the rights to ownership are also gone by now. Some progress has been recorded by foreign firms in the last year, but their efforts continue to be dwarfed by those of the Japanese abroad. Meanwhile, attempts to force western goods onto the Japanese through political action, e.g. by guaranteeing a certain share of the computer chip market to foreigners, send the wrong signals.

Given the different nature of partnerships and information sharing on the two

[8] That Japanese firms in fact report low profits is irrelevant, as this is motivated by the extremely high profit taxes in Japan.

sides, western firms can succeed in Japan only through a commitment to its market, getting to know the consumers and what it takes to succeed there. To neglect this task means to go down a dangerous path. Paradoxically, a continued lack of success for western firms in the Japanese home market will be equally dangerous for Japan itself. Widening trade and investment imbalances will sooner or later become intolerable for western politicians, undermining the world trading system and even the prospects for peace and security. Japan must become aware of these risks, and seriously consider how it can remove undue obstacles for foreigners. Continued progress for Japanese direct investment in the 1990s and beyond will eventually require that multinationals engage in increased exchange in both directions.

References

Abbeglen, J.C. and G. Stalk (1985), *Kaisha The Japanese Corporation* , New York: Basic Books.

Andersson, T. (1992a), "Approaches to Partnerships Causing Asymmetries between Japan and the West", *Working Paper 320,* Stockholm: Industrial Institute for Economic and Social Research (IUI).

Andersson, T. (1992b), "Investment Asymmetry between Europe and Japan", *mimeo,* Bank of Japan.

Andersson, T. and S. Burenstam Linder (1991), *Europe and the East Asian Agenda,* European Policy Unit at the European University Institute, Florence.

Aoki, M. (1988), *Information, Incentives and Bargaining in the Japanese Economy,* Cambridge: Cambridge University Press.

Aoki, M. (1991), "The Japanese Firm as a System: Survey and Research Agenda", paper presented at a conference on Japan in a Global Economy, September 5-6, Stockholm: Stockholm School of Economics.

Asanuma, B. (1988), "Japanese-Supplier Relationships in International Perspective: The Automobile Case", *Working Paper no. 8,* Kyoto: Kyoto University.

Asanuma, B. (1989)," Manufacturing-Supplier Relationships in Japan and the Concept of Relation-Specific Skill", *Journal of Japanese and International Economies,* 3, pp.1-30.

Asian Development Bank (1990), *Asian Development Outlook,* Manila.

Balassa, B. (1991), *Economic Policies in the Pacific Area Developing Countries*, London: Macmillan.

Caves, R. (1982), *Multinational Enterprise and Economic Analysis*, Cambridge: Cambridge University Press.

Clark, K.B., W. B. Chew and T. Fujimoto (1987), "Product Development in the World Auto Industry", *Brookings Papers on Economic Activity*, pp. 729-771.

Coulbeck, N.S. (1984), *The Multinational Banking Industry*, London: Croom Helm.

Dufey, G. (1990), "The Role of Japanese Financial Institutions Abroad", in C.H.E. Goodhart, and G. Sutija (ed.), *Japanese Financial Growth*, London: Macmillan.

Dunning, J.H. (1977), "Trade, Location of Economic Activity and the MNE: A Search for an Eclectic Approach"; in B. Ohlin, P.-O. Hesselborn and P.M. Wijkman, (eds.), *The International Allocation of Economic Activity: Proceedings of a Nobel Symposium Held at Stockholm*, 395-418, London: Macmillan.

Encarnation, D. (1992), *Rivals Beyond Trade: America versus Japan in Global Competition*, Cornell: Cornell University Press.

Feldman, R.A. (1990), "The Future of Japanese Banking", in C.H.E. Goodhart, and G. Sutija, (eds.), *Japanese Financial Growth*, London: Macmillan.

Fredriksson, T. (1992), "Policies Towards Small and Medium Enterprises in Japan and Sweden", *EFI Research Report*, Stockholm: Stockholm School of Economics.

Freeman, C. (1987), *Technology Policy and Economic Performance-Lesson from Japan*, London and New York: Printer Publishers.

Hamel, G., Y. Doz and C. K., Prahald, (1986), "Strategic Partnerships: Success or Surrender?", *Working Paper* Series 24, Center for Business Strategy, London Business School.

Imai, K (1990), "Japan´s Business Groups and the Structural Impediments Initiative", in K. Yamamura (ed.), *Japan's Economic Structure: Should it Change?* , Washington: Society for Japanese Studies.

Imai, K. (1991), "Globalization and Cross-border Networks of Japanese Firms", in T. Andersson, (ed.), *Japan: A European Perspective*, London: Macmillan.

International Monetaty Fund (1992), *International Financial Studies*, Washington.

Itoh, H. (1990), "Coalitions, Incentives and Risk Sharing", *mimeo*, Kyoto: Kyoto University.

ITTO (1991), "International Tropical Timber Organization, Pre-project Report on Incentives in Producer and Consumer Countries to Promote Sustainable Development of Tropical Forests". Prepared by the Oxford Forestry Institute in Association with the Timber Research and Development Association, Oxford.

JETRO (1990), "Current Situation of Business Operations of Japanese Manufacturing Enterprises in Europe", the 6th *Survey Report.*

Kojima, K. and T. Ozawa, (1984), "Micro- and Macro-economic models of direct foreign investment: Toward a Synthesis", *Hitotsubashi Journal of Economics,* 25, 1-20.

Krugman, P. (1984), "Import Protection as Export Promotion: International Competition in the Presence of Oligopolies and Economics of Scale" In H. Kierzkowski, (ed.), *Monopolistic Competition and International Trade,* Oxford: Clarendon Press, 180-193.

Krugman, P. (1987), " Is the Japan Problem over?" in Sato R., and P. Wachtel, (eds.), *Trade Frictions and Economic Policy, Problems and Prospects for Japan and the United States,* Cambridge: Cambridge University Press.

Kumazaki, M. (1992), "Lessons from the Deforestation of Southeast Asia's Forests", presented at the 2nd National Congress on Biodiversity, Instituto Florestal, Sao Paulo.

Lawrence, R.Z. (1987), "Imports in Japan: Closed Markets or Minds?", *Brookings Papers in Economic Activity*, 2.

Messerlin, P. A. (1989), "The EC Antidumping Regulations: A First Economic Appraisal, 1980-85", *Weltwirtschaftliches Archiv,* 125, 563-587.

Ministry of Finance (1988-1991), Kokusai Kinyu Kyoku Nenpo, Tokyo.

Ministry of International Trade and Industry (MITI) (1992), unofficial data.

Ministry of International Trade and Industry (MITI) (1991), *Successful Foreign-Affiliated Enterprises in Japan,* Vol. 2, International Affairs Division, Tokyo.

Naya, S. (1990), "Direct Foreign Investment and Trade in East and Southeast Asia", in R. W. Jones and A.O. Krueger (eds.), *The Political Economy of International Trade,* Cambridge: Basil Blackwell, 288-312.

Nester, W.D. (1990), *Japan's Growing Power over East Asia and the World Economy: Ends and Means*, London: Macmillan.

Odaka, K. (1990), "Sokusenryoku tositeno Chuto-saiyosha; Shokunou no Ippan-tsuyousei wo megutte", *mimeo*,Tokyo: Hitotsubashi University.

OECD (1992), *Main Economic Indicators*, Paris.

Okita, S. (1990), *Approaching the 21st Century: Japan's Role*, Tokyo: The Japan Time.

Ozawa, T. (1979), *Multinationalism, Japanese Style*, Princeton: Princeton University Press.

Saxonhouse, G., and R.M. Stern (1989), "An Analytical Survey of Formal and Informal Barriers to International Trade and Investment in the United States, Canada and Japan" in R.M. Stern (ed.), *Trade and Investment Relations among the US, Canada and Japan,* Chicago: University of Chicago Press.

Shigehara, K. (1990), "Comment on the Future of Japanese Financial Development", in C.H.E. Goodhart, and G. Sutija (eds.), *Japanese Financial Growth,* London: Macmillan.

Shinohara, M. (1972), *Growth and Cycles in the Japanese Economy*, Institute of Economic Research, Tokyo: Hitotsubashi University.

Shinohara, M. (1989), "High Yen, Overseas Direct Investment, and the Industrial Adjustments in the Asia-Pacific Area", in W. Klenner (ed.), *Trends of Economic Development in East Asia,* Berlin: Springer-Verlag.

Trevor, M. (1989), "Japanese Managers and British Staff, A Comparison of Relations and Expectations in Blue-Collar and White-Collar Firms", in K. Shibagaki and A. Tetsuo, *Japanese and European Management. Their International Adaptability,* Tokyo: Tokyo University Press, 164-181.

United Nations Centre on Transnational Corporations (UNCTC) (1983), *Transnational Corporations in World Development, Third Survey*, New York.

U.S. Department of Commerce (1987), *Survey of Current Business*, March, Washington.

U.S. Department of Commerce (1992), *Survey of Current Business*, March, Washington.

Vernon, R. (1966), "International Investment and International Trade in the Product Cycle", *Quarterly Journal of Economics*, 190-207.

Wakasugi, R. (1992), "Why are Japanese Firms so Innovative in Engineering Technology", *Research Policy* 21, 1-12.

World Bank (1990), *World Development Report*, New York.

Yasui, D.I., B. von der Osten, and S.-J. Park, (1989), *Japanisches Management in der Bundesrepublik Deutschland. Ergebnisbericht der zweiten Enquete-Untersuchung*, Berlin.

Chapter 9

Globalization and the Future Role of Small and Medium Sized Enterprises

Pontus Braunerhjelm

Introduction

A significant characteristic of "industrial organisation" in the postwar era, especially up to the 1980s, is the establishment of large international firms designed to mass-produce standardized goods. For a number of reasons, traditional wisdom has regarded production by smaller units as inferior, with small firms being expected to more or less wither away. However, since the beginning of the 1970s the increasing role of small and medium-sized enterprises (SMEs) in terms of employment and value added has prompted a revaluation of the importance of SMEs.[1]

The issue adressed here is the future of SMEs in a globalized economy, in particular the extent and direction of their foreign direct investments in the 1990s. Evidently different types of SMEs face different options and a large part of the smallest SMEs (micro-firms) will no doubt remain domestic, particularly in the service sector. For other SMEs, notably subcontractors with close links to one or a limited number of highly internationalized firms, the establishment of production units abroad may be a necessary requisite for survival. Strategic networks may also become more international, especially for high-tech firms, necessitating presence abroad.

The insulation from shocks in the international economy earlier enjoyed by SMEs has, to a large extent been eroded in the postwar era through technological advance and increased international interdependence. This vulnerability

[1] See Sengenberger, Loveman and Piore (1990), for the argument that this trend started already in the end of the 1960s for most of the industrialized world. See also Burns-Dewhurst (1986) and OECD Employment Outlook (1985). Cantwell and Radaccio (1990) shows that on average the size of multinational firms has decreased. Carlsson (1989) showed that the role of the Fortune 500 firms in the U.S. diminished in the 1980s. Also, Carlsson (1992) analyzes the causes of the shift towards small business internationally and explores the consequences for industrial structure and competitiveness.

influences industrial structures and the size distribution of firms. The question is then what prospects SMEs face in such a globalized, or regionalized, world. Furthermore, what strategies should SMEs adopt to succeed in the 1990s? How will the investment pattern and the distribution of investments between domestic and foreign markets be affected? The chosen strategy must build on the specific capabilities and characteristics of each individual firm and the setting in which it operates.

This chapter aims to shed light on these matters by studying SME performance during the last few decades and by defining the structural factors forming the capabilities and competitiveness of small firm production. Based on past performance of SMEs in the major industrialized economies, complemented with a case study of Swedish SMEs, the prospects and strategies for small firm engagement in foreign operations are discussed and summarized in Table 9.11. The presentation focuses on the manufacturing industry, since FDI is concentrated in that sector. Services often have a markedly local character although a large and growing part of the sevice industry is intimately interlinked with production. The following discussion emanates from a perspective of ongoing internationalization of the world economy, i.e. protectionistic waves due to a collapse of the GATT negotiations etc. will be disregarded.

The first section reviews the specific advantages and disadvantages, or competitiveness, traditionally associated with smaller batch production. Furthermore, the determinants of growth and the degree of internationalization are discussed. Thereafter the size distribution of manufacturing production over time in the industrialized world is considered. In the following section a case study of Swedish SMEs and subcontractors is presented where emphasis is on structural features rather than on evolution over time. The last section summarizes the main findings and discusses the prospects for the internationalization of SMEs in the 1990s.

Characteristics of SMEs

The key to understanding the future role of SMEs in an internationalized environment lies in defining the sources of their competitiveness. In particular, what are the capabilities of SMEs that overcome the drawbacks of being small? Mill claimed already in 1848 that a tendency towards large scale organization of businesses would lead to the demise of SMEs. This view was pursued, although for different reasons, by Marx and Schumpeter, and in the aftermath of the industrial revolution the share of employment in large units did indeed increase. Recently, however, the opposite opinion is on rise.

In fact, the revival of the SME sector has induced both economists and politicians to direct more attention towards this strand of economics. For instance, the European Community has declared SMEs as an area of priority. The present EC policy towards SMEs is a mixture of providing information (Euro-Info-Centres and BC-NET) and of making capital accessible (examples are the Venture and Consort Seed Capital program and the Eurotech Capital program). These are also the general areas where nations concentrate their eventual support to SMEs. For example, Japan and Germany are two countries that have had special legislation concerning SMEs since the beginning of the 1960s. Still, most countries have favored or focused on activities by large enterprises (LEs). One explanation is that the impact of LEs in terms of employment and investment effects is easier to observe, which may be attractive from a politician's point of view.

"Small is Beautiful"

In order to discuss the "beauty", or competitive advantages, of SMEs, a distinct definition of smallness is required. The problem is, however, that the definition of SMEs varies from country to country, not only with regard to the variables used, but also with regard to the level of these variables. The more generally accepted definition for small enterprises seems to be firms with less than 200 employees while the limit for medium-sized enterprises is set at 500 employees (Burns and Dewhurst 1986).[2]

What factors determine the size distribution of firms? Even though the question may appear somewhat naive it has occupied several economists over the years, particularly since economies of scale in production is a standard assumption in much of economic modelling. Yet, scale economies seem to become increasingly important for activities outside the actual production process. Examples of such activities are R&D, marketing, finance etc. from which several production units within a firm can extract benefits. Hence, a distribution of a large number of small establishments may be compatible with a market dominated by large firms.

---

[2] National definitions are generally based on the level of employment and vary substantially, not only between nations, but also between industries within the same nation. Within the EC SMEs are defined as firms with less than 500 employees, having fixed assets of less than ECU 75 million and where ownership by another firm is restricted to a maximum of one third.

One reason for the changing size distribution of firms is technological progress. On the one hand, production technology sets the limit for the operating units. As technology improves over time, different vintages apply to different scales. Hence, the distribution of firm size has a time aspect (Hjalmarsson 1991). Furthermore, the improvement of manufacturing technologies has revolutionized SME flexibility (Carlsson 1984, Carlsson and Taymaz 1993).[3] On the other hand, information technology also affects the plant size and the organisation of production within the firm. It gives access to information at lower costs, and also makes information easier to process and interpret, which weakens the scale argument in production. However, it could also be argued that the establishment of larger firms is facilitated since control and monitoring possibilities increase with improved information technology.

Another factor influencing size (and technology) is the characteristics of demand facing the firm. As pointed out by Taymaz (1989), if demand fluctuates with regard to product attributes, then firms should implement technologies geared towards flexibility in differentiating the product. However, if demand is volatile in terms of volume, then volume flexibility should be emphasized. Depending on the demand structure for different products, there is a trade-off between different types of flexibilities and technologies which influences the size of firms and plants. Hence, from a static point of view, the given technology, the demand pattern and the set of production factors are the main determinants of the distribution of firm size. Over time, technological progress, R&D achievements and changes in consumer preferences influence the distribution of SMEs and LEs.

A somewhat different question–although important in a context of internationalization–is whether firms stay small or eventually grow large. First, very few firms experience a smooth growth, rather a preponderant feature is recurrent crises, induced learning and the development of firm-specific knowledge and niche production (Eliasson 1991a, Arthur, Hendry and Jones 1991). Firms with R&D facilities also seem to experience much higher growth than non-R&D- intensive firms, although the evidence is a bit fragmented (Kamien and Schwartz 1975, Rothwell and Zegweld 1982, Drucker 1986). In an extensive survey undertaken by Pratten (1991), the most important factor is argued to be time: it simply takes time to grow. Others claim that sophisticated production technology must be complemented with stable and advanced customer demand, requiring a relevant network (Arthur, Hendry and Jones

[3] See also Sabel (1983) and Piore and Sabel (1984).

1991, NUTEK 1991a). Still, as shown in several studies (Jagrén 1988, Davidsson 1989), only a very limited number of firms survive and become LEs.

To explain the SME success, a number of sources of diseconomies of scale have been suggested that may offset potential economies of scale. These offsetting factors are, for example, limited supply of strategic factors, decreasing efficiency of factors as scale increases, disproportionally increasing costs of management due to coordination and monitoring costs, decreasing motivation and increasing selling and distribution costs. Especially the scarcity of human capital and entrepreneurial skill is regarded as a constraint to growth (Lucas 1978, Brock and Evans 1986). In addition, it has also been suggested that growth is simply not the prime goal of SMEs, rather the objective is related to private motives such as independence and exploiting own ideas (SIND 1991). Deterrents to growth are also small home country markets and difficulties in raising the capital necessary for expansion. Especially the latter factor has been viewed as a major obstacle to growth (Penrose 1956, Horwitch and Pralahad 1976, Buckley 1986).[4]

Internationalization

Under the auspicies of GATT, on a global level, and supplemented with regional trade arrangements, the evolution of international trade policies has led to a substantial dismantling of trade barriers in the last forty years and to a considerable internationalization of the world economy. As a consequence, firms are more sensitive to changes in international competition–notably the entrance of new actors–and more vulnerable to changes in macroeconomic disturbances (Oxelheim 1990). A more volatile environment requires firms to react swiftly to changing conditions. Large firms have also long ago recognized the importance to act from a global perspective. As deregulation and diminution of protectionistic measures proceed, pressure is also put on SMEs to incorporate more global concern into their strategies.

First, the meaning of internationalization has to be defined. Its general meaning it alludes to a wide range of international penetration and commit-

[4] Financial constraint is habitually regarded as a severe bottleneck for SMEs. Some studies, however, point in another direction. Lindquist (1991), for instance, in her study on small Swedish high-tech firms, finds little support for financial constraints and similar results are reported for English SMEs (Burns and Dewhurst 1986). The ongoing integration of financial markets also favors SMEs. However, during the transition from regulated to integrated markets it possible for financial institutions to charge SMEs higher costs by exploiting information differences (Oxelheim 1993).

ment, from exports to sales agents and wholly-owned production units abroad. Internationalization by SMEs predominantly takes the form of exports, while setting up subsidiaries abroad is less common. Furthermore, export performance by SMEs differs widely among countries. The explanation is related to differencies in size of the home country markets, the structure of the industry, governmental policies etc.[5]

A theoretical rationale for internationalization has been provided by Hymer (1961), Buckley and Casson (1976), Williamson (1975, 1985), Caves (1982), and others.[6] In short, the argument is that the lack of markets for firm-specific assets or knowledge induces firms to internalize production in wholly-owned subsidiaries abroad. Arm's length contracts are not possible since they may erode the firm-specific advantage through opportunistic behavior and therefore firms prefer to expand through FDI rather than through cooperative arrangements such as licensing.

One particular branch of the above theory is the behavioristic approach to explaining internationalization which is often regarded as particularly relevant for SMEs (Aharoni 1966, Johanson and Vahlne 1977). A sequential process is visualized, where close markets– close in terms of geographical and cultural distances–are first exploited. Expansion to other markets then gradually proceeds, both in terms of markets and means of internationalization, i.e. export agents are substituted for sales affiliates, for example, and finally producing subsidiaries are established.

A more novel framework is introduced by Porter (1980, 1990). He conceptualizes factors that generate firm-specific skills and abilities in the so-called "diamonds", which explicitly enumerate six factors that determine the competitiveness of firms of different nations. Since "diamonds" differ among countries, trade and internationalization take place. Porter stresses that production factors are partly created and attributes the most important role to these factors in sustaining competitiveness on the firm level. The interlinks to the industrial network approach are close, where emphasis is on the establishing and developing of networks in the internationalization process (Arthur, Hendry and Jones 1991, Johanson and Mattson 1988).

---

[5] Government policies have for example played a vital role in the internationalization of Japanese SMEs during the 1980s (Fredriksson 1992).

[6] See also Dunning's (1977) eclectic approach. This approach is also known as the OLI theory, where O stands for ownership advantages (firm level), L denotes location advantages (country level) and I represents internalization (firm specific assets).

To summarize, the theories outlined above all stress the importance of developing some firm-specific asset or unique product that leads to competitive capabilities which can be exploited abroad. Firms of different sizes are associated with specific advantages as well as disadvantages. Therefore, firms are likely to cooperate and coexist, fulfilling different and complementary tasks, a conclusion forwarded already by Marshall (1890). One indication of such co-existence is that, on average, profit levels of SMEs match large firms quite well and even surpass them in some cases (Aiginger and Tichy 1984, Burns and Dewhurst 1986, Braunerhjelm 1991a).[7] The specific strongholds of SMEs are customization and prompt delivery, paired with flexibility and related services. Furthermore, small units are claimed to attain higher cost efficiency as well as having flatter, non-bureaucratic organisations and highly motivated personnel (Tichy 1989, Pratten 1991). As technologies during the last decades have been adapted to suit small scale production, SMEs are often better equipped to encounter heterogeneous and volatile demand with their closer and more direct links to the market. But new technology also imposes constraints on the SMEs due to increased demand for human capital encompassing the knowledge required to handle the more advanced technology.

The disadvantage of small-size production traditionally relates to the financial side, in addition to scarcity of management and marketing knowledge. Difficulty in obtaining necessary financing also puts constraints on other strategic activities crucial for growth, such as marketing, which may induce a vicious circle. Research is also an area where SMEs are generally weak compared to large firms, while product development is regarded as an area where SMEs are competitive.

The Role of SMEs in Industrialized Countries

Before the future role of SMEs in internationalization and FDI activities can be assessed, past behavior of SMEs must be considered. How have SMEs evolved internationally and where is the impact of SMEs most notable? First, ever since Birch's (1979) study on SMEs–where it was concluded that approximately 80 percent of employment growth emanated from SMEs–

[7] One explanation forwarded on the impressive profit performance by SMEs relates to different managerial organisations in SMEs and LEs. The former are claimed to be managed by owners, who are more inclined towards maximizing profits than hired management.

attention has been directed towards employment effects.[8] This attention covers both quantitative and qualitative aspects. The latter refers to the possibilities for entrepreneurs to exploit their ideas, the freedom of employees to choose between organisations, for example.

Another important aspect of past behavior is the contribution to technological development, and thereby to growth and dynamics, where opinions differ widely concerning the role of SMEs (Kamien and Schwartz 1975, Doctor, Van der Haorst and Stokman 1989). Adherents to Schumpeter would argue that large firms are the main promoters of "creative destruction" and technological progress, while for instance Rothwell and Zegweld (1982) claim that the efficiency of R&D is higher in SMEs and also that the innovation rate is proportionally much higher in smaller firms. A third view is that SMEs are primarily involved in the development and modification of existing technology whereas more research orientated activities are undertaken by large firms, i.e. the two categories complement each other (Abernathy and Utterback 1978, Utterback and Reitberger 1982 and Pratten 1991). The two latter views imply a larger potential for FDI activities by SMEs.

The development of SMEs in the industrialized world–primarily in terms of employment shares–has recently been investigated in two studies, covering altogether 10 countries (Sengenberger, Loveman and Piore 1990, Burns and Dewhurst 1986). In addition, some extensive country studies have been undertaken, Evan's (1991) report on SMEs in the U.S. for instance. All studies report that SMEs have increased in importance in spite of bottlenecks in finance, and managerial know-how.[9]

In Sengenberg et al. (1990), the authors set off with the following statement.

> "Just a decade ago the idea that small enterprises might be seen as the key to economic regeneration, and a road to renewed growth of employment and the fight against mass unemployment, may have seemed eccentric or even absurd. Today this view seems much less far fetched. On the contrary, many observers from different traditions and political orientations embrace the idea, though they may disagree on why and how small firm expansion and dynamism have arisen."

---

[8] Birch's results are confirmed, and even reinforced, in a later study (Birch 1987).

[9] For a different view on the U.S., see Brown, Hamilton and Medoff (1990). The authors claim that the alleged success of SMEs cannot be empirically verified.

In all the countries covered in the studies mentioned above, an apparent shift towards smaller units of production in terms of employment in the postwar period is reported.[10] Moreover, in all countries–with one exception–this development coincides with a loss of the LEs' part of manufacturing employment. It is also remarkable how robust these findings are despite the differences among countries with regard to industrial structure, institutional setting, size distribution, legal framework, tradition and history. However, although the trend is similar in various countries, the extent of SME growth differs quite substantially among the countries. Tables 9.1 and 9.2 show how the employment share of small enterprises and establishments have evolved during the last three to four decades. Most countries seem to have experienced a shift towards smaller units in the late 1960s or in the beginning of the 1970s. This is particularly evident for establishment data on the total economy (Table 9.2).[11]

As mentioned above, SMEs are most important in the service sector and the size distribution in the total economy may therefore be influenced by the expansion of the service sector. However, this compositional shift explains only part of the shift to smaller production units (Sengenberg et al. 1990). As shown in Tables 9.3 and 9.4, even if the manufacturing sector is isolated, the tendency towards smaller units remains, even though it is weaker (with the exception of Switzerland). If establishment size is studied, the pattern is more clearcut (Tables 9.2, 9.4).

A picture of a movement towards decentralized organisation structures emerges since both enterprise and establishment sizes are diminished. Furthermore, the authors argue that size in itself is not decisive for performance but rather the organisation of production and the underlying structure in terms of policies, networks etc., thus supporting the theoretical approach of Porter (1980, 1990). There is no evidence that sectoral or cyclical factors determine the expansion of SMEs. Instead, the expansion of SMEs seems to be connected with increased heterogeneity in consumer demand and the implementation of new technology, allowing flexibility and high quality production.

---

[10] The countries are Denmark, France, Italy, Japan, Switzerland, The Republic of Ireland, The United Kingdom, The United States and West Germany. The same pattern is observed in Canada (Larouche 1989).

[11] Data on establishments are often more reliable than firm data. In Sengenberger's et al. study, data have sometimes been collected from different sources which may influence the time series. In Tables 9.1-9.4, small implies less than 100 employees while medium refers to less than 500 employees, if nothing else is stated.

Table 9.1. Employment Shares by Enterprise Size, Time Series for the Total Economy.

Japan	**1965**	**1968**	**1971**	**1974**	**1977**	**1982**	**1985**
Small	53.7	55.0	55.9	57.0	58.9	60.0	
Medium*			70.0	70.4	72.2	73.1	73.0
United States	**1958**	**1963**	**1967**	**1972**	**1977**	**1982**	
Small	41.3	39.9	39.9	41.3	40.1	45.7	
Medium	55.1	52.9	53.2	53.5	52.5	58.7	
France			**1971**		**1979**		**1985**
Small			39.0		43.4		46.2
Medium			57.4		60.7		64.5
W. Germany	**1961**		**1970**				
Small**	54.9		52.3				
Italy	**1951**	**1961**	**1971**			**1981**	
Small	60.2	63.5	61.6			69.3	
Medium	73	77.1	74.4			81.5	
Switzerland	**1955**	**1965**		**1975**			**1985**
Small***	52.5	45.4		46.1			46.3
Medium	82.0	78.9		77.4			73.4

* 1-300 employees ** 1-200 employees *** 1-50 employees

Source: Sengenberger et al. (1990).

Burns and Dewhurst (1986) report similar results, where all countries except one belong to the EC. Irrespective of whether countries are small or large, a pattern of growing SMEs sectors is quite evident. Their results contrast with the general assumption that the harmonization within EC has primarily benefited LEs. Moreover, the process of concentration observed in the 1950s and 1960s has, according to the authors, not only ceased, but also been reversed.

Finally, the evolution of the small firm sector in the U.S. will briefly be discussed. In a comprehensive study by Evans (1991) on U.S. small firms (less than 100 employees) it is shown how their share of employment started to rise in the early 1970s after a continuous decline since the industrial revolution. Evans sets forth the following six conceivable hypotheses explaining this remarkable SME evolution:

Table 9.2. Employment Shares by Establishment Size, Time Series for the Total Economy.

Japan		**1969**	**1972**	**1975**	**1978**	**1981**	
Small		70.1	71.5	73.8	76.1	77.1	
Medium*		83.1	84.2	85.6	87.5	88.3	
United States	**1962**	**1965**	**1970**	**1975**	**1978**	**1982**	**1985**
Small	51.3	51.5	49.5	54.0	54.4	55.1	55.9
Medium				76.9	77.7	78.6	79.8
W. Germany			**1977**	**1979**	**1981**	**1983**	**1985**
Small			47.0	47.9	48.3	49.7	49.6
Medium			70.4	71.1	71.4	72.3	72.3
Italy	**1951**	**1961**	**1971**			**1981**	
Small	67.2	61.6	69.3			72.4	
Medium	82.6	82.2	85.0			87.3	
Switzerland				**1975**			**1985**
Small				66.2			69.3
Medium				88.2			89.0

* 1-300 employees

Source: Sengenberger et al. (1990)

* Technological change favoring small firms, e.g. lower computer costs.
* The integration of the world economy and the emergence of more competitive manufacturing in LDCs have caused a greater variability in sales and exchange rates favoring adaptive and flexible small firms.
* Increased participation of women has decreased average wages which may have enhanced the competitiveness of small firms.
* Consumer tastes have changed, so that specialty products are more frequently demanded at the expense of mass-produced standard goods, the so-called "boutique" effect.
* Entry barriers has relaxed.
* The propensity to start firms have increased and, since firms tend to be small in their initial phase, their number has increased. Such increased startup propensity can be traced to increased returns to entrepreneurs and increasing unemployment.

Table 9.3. Employment Shares by Enterprise Size, Time Series for the Manufacturing Sector.

Japan*	**1955**		**1972**	**1975**	**1979**	**1983**	
Small	57.0		43.0	45.0	49.0	47.0	
Medium	85.0		63.0	65.0	68.0	67.0	
United States	**1958**	**1963**	**1967**	**1972**	**1977**	**1982**	
Small	20.6	19.1	16.3	16.2	16.2	17.6	
Medium	37.1	34.5	30.4	28.9	29	30.3	
France			**1971**		**1979**		
Small			26.4		28.6		
Medium			49.5		50.6		
W. Germany**	**1963**		**1970**	**1976**	**1980**	**1983**	**1984**
Small	14.0		12.5	13.1	15.4	16.0	16.2
Medium	39.6		37.3	38.0	40.4	40.8	41.1
Italy***	**1951**	**1961**	**1971**			**1981**	
Small	50.5	53.2	50.5			55.3	
Medium	67.4	72.0	69.2			73.9	
Switzerland		**1965**					**1985**
Small		34.8					29.7
Medium		71.0					69.4
United Kingdom			**1971**	**1975**	**1978**	**1981**	**1986**
Small			15.5	16.8	17.3	20.3	22.0

* In 1955 "small" is defined as 5-99 employees and "medium" size as 5-999 employees. ** Handicraft is included in the figures for 1980, 1983 and 1985. *** Small is defined as 1-49 employees.

Source: Sengenberger et al. (1990).

Table 9.4. Employment Shares by Establishment Size, Time Series for the Manufacturing Sector.

Japan	**1957**	**1962**	**1971**	**1977**	**1980**	**1982**	**1984**
Small	59.0	52.0	51.0	56.0	58.0	56.0	55.0
Medium*	73.0	68.0	67.0	71.0	74.0	72.0	72.0
United States			**1974**	**1978**	**1980**	**1982**	**1985**
Small			24.4	25.3	25.2	26.9	27.6
Medium			57.2	58.3	58.2	59.6	61.4
France	**1954**	**1966**		**1974**		**1981**	
Small	52.0	48.0		45.0		47.0	
Medium	75.0	74.0		72.0		73.0	
W. Germany**	**1963**		**1970**	**1976**	**1980**		**1984**
Small	20.0		18.5	19.6	18.3		18.6
Medium	48.2		46.6	48.3	47.6		48.5
Italy	**1951**	**1961**	**1971**			**1981**	
Small	54.2	56.9	54.6			59.1	
Medium	74.6	78.5	76.9			80.3	
Switzerland	**1955**	**1965**			**1975**		**1985**
Small	43.6	37.8			38.4		33.3
Medium	80.1	76.8			78.3		77
United Kingdom	**1954**	**1963**	**1970**	**1975**			**1983**
Small	24.2	20.2	18.4	19.7			26.2
Medium	56.5	50.9	45.4	45.0			53.2

* "Medium" is defined as 100-299 employees. ** After 1976 the figures include the handicraft sector.

Source: Sengenberger et al. (1990)

Evans supplements his statistical description with case studies of five industries assumed to be of specific relevance for the small firm phenomena. He concludes that two effects have dominated small firm growth: changes in technology and demand.

With regard to technology, a Schumpeterian effect of creative destruction is claimed to have opened up entry possibilities for small firms. The case studies show that this effect has occurred either by decreasing the cost of entering or by diminishing the minimum efficient scale of production. Technological progress has also facilitated the implementation of high quality technologies in smaller units.

The demand effect has favored production of "customized" goods which is an area where SMEs often have a competitive advantage.[12]

The Case of the Swedish SME sector

The purpose of this section is to describe how structural factors within the Swedish SME sector influence the prospects for their internationalization in the 1990s. To this end, a comparison will be made between Swedish large firms (MNFs and domestic firms) and SMEs with regard to:

* Specialization in production, niches.
* Level of competence.
* Internationalization.

The first two factors are crucial determinants of the third. Furthermore, firms which are already international are assumed to be better prepared to embark on strategies requiring overseas production. It is argued that the information captured in these structural factors can be generalized to other countries in order to derive the potentials for FDI.

Being a highly industrialized country with a diversified industry and a long-standing tradition of free trade policies, Sweden is an excellent candidate for a case study of SME internationalization. About 30 percent of GNP, or more than 50 percent of industrial production is exported. Although the Swedish

---

[12] Toffler (1985) reached the same conclusion. The other conceivable factors put forward by Evans to explain the emergence of SMEs attain little support and are rejected.

economy is dominated by comparatively few and large MNFs, the SMEs share of manufacturing employment amounts to approximately 50 percent (Lindquist 1991). It indicates a high dependence of many SMEs on the large Swedish firms. Considering that most large Swedish firms stepped up their internationalization considerably during the 1980s–EC being the main reciepient of Swedish FDI–a new situation is implied for the SMEs.

For obvious reasons, and in stark contrast to the ample studies on the internationalization of Swedish large firms (Swedenborg 1979, 1988), less attention has been directed towards SMEs. However, in a recent study Lindquist (1991) focuses on the internationalization of small technology-intensive Swedish firms.[13] It is concluded that technology-intensive firms experience a more rapid internationalization process than other SMEs, due to a combination of a limited range of products, few customers in the home country, high R&D costs and short product cycles. Consequently, technology acts as both a push and a pull factor. Foreign direct investment is also higher in R&D intensive firms due to reasons of proprietary control and the associated appropriability problems, supporting Hymer's et al. theory (see, e.g. Hymer 1961).[14] Another distinguishing feature of internationalized SMEs in Lindquist's study is a comparatively higher level of complexity, a higher software content and a high preparedness for customer adaptation.

According to Lindquist, foreign markets are often selected on the basis of a strategic consideration like access to advanced customers, market potentials, the competitive situations, demographic and skill factors, hence opposing the predictions forwarded by the behavioristic school (Aharoni 1966 et al.). In Lindquist's study, this is reflected in a much higher representation of Swedish SMEs in Japan and the U.S. than in many neighboring countries.

The rest of this section relies heavily on an IUI survey directed to 230 SMEs in Sweden during 1990, supplemented by in-depth interviews with 20 firms. The sample of 230 firms consisted of two subsamples: one consisting of a random sample of 100 small firms (less than 200 employees) belonging to the

---

[13] SMEs and internationalization are also studied by Ghauri and Kumar (1989), Miesenbock (1989), Kothari (1989) and others.

[14] For a discussion of the appropriability problem see for example Williamson (1975), Magee (1977) and Teece (1983).

Table 9.5. Average Employment, Turnover and Rates of Return for Small Firms and Subcontractors, 1989

	Employment	Turnover (million SEK)	Rate of return on total capital	Gross margin (%)
Small firms	53	30	n.a.	9
Subcontractors	220	100	9.9	7.3

Source: Braunerhjelm 1991a.

engineering industry and one consisting of a random sample of medium-sized subcontractors.[15] Together they are referred to as SMEs. The separation between subcontractors and small firms is motivated by the particular circumstances subcontractors are expected to encounter as their customers become more internationalized, e.g. just-in-time deliveries gain in importance, etc.[16] The underlying population for subcontractors is dispersed over several industries, although heavily concentrated in the engineering industry (particularly the transport industry). Some characteristics of the respective groups are revealed in Table 9.5.

Production specialization by SMEs

In the survey, firms were asked to identify themselves among six different production segments:

* Simple processing of raw material
* Contractual production of simple components
* Other production of simple components
* System production, sophisticated components
* Investment goods
* Other goods (consumer goods)

The distribution of production in the subcontracting industry is shown in Figure 9.1a. It illustrates that approximately 75 percent of production can be

---

[15] Small firms are defined as firms employing between 20 and 200 persons while large firms consequently have more than 200 employees. Subcontractors are defined as producers of intermediate goods exposed to international competition (to avoid firms from the sheltered part of the economy) where at least 20 percent of production goes to one customer.

[16] See also Dunning in this volume.

Figure 9.1a. Production of Swedish Subcontractors Distributed by Different Product Groups, 1990

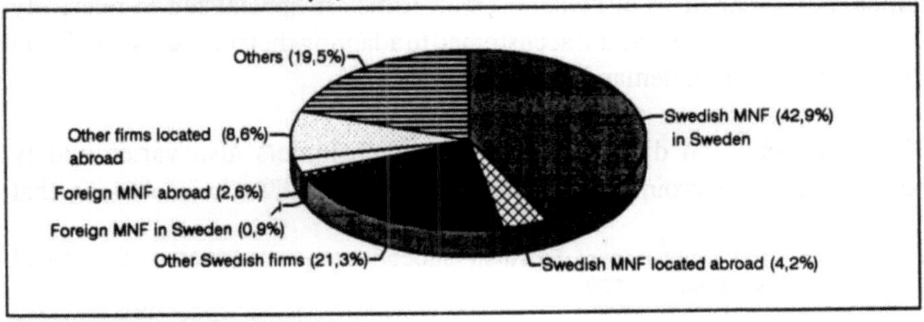

Source: Braunerhjelm (1991a)

categorized into the segment of simple component or raw material production. Only 5,9 percent of production belongs to the advanced systems segment, while roughly 16 percent of production can be attributed to the investment goods segment.[17]

Looking at the specialization pattern for small firms it is evident that these are much less inclined to simple components production (Figure 9.1b). Together with the processing of raw material it only amounts to 43 percent of production while advanced systems production is twice as large as for the subcontracting group. Yet, striking is that production of investment goods, often customized according to specific customer demand, reaches almost 40 percent. This indicates a more vulnerable situation for the subcontracting industry, where dependence on few customers is much more pronounced, and where firms are

Figure 9.1b. Production of Small Swedish Firms Distributed on Different Product Groups, 1990.

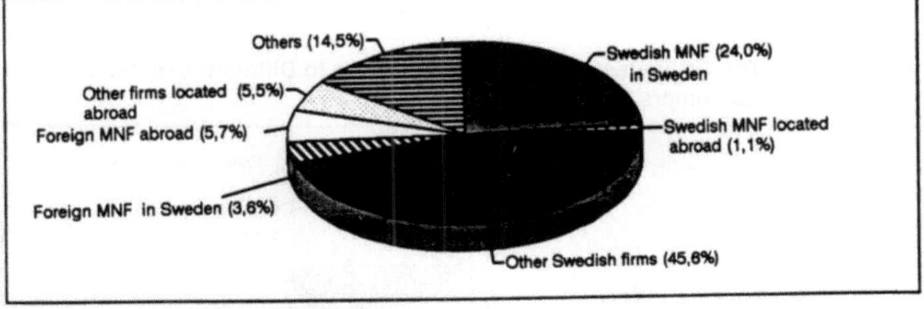

Source: Braunerhjelm (1991a)

[17] Admittedly investment goods are not typical subcontractor products. However, since several firms are producing both investment goods and intermediate products it was decided that this category should be incorporated.

primarily involved in simple component production which could easily be imitated by other firms elsewhere. Small firms are specialized in relatively more sophisticated goods, and accustomed to adapting their products according to specific customer demand.

The dependence on different categories of customers also varies widely between the two groups. From Figures 9.2a and 9.2b it is obvious that

Figure 9.2a. The Deliveries of Swedish Subcontractors to Different Groups of Customers, 1990.

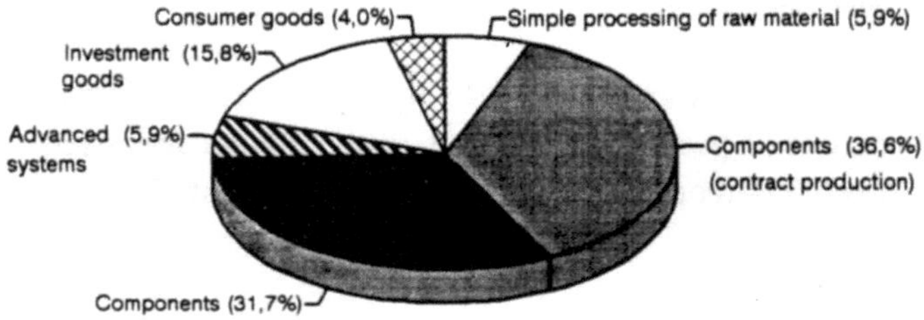

Source: Braunerhjelm (1991a).

subcontractors have a considerably closer link to large Swedish MNFs. In a process of intensified internationalization of the customer firms, subcontractors encounter special requirements in their adaptation to the new conditions. They have to ponder whether they themselves should internationalize, i.e. follow their customers and set off a bandwagon effect, or seek alternative ways to serve their customers. An internationalization process is coupled with considerable financial risks and requires special competences, a matter which will be elaborated further below.

Figure 9.2b. The Deliveries of Small Swedish Firms to Different Groups of Customers, 1990.

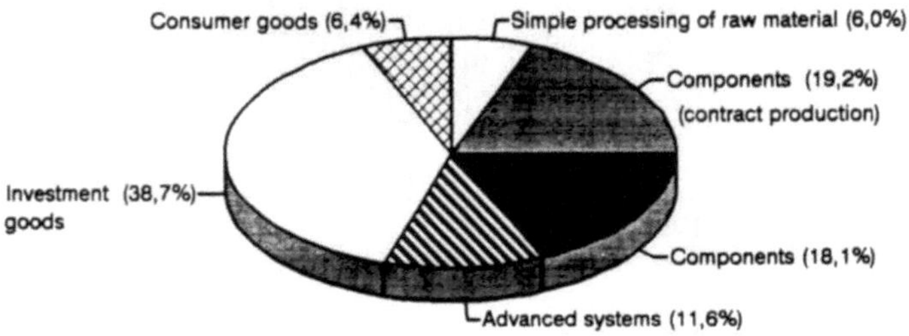

Source: Braunerhjelm (1991a).

Again, the group of small firms seems to be in quite a different position as depicted in Figure 9.2b. The dependence on Swedish MNFs is much less pronounced and the major part of customers belong to non-MNFs which are locally situated. Although many of these will also be affected by a global or regional deregulation, as the EC 1992 program, the probability of maintaining such customers is much higher, especially since products of small firms are often customized and after sales-services constitute an important ingredient in the package sold. In addition, local firms may have access to a local network which could be of value for customers.

The type of customer differs markedly among producers of different intermediate products, and in Figures 9.3a and 9.3b a clear pattern emerges. In the subcontracting group the producers of components sell up to 80 percent of their production to Swedish MNFs. For producers of more sophisticated systems and investment goods, the role of Swedish MNFs diminish substantially. Notably, most of the exports are within the group producing systems, suggesting that these firms have developed a certain production niche–on which they base their international competitiveness. Exports by smaller firms are generally lower and the small system producers are closely tied to the Swedish MNFs. Hence, one interpretation is that the small system producers initially supply the large, advanced customers on the home market and, as they expand,they turn to the international market. Such a development could be explained by a lack of knowledge of the foreign market and the attempt to reduce risks and costs by taking advantage of their customers' relations etc, which conforms to the network approach (Håkansson 1982, Spencer and Valla 1989, Arthur et al. 1991).[18] Hence, acquiring and developing special competence and know-how, i.e. niche production, seems to be the key to export success.

Competence

The questionnaire sent out to firms also contained questions concerning the competence level. Scholars in business economics have often attributed lack of competence in especially management as the main explanation of inferior business performance.

---

[18] See also SIND (1990a,b) for similar conclusions.

Figure 9.3a. The Composition of Customers in Different Subcontraction Production, 1990.

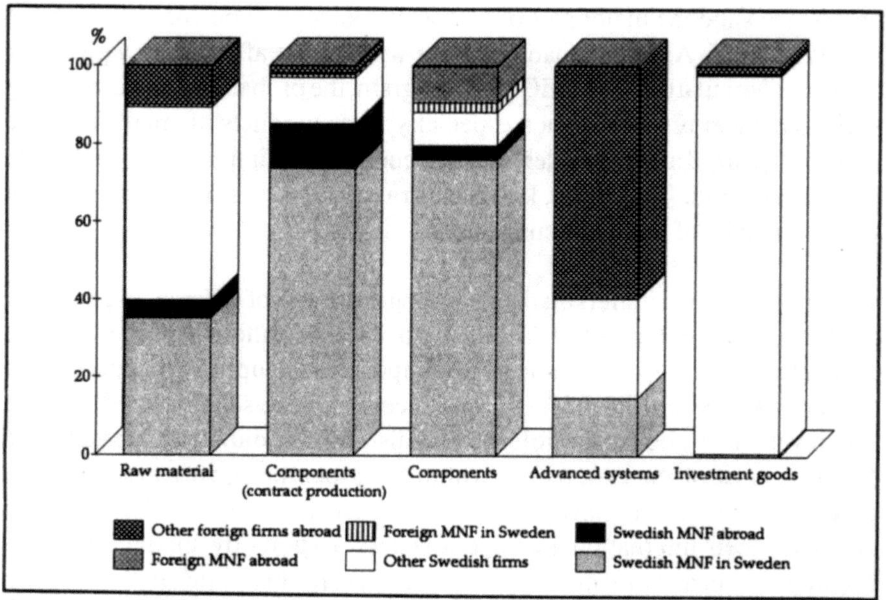

Source: Braunerhjelm (1991a).

Figure 9.3b. The Composition of Customers in Different Small Firm Production, 1990.

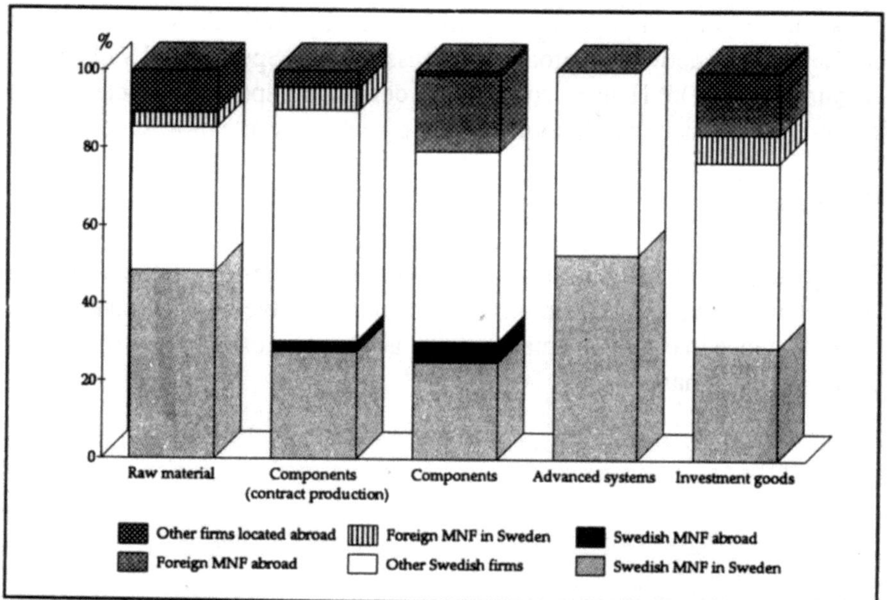

Source: Braunerhjelm (1991a).

Table 9.6. R&D, Marketing, and Education Expenditures as Percentage of Total Costs in Small Firms, Subcontractors and Large Firms, 1989.

	R & D	Marketing	Education
Small firms	0.8	4	0.3
Subcontractors	1.5	3	2
Large firms	9	5	2

Source: Braunerhjelm (1990, 1991a).

Competence is a multi-dimensional concept and there is no generally accepted definition.[19] Competence can be in production, marketing, organisation, distribution, R&D etc., i.e. in all the elements that constitute the ability to run a business successfully. It will always be tacit to a certain extent, partly related to entrepreneurial capacity, but also due to luck and other non-measurable factors. In the long run competence should be revealed in a firm's ability to sustain a high level of profit. Despite the difficulties associated with the measurement of competence, data on a limited number of competence variables have been collected. These data were R&D expenditures, marketing and education expenditures and, finally, the composition of the labor force within firms. The distribution and level of profits within and among the different groups of firms will also be shown.[20]

In Table 9.6 the average outlays on R&D, marketing and education–as reported in the firms' financial statements–are given. The difference between large firms and SMEs is striking. R&D expenditures are six times higher in large firms than in subcontractors and about 11 times higher than in small firms. In marketing, although for the majority of large firms only domestic marketing expenditure is included, large firms display the highest expenditures, especially in comparison to subcontractors. This reflects the close links that subcontractors often have to a limited number of customers which makes marketing efforts less urgent. Education costs are more evenly dispersed among firms of different size, even though the SMEs report the smallest figures. On the other hand, as the in-depth interviews with the firms reveal, less formal "on-the-job" training seems to be particularly important in the group of small firms.

---

[19] For a discussion of business competence, its composition, and the evolution of the concept in the economic literature, see Carlsson and Eliasson (1991).

[20] Data on LEs emanates from a survey of 260 firms in 1989 (Braunerhjelm 1990).

Table 9.7. The Skill Composition of the Labor Force in Small Firms, Subcontractors and Large Firms, 1990.

	Small	Subcontractors	Large firms (1989)
Executive staff	5	3	2
Specialists, middle management	9	7	11
White collar	16	15	29
Skilled worker	46	35	25
Unskilled worker	24	40	33
Total	100	100	100

Source: Braunerhjelm (1990, 1991a).

Table 9.7 pictures the differences in composition of labor forces among three groups of firms. The five categories are ranked in descending order with regard to competence, defined as their profession status, informal training and education. Notably, large firms have more than 40 percent of their labor force in the three high-skill categories whereas subcontractors are dominated by the least-skilled employees.

The higher proportion of service-related employees in the LEs could of course be due to exaggeratedly bureaucratic organisations. However, a more plausible interpretation is that large firms working in highly competitive international markets, are dependent on a large and sophisticated internal "service" sector. This sector is nececessary to sustain and upgrade. It is within these service activities that strategic competences and competitiveness are created. Areas like marketing, finance, computer knowledge, logistics, and R&D, are of crucial importance. If these functions are necessary for international competitiveness, then the gap between large firms and subcontractors is particularly obvious. Note that the small firms are more abundantly endowed with skilled personnel than are subcontractors. As shown in other studies, only a minor part of large firm employees are involved in the actual production of the goods (Eliasson 1991b).

Figure 9.4. Rate of Return over the Interest Rate (epsilon) of Small Firms, Large Firms and of Subcontractors, 1988

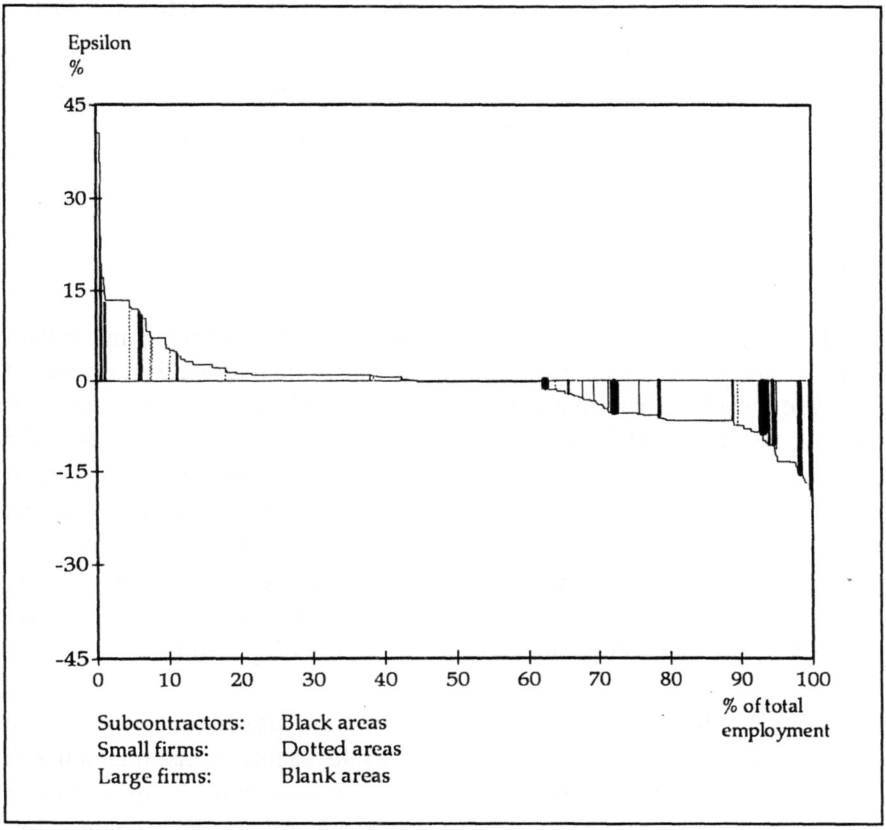

Source: Braunerhjelm (1991a).

Profits could also be regarded as a measure of competence and the distribution of firms of different size can be represented in a Salter diagram (Figure 9.4).[21] The firms are ranked such that the firms exhibiting the highest profit rates are situated in the left area of the figure.[22] It is apparent that the smaller firms and the larger firms are distributed in a similar way, whereas subcontractors are overrepresented in the lower right end, displaying comparatively weaker profitability than the other groups. Hence, again subcontractors seem to be in a worse position compared to LEs and the group of small firms.

[21] Profits are defined as the real rate of return over the real interest rate on long-term bonds.

[22] Since each firm is represented by a pillar where the width of the base is determined by the number of employees and the heigth of the level of profit, the smallest firms becomes extremely tiny (the dotted areas). (see, Salter 1966).

Table 9.8. Number of Swedish Small MNF with Production Units Abroad.

Year	1965	1970	1974	1978	1986	1990
Number of firms	8	7	9	15	18	23

Source: IUI surveys 1965, 1970, 1974, 1978, 1986, 1990

Internationalization

Has the long standing tradition of free trade policies in Sweden encouraged internationalization by the Swedish SMEs? Such internationalization would facilitate the adjustment to a more integrated world. However, the degree of internationalization of the Swedish SMEs is generally quite low, in particular with regard to FDI. Still, over the last 28 years the number of Swedish small firms (less than 200 employees) with production units abroad has almost tripled (Table 9.8). On average, Swedish SMEs account for approximately 7 percent of total Swedish exports. Measured as a percentage of total sales by SMEs, the figure amounts to 20 percent, where the most important market consists of the member countries of the EC (excluding Denmark).

In the present study, internationalization aspects are limited to exports and the establishment of subsidiaries abroad as data on sales agents, licenses, agreements with distribution chains and franchising are not available.[23] Some evidence concerning plans for future establishment abroad will also be accounted for.

The Tables 9.9a and 9.9b reveal that the EC is by far the most important export market followed by the market category "rest of the world", while the Nordic countries receive the smallest share of SMEs' export. This is consistent with Lindquist's (1991) findings and contradicts the sequential approach described above (Aharoni 1966 and others). Interestingly enough, the export share to the EC has increased for subcontractors during 1988-1990 while remaining constant for the smaller firms. One interpretation is that the massive FDI

[23] Some regional studies show that Swedish small firms began to internationalize themselves in response to the EC 1992 programme. In a study of Southeastern Sweden it was shown that over 60 percent of the small firms had taken some action to promote export of their products, ranging from contacts with sales agents to the establishment of production units abroad. The most frequent measure was participation in different fairs and similar events. The smaller the firms, the less measures had been taken (Andersson 1991, Karlsson-Larsson 1991).

Table 9.9a. The Distribution of Swedish Subcontractors' Exports to Different Regions, 1988-1990.
Percentage

	EC	Nordic countries (except Denmark)	Rest of the World
1988	59	17	24
1989	59	15	26
1990	64	16	20

Source: Braunerhjelm (1991a).

Table 9.9b. The Distribution of Swedish Small Firms' Exports to Different Regions, 1988-1990.
Percentage

	EC	Nordic countries (except Denmark)	Rest of the World
1988	44	20	36
1989	41	24	35

Source: Braunerhjelm (1991a).

undertaken by Swedish MNFs during the 1980s in the EC, has had a pull effect on exports from the domestically located subcontractors. This is also confirmed by total sales remaining more or less constant during the period. Note also that exports to the rest of the world have fallen during the same period. In the short run it is difficult to change existing delivery structures, although in the long run these firms will be exposed to competition from firms located abroad. However, it also opens up possibilities for subcontracting firms to proceed and intensify their internationalization, since this is a relatively inexpensive way to establish contacts with other firms and markets.

As far as production abroad is concerned, the smallest firms have virtually no foreign establishments, while subcontractors report that the overwhelming part (99 percent) of production is located within Sweden. Likewise, employment is to 95 percent tied to Sweden, where the discrepancy between produc-

Table 9.10. Distribution of Swedish Subcontractors' Production in Different Regions, 1988-1992 .
Percent

	Production			Employment	
	Sweden	Nordic countries	EC	Sweden	Abroad
1988	99	0.5	0.5	95	5
1989	99	0.5	0.5	95	5
1990	99	0.5	0.5	n.a.	n.a.
1992 (planned)	98	0.5	1.5	n.a.	n.a.

Source: Braunerhjelm (1991a).

tion and employment is explained by more sales employees abroad. Regarding planned future activities, a modest increase in foreign market is reported (Table 9.10).

This section has focused on three strategic factors: specialization, competence and internationalization, with the aim of detecting strengths and weaknessess in the Swedish SME sector. It is argued that these structural factors reveal the potentials for internationalization and FDI and, moreover, can be generalized to other countries. What conclusions can then be drawn from the case study?

Overall, and in accordance with earlier empirical studies and the theoretical approach emphasizing firm-specific assets, it seems as if firms with some unique capability or competence are most successful on the international market. More specifically, subcontractors are stuck with problems of a more structural character than small firms in general. Subcontractors are more deeply involved in production of relatively simple components that do not require any particular skill or knowledge, they are more dependent on Swedish MNFs, and their degree of internationalization is quite low. The latter characteristic is also true for the smaller firms but, since their customers are already more local, it is of less concern. Moreover, subcontractors employ by far the largest proportion of unskilled labor and display a lower profit performance than the other groups. The problems for subcontractors are further aggravated by their customers' attempt to outsource part of the R&D activities and at the same time demanding price-cuts. To embark on internationalization, or to move production into more specialized and sophisticated segments, is a very delicate task under these circumstances. Both activities are risky and costly, especially if they coincide with a business recession. Many Swedish subcontractors have also been squeezed out of the market because their customers have been dissatisfied not only with prices, but also with quality.

Prospects for Small Firms and Subcontractors in the 1990s: Some Concluding Remarks

The 1960s and 1970s were characterized by the establishment of large scale production units, designed to mass-produce standardized goods. Organization of production followed Tayloristic and Fordistic principles, resulting in bureaucratic and hierarchic structures. Strategies to develop and sustain the competitive edge of firms were predominantly geared to lowering costs while less attention was paid to differentiation and quality. During the 1980s a phase of increased internationalization began, which led to stronger interdependence across national borders as firms became more global. At the same time demand shifted towards more differentiated, high quality products. As internationalization proceeds through the dismantling of trade barriers, continued integration efforts, improved and less expensive transportation systems, competition can be expected to increase and to extend to more sectors in the 1990s. Traditional home-market orientated firms in industrialized countries will, hence, become more exposed to foreign competiton.

Yet, the last two to three decades have also been characterized by an impressive revival of SMEs in terms of employment shares, creation of value added and profit levels. The demand effect of rising income has stimulated production of cheaper differentiated, customized products at the expense of homogeneous, mass-produced and less expensive products. Not only can a "boutique" effect–through heterogenous consumer preferences–be detected, but there is also a shift toward more services, which favors SMEs production. Furthermore, new technology, in particular information technology, yields new business opportunities. Since firms tend to be small at the start, it follows that technological shifts can spur entrance of SMEs and thereby increase their proportion in industrial production. In addition, as argued by for example Gibb (1992), the potential for disaggregation in LEs is enormous. The arguments for such "externalization" of more peripheral production by LEs have, in its short-hand version, been called the KISS-factors (Keep It Simple and Small), while more detailed versions of externalization include efficiency and cost factors in addition to attempts to unleash more of the entrepreneurial spirit. Hence, income effects, technological progress and externalization can be expected to continue to support this trend towards small units.

In view of the development of SMEs in industrialized countries in the last decade–and of the case study of a highly internationalized country (Sweden)–what can be said about the future internationalization of SMEs and their engagement in FDI? Furthermore, what strategies should–or must–they adopt to survive in the intensified competitive situation expected in the 1990s? Obviously, FDI activities depend on firm-specific factors as well as ties and networks between firms and the markets in which they operate. The avenue chosen will depend on the capability and characteristics of each particular firm. Some conceivable strategies are illustrated in Table 9.11.

The matrix naturally does not cover all conceivable strategies or combinations of strategies, rather it presents some of the main alternatives. Moreover, although the matrix gives a static impression, it also encompasses dynamic

Table 9.11. Strategies for Small Firms and Subcontractors in the 1990s.

Strategy / SMEs	Internationalize		Niches, know-how, technology		Remain local	
	FDI	Export	Network	R&D	Local hero	Foreign master
Advanced subcontractors	X	X	X	X		
Other subcontractors	X		X			X
Advanced small firms	X	X	X	X		
Other small firms			X		X	X

effects. Hence, several of the strategies in the matrix imply growth of the firms. In fact, firms may grow out of their definition, turning into large enterprises. With these caveats in mind, the matrix suggests that advanced subcontractors, producing systems or operating within niches should embark on FDI as their customers establish production abroad in order to stay close to their market and to facilitate communication. FDI can also facilitate access to important networks which, in addition to the ongoing R&D is decisive for upgrading and sustaining their skill level. However, depending on the degree of specialization or volumes produced, export may also be an adequate strategy for some of the advanced subcontractors.

For simple assembly of low-tech components, FDI is required in markets where production costs are competitive.[24] Otherwise such production can easily be taken over by firms in those countries. For neither of the two types of subcontractors is the "local hero" alternative, i.e. to gain a strategic position on the local market, a viable strategy. The advanced producers have to spread their R&D costs across a much larger market, while less advanced producers will be beaten out by cheaper foreign supply. Surrending to a "foreign master" and becoming a "secondary" subcontractor may however be a relevant strategy. Especially the less advanced producers will get involved in such types of mergers and acquisitions. For small firms the options are almost identical although the "local hero" possibility is probably a more relevant strategy, especially for the less advanced. In this adjustment process a large number of SMEs will fail and exit from the market, either due to take-overs or because of closings.

In all the strategy options, the formation of networks (broadly defined) is regarded as vital for success. Networks are claimed to increase flexibility, induce a higher sensitivity to the price mechanisms and to enhance learning (Asanuma 1991, Westney 1991). As networks, and network externalities, are judged to become strategically more important, they will also influence the pattern of FDI. Clustering is likely to occur since the location of large customer firms will be more influenced by such non-traditional factors such as the regional composition of firms, skill levels and education, which induce SMEs to undertake FDI in certain areas. This is already taking place in Europe. Examples are the clustering of biotech firms in the south of France and the regional clustering of part of the engineering tool industry in Germany. Hence, FDI will be directed to areas where the capability of the respective firm can be

[24] Compared with the textile industry where the more labor intensive stages in the production process have been relocated to countries where labor is relatively cheap.

matched by complementary regional capabilities. From such clustering of specific capabilites and competences, a pattern of regional comparative advantage is likely to emerge.

With regard to the subcontracting industry, the adjustment and reorganization in the U.S. in the last decade sets an interesting example. In the U.S., deregulation of the transportation market and increased local presence by Japanese subcontractors - a development which is now also taking place in Europe - prompted a reorganisation of the subcontracting industry. The prime reason for the Japanese subcontractors to establish production in the the U.S. was protectionistic threats. Japanese car producers took up production in the U.S. to evade export quotas, but they maintained a substantial share of import of components from Japan which induced a discussion of whether or not so-called "screw-driver" production–i.e. assembly of imported components–should fall within the export quotas (compare the present discussion within the EC). As a result, Japanese subcontractors followed suit and today approximately 300 Japanese subcontracting firms are represented in the U.S.[25] Through their presence, and their habit of undertaking part of the R&D themselves, they increased the pressure on the domestic U.S. subcontracting firms to restructure. The difference between the U.S. and the European subcontracting industry can be illustrated by the fact that the U.S. today has 5 producers of exhaust systems whereas Europe has 18. There are many similar examples and they indicate the extent of the adjustment process to come in Europe.

A related question–and decisive for future FDI by SMEs–is of course whether or not the success of SMEs will continue. Obviously, size is by no means a guarantee for economic superiority. The most frequent explanations for the decreased importance of size relate to exogenous turbulence on the international markets, instability of demand, and technological achievements which have lowered the cost of capital. According to several scholars in business economics, these trends can be expected to continue in the 1990s, where the base for competitiveness of firms continues to shift from low costs to quality, flexibility and innovations.[26] As evident from the case study and several other investigations, firms with specific knowledge and capabilities are best equipped to internationalize. The speed of learning will become a key factor as lead times

---

[25] In 1990 the number of Japanese manufacturing companies within the EC increased by 147 to a total of 676 whereof 34 could be classified as subcontractors.

[26] See Grant (1991) for a survey.

shorten and the speed of technological progress is intensified. These dynamic sources will shape the future success or failure of firms, and the skill level of employees will become even more important. Networks will become increasingly complex and extended, and substitute for traditional structures of vertical integration. As a result, firms will be organized in a more "fleet-of-foot" manner, designed to respond quickly to changes in local production conditions by relocating to other regions or countries. Furthermore, non-traditional resources such as level of education, R&D and potential and existing networks, will increasingly govern locational decisions by firms in the 1990s.

Most of this is promising news for the smaller firms in the 1990s. The "boutique" effect is likely to continue–assuming that income does not fall–where SMEs respond to local differences in preferences. Furthermore, flexibility of SMEs enables swift reactions to changes in demand, and in addition, the local presence often certifies that service and maintenance can be supplied adequately. As international competition intensifies, SMEs can exploit their strength of having small, flat, and flexible organisations, promoting high "economies of learning". All these factors seem to favor SME production, although there are some caveats to this story. First, the past evolution of SMEs is blurred by the fragmented knowledge about the lifecourse of firms and its effect on the distribution of firm size. If mainly LEs exit from market it would render the impression that SME participation increases. Related to this is the question of "externalization", networks and how subsidiaries are treated in the statistics. Furthermore, it should be noted that the change in size distribution is measured in terms of employment. Obviously, if a large firm substitutes labor for more capital intensive techniques, while production remains constant, it is hard to argue that the firm has diminished in size (Carlsson 1992, Carlsson and Taymaz 1993). Hence, employment measures should perhaps be complemented with other measures.

There are also threats of another nature to SMEs, for example the indications that large firms re-organize to capture some of the advantages associated with SMEs production (Grant 1991, Buckley and Casson 1992). One aspect of this, using Porter's terminology, is multi-domestic production, implying that large firms establish production plants in a large number of countries where the objective is to adapt to specific local requirements–become local–by establishing flexible and relatively small units. At the same time, R&D, marketing and other strategic and costly activities are concentrated to exploit economies of scale. Sometimes basic component production can also be concentrated to a few units, leaving the local adaptation to the respective plant. Hence, large firms may embark on strategies combining economies of scale and economies of scope, where the latter are derived from a multi-plant organisation of production. This would probably discourage FDI by SMEs.

To conclude, the success of SME production in industrialized countries is expected to continue in the 1990s, although perhaps at a lower rate. International deregulation will foster intensified competitive pressure in traditionally sheltered areas, implying that an adjustment process–where internationalization will be one ingredient–is inevitable for a large part of the SME sector. However, although trade liberalization carries on smoothly in different parts of the world (EC, NAFTA, LAFTA etc.), the prospects for global deregulation are less evident. The threat of regionalization, should trade barriers be erected or maintained between the Triad powers of Europe, Japan and USA, cannot at present be neglected. Regionalization includes tariff-jumping FDI, as EC experience with Japanese investment in the last years shows.

The extent of FDI by SMEs can only be assessed in qualitative terms–it is likely to increase–while quantitative predictions will be extremely shaky. Yet, something can be said about the direction. Subcontractors producing sophisticated components or systems will establish foreign subsidiaries where they expect network externalities to materialize and where customer firms locate. This will encourage clustering in areas where factor markets (notably skilled labor) or product markets are especially attractive, i.e. in the industrialized countries. Low-tech subcontracting production will have to relocate production to areas where production costs are competitive, indicating increased FDI in Eastern Europe and other semi-developed countries.

For SMEs in general, producing in a high-tech niche, the necessity to exploit network externalities from advanced customers and suppliers–often scattered all over the world–will induce increased FDI. This FDI will be concentrated in Europe, U.S. and Japan. To promote the right setting, or investment climate, for LEs, it is quite conceivable that countries will increase their efforts in the future to attract relocation of strategically important SMEs. Whether or not less advanced SMEs engage in FDI depends on the characteristics of their customers, especially if they are local or dispersed and if they demand customized products. Structural characteristics–and strategic actions taken today–such as specialization in production, internationalization and competence, will set the future path for SMEs.

References

Abernathy, W. and J. Utterback (1978), "Patterns of Industrial Innovation", *Technology Review*, Vol 80, pp 41-47.

Aharoni, Y. (1966), *The Foreign Investment Decision Process*, Ma: Division of Research, Graduate School of Business Research, Harvard University.

Aiginger, K. and G. Tichy (1984), "Die Grösse die Kleine", *mimeo*, University of Graz, Austria.

Andersson, P. (1991), "EGs inre marknad 1992 - Planerade eller vidtagna åtgärder bland småföretagen i Kronoborgs län", *mimeo*, Växjö University, Sweden.

Arthur, M., C. Hendry and A. Jones (1991), "Learning From Doing: Adaptation & Resource Management in the Smaller Firms", *mimeo,* Presented at the 11th Annual Strategic Management Society International Conference, University of Warwick, England.

Asanuma, B. (1991), "Coordination between Production and Distribution in a Globalized Network of Firms: Assessing Flexibility Acheived in the Japanese Automobile Industry", *mimeo*, Presented at the conference "Japan in the Global Economy", The Stockholm School of Economics, Stockholm, Sweden.

Birch, D. (1979), *The Job Generation Process*, Cambridge: MIT University Press.

Birch, D. (1987), *Job Generation in America*, New York: Free Press.

Braunerhjelm, P. (1990), *Svenska industriföretag inför EG 1992 - Planer och förväntningar*, (Swedish Industrial Firms afore EC 1992 - Plans and Expectations), Stockholm: The Industrial Institute for Economic and Social Research (IUI).

Braunerhjelm, P, (1991a), "Svenska underleverantörer och småföretag - Struktur, internationalisering och kompetens" (Swedish Subcontractors and SMEs - Specialization, Internationalization and Competence), *Research Report No. 38*, Stockholm: The Industrial Institute for Economic and Social Research (IUI).

Braunerhjelm, P. (1991b), "Svenska underleverantörer och småföretag i det nya Europa", (Swedish Subcontractors and SMEs in the New Europe), *The Journal of the Economic Society of Finland*, No 4, pp 219-228.

Brock, W. and D. Evans (1986), *The Economics of Small Business*, New York: Holmes & Meier.

Brown, C., J. Hamilton and J. Medoff, (1990), *Employers Large and Small*, Cambridge MA and London: Harvard University Press.

Buckley, P. (1986), "Foreign Direct Investment by Small and Medium Sized Enterprises: The Theoretical Background", *mimeo*, Presented at the conference "Project on Transfer of Technology to Developing Countries by Small and Medium Sized Enterprises", Nürnberg, Germany.

Buckley, P. and M. Casson (1976), *The Future of the Multinational Enterprise*, London: MacMillan.

Buckley, P. and M. Casson (1992), "Organizing for Innovation: The Multinational Enterprise in the Twenty-first Century", in P. Buckley and M. Casson (eds.), *Multinational Enterprises in the World Economy*, Aldershot and Brookfield: Edward Elgar Publishing Ltd.

Burns, P. and J. Dewhurst (1986), *Small Business in Europe*, London: Macmillan.

Cantwell, J. and S. Raddacio (1990), "The Growth of Multinationals and the Catching Up Effect", *Economic Notes*, Vol 1, pp 15-27.

Carlsson, B. (1984), "The Development and the Use of Machine Tools in Historical Perspective", *Journal of Economic Behavior and Organization*, Vol. 5, pp 90-111.

Carlsson, B. (1989), "The Evolution of Manufacturing Technology and Its Impact on Industrial Structure: An International Study", *Small Business Economics*, Vol. 1, pp 21-37.

Carlsson, B. (1992), "The Rise of Small Business: Causes and Consequences", in W.J.Adams, (ed.), *Singular Europe: Economy and Polity of the European Community after 1992*, Ann Arbor: University of Michigan Press (forthcoming).

Carlsson, B. and G. Eliasson (1991), "The Nature and Importance of Economic Competence", *Working Paper No. 294*, The Industrial Institute for Economic and Social Research (IUI).

Carlsson, B. and E. Taymaz (1993), "Flexible Technology and Industrial Structure in the US", *Small Business Economics*, forthcoming.

Caves, R (1982), *Multinational Enterprises and Economic Analysis*, New York: Cambridge University Press.

Davidsson, P. (1989), *Continued Entrepreneurship and Small Firm Growth*, Stockholm: EFI.

Doctor, J., R. Van der Haorst, and C. Stokman (1989), "Innovation Processes in Small- and Medium-sized Companies", *Entrepreneurship and Regional Development*, Vol. 1, pp 33-53.

Drucker, P. (1986), "The Changing World Economy", *Foreign Affairs*, Vol 64, Spring, pp 768-79.

Dunning, J. (1977), "Trade, Location of Economic Activities and the MNE: A Search for an Eclectic Approach", in B.Ohlin, P-O.Hesselborn, and P-M.Wijkman (eds.), *The International Allocation of International Production*, London: Macmillan.

Dunning, J. (1992), "International Direct Investment Patterns", in L.Oxelheim, (ed.), *The Global Race for Foreign Direct Investment: Prospects for the Future*, Springer–Verlag.

Eliasson, G. (1991a), "Modelling the Experimentally Organized Economy - Complex Dynamics in an Empirical Micro-Macro Model of Endogenous Growth", *Journal of Economic Behaviour and Organization*, Vol. 16, pp 153-182.

Eliasson, G. (1991b), "The Firm As a Competent Team", *Journal of Economic Behaviour and Organization*, Vol. 13, pp 273-89.

Evans, D. (1991), *Industry Dynamics and Small Firms in the United States*, Report for the US Small Business Administration, NERA, Cambridge, USA.

Fredriksson, T. (1992), "Policies Towards Small and Medium Enterprises in Japan and Sweden", *EFI Research Report*, April.

Ghauri, P. and P. Kumar (1989), "An Empirical Investigation of Factors Influencing Export Behaviour of Smaller Swedish Firms", in G.Avlonitis, N.Papavasiliou and A.Kouremenos (eds.), *Marketing Thought and Practice in the 1990's*, Proceedings of the XVIII Conference of the European Marketing Academy, Athens, Greece.

Gibb, A. (1992), "Revisiting Smallness", *mimeo*, Presented at the "The 7th Nordic Conference on Small Business", Turkko, Finland.

Grant, R. (1991), *Contemporary Strategy Analysis*, Oxford: Basil Blackwell.

Hjalmarsson, L. (1991), "Competition Policy and Economic Efficiency: Efficiency Trade-Offs in Industrial Policy", in Y.Bourdet, (ed.), *Internationalization, Market Power and Consumer Welfare*, London: Routledge.

Horwitch, M. and C. Pralahad (1976), "Managing Technological Innovation - Three Ideal Modes", *Sloan Management Review*, Vol. 17, pp 77-89.

Hymer, S. (1961), *The International Operations of National Firms: A Study of Direct Foreign Investment*, Cambridge: MIT University Press.

Håkansson, H. (1982), *International Marketing and Purchasing of Industrial Goods. An Interaction Approach*, Chichester: John Wiley.

Jagrén, L. (1988), "Företagens tillväxt i ett historiskt perspektiv", in Örtengren, J, (ed), *Expansion, avveckling, företagsvärdering i svensk industri*, Stockholm: The Industrial Institute for Economic and Social Research (IUI).

Johanson, J. and L.-G. Mattson (1984), "Internationalization in Industrial Systems - A Network Approach", Presented at the conference "Prince Bertils Symposium on Strategies in Global Competition", Stockholm School of Economics, Stockholm, Sweden.

Johanson, J. and J.-E. Vahlne (1977), "The Internationalization Process of the Firm - A Model of Knowledge Development and Increasing Foreign Market Commitments", *Journal of International Business Studies*, Vol. 8, pp 23-32.

Kamien, M. and N. Schwartz (1975), "Market Structure and Innovation: A Survey", *Journal of Economic Literature*, Vol. 13, pp 1-37.

Karlsson, C. and J. Larsson (1991), "A Macroview of the Gnosjö Entrepreneurial Spirit", *mimeo*, Jönköping International Business School, Jönköping.

Kothari, V. (1989), "Overseas Strategies of Small Business - A Longitudinal Study", in Avlonitis, G., N.Papavasiliou and A.Kouremenos (eds.), *Marketing Thought and Practice in the 1990's*. Proceedings of the XVIII Conference of the European Marketing Academy, Athens, Greece.

Larouche, G. (1989), "Petites et moyennes entreprises au Quebec: Organisations Économique, croissance de l'emploi et qualité du travail", *mimeo*, Institut Internationales d'Etudes Sociales, Geneva, Switzerland.

Lindquist, M. (1991), *Infant Multinationals. The Internationalization of Young, Technology-Based Swedish Firms*, Stockholm: IIB.

Lucas, R. (1978), "On the Size Distribution of Business Firms", *Bell Journal of Economics*, Vol. 9, Autumn, pp 508-523.

Magee, S. (1977), "Information and the Multinational Corporation: An Appropriability Theory of Foreign Direct Investment", in J. Bhagwati (ed.), *The New International Economic Order: The North-South Debate*, New York and London: MIT University Press.

Marshall, A. (1890), *Principles of Economics*, London, England.

Miesenbock, K. (1989), "Small Businesses and Exporting: A Literature Review", *International Small Business Journal*, Vol. 6, pp 42-61.

Mill, J. (1848), *Principles of Political Economy*, (Reprinted 1985), New York: Penguin Books.

NUTEK (1991a), *Att skapa livskraft*, B1991:4, Stockholm.

NUTEK (1991), *Medium-Sized Industrial Firms*, B1991:3, Stockholm.

Oxelheim, L. (1990), *International Finacial Integration*, Heidelberg: Springer-Verlag.

Oxelheim, L. (1993), *Financial Markets in Transition: The Globalization of Small National Financial Markets*, London: Routledge, forthcomimg.

Penrose, E. (1956), "Foreign Investment and Growth of the Firm", *Economic Journal*, Vol 66, pp 220-235.

Piore, M. and C. Sabel, (1984), *The Second Industrial Divide: Possibilities for Prosperity*, New York: Basic Books.

Porter, M. (1980), *Competitive Strategy*, New York: Free Press.

Porter, M. (1990), *The Competitive Advantage of Nations*, London and Basingstoke: Macmillan.

Pratten, C. (1991), "The Competitiveness of Small Firms and the Economies of Scale", *mimeo*, University of Cambridge, England.

Rothwell, R. and W. Zegweld (1982), *Innovation and the Small and Medium Sized Firm - Their Role in Employment and in Economic Change*, London: Francis Pinter.

Sabel, C. (1983), "Italian Small Business Development: Lessons for US Industrial Policy", in J. Zysman and L. Tyson (eds.), *American Industry in International Competition*, New York: Cornell University Press.

Salter, W. (1966), *Productivity and Technological Change*, New York and London: Cambridge University Press.

Sengenberger, W., G. Loveman and M. Piore (1990), *The Re-emergence of Small Enterprises: Industrial Countries*, Geneva: ILO.

SIND (1990a), *Att utveckla produkter i småföretag*, SIND 1990:5, Stockholm.

SIND (1990b), *Riskkapitalet och de mindre företagen*, SIND 1990:3, Stockholm.

SIND (1991), *Nyföretagande i Sverige - vilka, hur och varför?*, SIND 1991:6, Stockholm.

Spencer, R. and J.-P. Valla (1989), "The Internationalization of the Industrial Firm: An International Development Network Approach", in R.Luostarainen, (ed.), *Dynamics of International Business*, Proceedings of the XV Conference of the European International Business Association, Helsinki, Finland.

Swedenborg, B. (1979), *The Multinational Operations of Swedish Firms. An Analysis of Determinants and Effects*, Stockholm: The Industrial Institute for Economic and Social Research (IUI).

Swedenborg, B. (1988), *Den svenska industrins utlandsinvesteringar 1960-1986*, Stockholm: The Industrial Institute for Economic and Social Research (IUI).

Taymaz, E. (1989), "Types of Flexibility in a Single Machined Production System", *International Journal of Production Research*, Vol. 27, pp 1891-1899.

Teece, D (1983), "Technological and Organisational Factors in the Theory of the Multinational Enterprise", in M.Casson, (ed.) *The Growth of International Business*, London: Allen & Unwin.

Tichy, G. (1989), "The Size of Firms and Economic Performance", *Research Memorandum*, University of Graz, Austria.

Toffler, A. (1985), *The Adaptive Corporation*, New York: Bantam Books.

Utterback, J and G. Reitberger (1982), *Technology and Industrial Innovation in Sweden - a Study of New Technology-Based Firms*, Center for Policy Alternatives, MIT, Cambridge and National Swedish Board for Technical Development, Stockholm.

Westney, (1991), "The Evolution of Industrial R&D in Japanese Firms", *mimeo*, presented at the Conference "Japan in the Global Economy", Stockholm: The Stockholm School of Economics.

Williamson, O. (1975), *Market and Hierarchies: Analysis and Antitrust Implications*, New York: Free Press.

Williamson, O. (1985), *The Economic Institutions of Capitalism*, New York: Free Press.

About the contributors

Kjell Andersen is Norwegian. He graduated in economics at the University of Oslo in 1950. After two years as research associate at the Institute of Economics at the University of Oslo and two years in the Ministry of Finance, he joined the OECD secretariat in 1954. He was Director of the Economics Department since the early 1970s, and remained with the OECD until retirement age in 1988. During much of this later period he was chairman of the OECD forecasting group. Since 1988 he has held the position of Special Adviser at the Norwegian Delegation to the OECD.

Thomas Andersson is a Senior Research Fellow at the Industrial Institute for Economic and Social Research (IUI), Stockholm, since 1990. He is also associated with the Stockholm School of Economics, at which he earned his Ph.D. in 1989. He has been Visiting Scholar at the Bank of Japan, Hitotsubashi University, Harvard University, the East-West Center, Honolulu, and Universidade de Sao Paulo. His research concerns various aspects of international economics, including trade, foreign direct investment and the environment. His publications include *Multinational Investment in Developing Countries, a study of nationalization and taxation* (Routledge), *Japan: A European Perspective* (Macmillan), and *Europe and the East Asian Agenda*, Jean Monnet Chair Papers at The European Policy unit at the European University Institute, Florence.

Pontus Braunerhjelm is a member of the research staff of the Industrial Institute for Economic and Social Research (IUI), Stockholm. He has a background from The Graduate Institute of International Studies, Geneva, to which he is still attached. His research focuses on firm dynamics, in particular the creation of firm specific advantages, and the macroeconomic implications of the increasingly mobile multinational firms. At present he is involved in a project analyzing the macroeconomic implications of the large Nordic firms' adjustments to the completion of the EC internal market, as well as an EC funded comparative study on small firm dynamics in the EC countries, Japan and the U.S. Pontus Braunerhjelm has published many articles and books in these research areas.

Thomas L. Brewer is Associate Professor of International Business at Georgetown University in Washington, DC. He is the author of a World Bank study titled *Foreign Direct Investment in Developing Countries.* His research has also appeared in the *Journal of International Business Studies,* the *Columbia Journal of World Business,* the *Journal of Money, Credit and Banking,* the *Asia-Pacific Journal of Management,* and the *Journal of Comparative Economics.* He has been a consultant to the World Bank, the Overseas Private Investment Corporation, the Internal Revenue Service, Price Waterhouse and other organizations in the private and public sectors. He is a member of the industry advisory committee on Japanese-U.S. trade in automotive parts of the U.S. Department of Commerce.

Gunter Dufey is Professor of International Business and Finance at The University of Michigan Business School in Ann Arbor. After attending schools in Germany and France, he obtained advanced degrees from the University of Washington, Seattle WA. His research and teaching focuses on issues in international financial markets and the financial management of multinational firms.

John Dunning is currently Emeritus Professor of International Business at the University of Reading (U.K.), and State of New Jersey Professor of International Business at Rutgers University (U.S.). He is also Senior Economics Adviser to the Transnational Corporations and Management Division of the Department of Economic and Social Development, and Chairman of a London based consultancy, Economist Advisory Group (EAG).

Lars Oxelheim is Professor of International Business at the University of Lund. He is also a Senior Research Fellow at the Industrial Institute for Social and Economic Research in Stockholm. For the period 1988-92, he was Professor of finance at the School of Economics and Commercial Law, Gothenburg University. His current research interest is in the area of corporate decision-making in an increasingly integrated world. His recent books in this area include *Macroeconomic Uncertainty –International Risks and Opportunities for the Corporation* (with Clas G. Wihlborg) (Wiley), *International Financial Integration* (Springer Verlag), and *Financial Markets in Transition-the Globalization of Small National Financial Markets* (Routledge, forthcoming).

Richard J. Sweeney is the Sullivan/Dean Professor of International Business and Finance in the School of Business Administration at Georgetown University. Previously, he was the Stone Professor of Money and Finance at Claremont McKenna College and The Claremont Graduate School. He has served on the faculty at UCLA and Texas A&M, and has visited at the University of Virginia, the Tuck School at Dartmounth College, and the Gothenburg School of Economics, Sweden. He served at the United States Department of the Treasury as Deputy Director of the Office of International Monetary Research. Sweeney's research is in financial and monetary economics, and public policy, with a particular interest in international aspects. Sweeney has more than 75 published scientific papers, included in the Journal of Finance, the Journal of Financial and Quantitative Analysis, Economic Inquiry, and the American Economic Review. He has been involved as an author or editor in nine books. The latest are *Wealth Effects and Monetary Theory* (Basil Blackwell, 1988) and *Profit-Making Speculation in Foreign Exchange Markets*, written with Patchara Surajaras (Westview Press, 1991). He has been an editor of Economic Inquiry since 1984, and serves on the boards of a number of other journals.

Ingo Walter is the Charles Simon Professor of Applied Financial Economics at the Stern School of Business, New York University, and also serves as Director of the New York University Salomon Center, an independent academic research institute founded in 1972 to focus on financial institutions, instruments and markets. He also holds a joint appointment as Swiss Bank Corporation Professor of International Management, INSEAD, Fontainebleau, France.

MIX
Papier aus verantwortungsvollen Quellen
Paper from responsible sources
FSC® C105338

If you have any concerns about our products,
you can contact us on
ProductSafety@springernature.com

In case Publisher is established outside the EU,
the EU authorized representative is:
Springer Nature Customer Service Center GmbH
Europaplatz 3, 69115 Heidelberg, Germany

Printed by Libri Plureos GmbH
in Hamburg, Germany